What is truth?
Truth is something so noble that if
God would turn aside from it,
I would keep to the truth
and let God go...
Meister Eckhart

that's the truth.
here's to friendship
and to truth
Nichole

Healing the Soul after Religious Abuse

Recent Titles in
Religion, Health, and Healing

Among the Healers: Stories of Spiritual and Ritual Healing around the World
Edith Turner

Kabbalah and the Spiritual Quest: The Kabbalah Centre in America
Jody Myers

Religion and Healing in Native America: Pathways for Renewal
Suzanne J. Crawford O'Brien, editor

Faith, Health, and Healing in African American Life
Stephanie Y. Mitchem and Emilie M. Townes, editors

Healing the Soul
after Religious Abuse

The Dark Heaven of Recovery

Mikele Rauch

RELIGION, HEALTH, AND HEALING
Susan S. Sered and Linda L. Barnes, Series Editors

Westport, Connecticut
London

Library of Congress Cataloging-in-Publication Data

Rauch, Mikele.
   Healing the soul after religious abuse : the dark heaven of recovery / Mikele Rauch.
       p. cm. — (Religion, health, and healing, ISSN 1556–262X)
   Includes bibliographical references and index.
   ISBN 978–0–313–34670–5 (alk. paper)
  1. Spiritual healing.   2. Psychology, Religious.   3. Psychological abuse.
4. Manipulative behavior.   5. Religious fanaticism.   I. Title.
   BL65.M4R38   2009
   201'.7622—dc22   2008045544

British Library Cataloguing in Publication Data is available.

Library of Congress Catalog Card Number: 2008045544
ISBN: 978–0–313–34670–5
ISSN: 1556–262X

First published in 2009

Praeger Publishers, 88 Post Road West, Westport, CT 06881
An imprint of Greenwood Publishing Group, Inc.
www.praeger.com

Printed in the United States of America

The paper used in this book complies with the
Permanent Paper Standard issued by the National
Information Standards Organization (Z39.48–1984).

10 9 8 7 6 5 4 3 2 1

For Sarada

Contents

Series Foreword

The Religion, Health, and Healing series brings together authors from a variety of academic disciplines and cultural settings in order to foster understandings of the ways in which religious traditions, concepts, and practices frame health and healing experiences in diverse historical and social contexts. Exploring the many ramifications of the roles played by religious traditions in the lives of adherents, volumes in the series include cases in which the authority invested in religious leaders and teachers is used to heal, as well as cases in which that authority is distorted and used to wound those who have come for help and healing. The present volume provides insight into what author Mikele Rauch characterizes as the wounding of the soul in religious communities around the United States.

Other books in this series have explored the word "healing" as a multidimensional and multifunctional concept, especially in religious settings. It can mean the direct, unequivocal, and scientifically measurable cure of physical illnesses. It can mean the alleviation of pain or other symptoms. It can also mean coping, coming to terms with, or learning to live with that which one cannot change (including physical illness and emotional trauma). Healing can mean integration and connection among all the elements of one's being, reestablishment of self-worth, connection with one's tradition, or personal empowerment. It can also involve the pursuit of justice and equity as a process of resisting the forces that generate social ills. Healing can be about repairing one's relationships with friends, relations, ancestors, the community, the world, the Earth, and/or God. It can refer to the development of a sense of well-being or wholeness, whether emotional, social, spiritual, physical, or in relation to other aspects of being that are valued by a particular group. Healing can be about purification, repenting from sin, the cleaning up of one's negative karma, entry into a path of "purer," abstinent, or more moral daily living, eternal salvation, or submission to God's will.

But when the very tradition from which a person has sought one or more of these forms of transformation—in which he or she has invested trust, hope, and the care of the soul—betrays, exploits, and violates that trust, the very antithesis of healing is the result. Because it is the soul that is at stake, the hurt goes all the deeper, and the healing becomes all the more complicated.

Written for lay people, clergy, and professionals working with those who have suffered religious abuse, this book draws on Rauch's own years of confronting her personal experience and of working as a therapist with others who have suffered related abuse. She draws on their stories of affliction, as well as their insights and wisdom, coupled with her own, to explore how religious authority cuts in different directions.

We hope that, by facilitating the publication of studies of diverse healers, healing communities, and healing practices, we will offer readers tools to uncover both the common and the uncommon, the traditional and the innovative, and the individual and the communal ways in which Americans engage with, find meaning in, and seek to embrace, transcend, or overcome affliction and suffering. To these works, we add the voice of Mikele Rauch and those whose stories she has brought before us.

Susan S. Sered and Linda L. Barnes

Acknowledgments

In musical composition, one note will lead to a sequence of tuplets that then can develop from a score to a symphony. There is a similar phenomenon in writing. The color, the sound, the picture of a single word can drive the writer through a spiral of thoughts, working into a fever of sentences until the end of a paragraph, a chapter, or a book.

What drove the words of *Healing the Soul after Religious Abuse* are the stories of those people who pitch such a fever. They give fire to what it means to live a spiritual life within or without religion, perhaps with and without their original notion of God.

There are many others to whom I am indebted. This book could never have been what it is without their contribution.

First and foremost, thank you to the fiercely graced souls who participated in the interview process and whom I mention by the pseudonyms you have given yourselves: Adam, Beth, Chris, Coach, Delicia, Diana, Eleanor, Francis, Irit, Jacob, Joseph Sainsbury, Kate, Keith, Naomi, Patrice, Rasan, Shimon, William, Victor, and Will Michaels. Your stories are seared into my heart. I only hope to do justice to what you so generously and bravely shared with me.

Thank you, Linda Barnes, my wonderful and observant editor. You saw a book in me before I did. I am still flabbergasted that you listened to the words behind my words and then challenged me to actually write them.

Thanks so much to Suzanne Staszak-Silva, my patient senior editor at Praeger/Greenwood Press. You walked me through the maze of publication with kindness and patience, especially late in the game, as we wrestled with the details. Thank you to Erin Ryan and the staff at Apex for careful editing and technical consultation.

To those who shared stories or expertise—and those who have asked to remain anonymous for professional reasons—I am privileged to say thank you:

Charles Bailey, Lee Beckstead, Suzanne Bessenger, Bill Clark, Charles Coe, Patricia Dunn, Peter Danzig, Mary Danzig, Dale English, Thom Harrigan, Johanna Hurley, Janet Jackson, Kevin MacParland, Yisrael Moskovitz, Hana Shiloach Nasser, Riad Nasser, and Kimothy Van Horn. The book would not—could not—be what it is without your important contributions.

Thank you, Huston Smith, the model of religious pluralism, spiritual ac-tivism, and all that is best in spiritual life. You once asked me if I was a writer—and, in your presence, it was a challenge to claim that title for myself. You encouraged me to write this book—and to write courageously. Thank you for your counsel. I hope I have done justice to the task.

Thank you to Richard Sipe and to Jill Gannon for publishing advice and support early in the project. Thank you Carol Flinders for wise advice and encouragement at the eleventh hour. Special thanks to Mike Lew for your exceptional and thoughtful input about the manuscript.

Thank you, Andy Ghahramani, my transcriber: you were faithful to the words of the interviewees through miles of cassette tape and the wonders of Garage Band.

Thanks to the following for immeasurable friendship through dark and light heavens: Charlotte Wheeler, Gail Wetmore, John Mudd, Baris Gok-turk, Denise Ballnick, Melissa Johnson, Noam and Florence Sender, Ellen Yaffa, Sharon Cockroft, Ellen Kaplan, Beverly Bader, John Finley, Mache Finley, Jon and Ana Monday, Jan Zaremba, Christine Freize, Carter Um-barger, John Peters, Ed and Mary Lynne Jensen, Carol Flinders, Barbara Ci-cone, Kurt Kuss, Lin Larsen, Mary Beth Melton, Josef L'African, Richard Humphreys, Sheri Espar (one word or observation was often just enough to redirect me), Judith Cooper (for the gift of Innana and Erishkigol as we walked around the sacred waters of Walden Pond on a cold spring day), and Deepti Zaremba (for a keen eye for detail and clear writing advice).

Thanks to the Tuesday group in Pasadena, California: Janet Jackson, Carol Filutz, and especially Ellen Tan and Kathleen Moore Alpaugh. Since 1990, we have shared the thick and thin of our personal stories and professional lives with love, tears, and laughter.

Thanks to my sisters and colleagues at Brookline Psychological Services: Karen Rosen, Cheryl Abel, and Sabina Garinko. A special thanks to Diane Kwasnick for your steadfast support and confidence in me. And thank you, Ginny Byron: you have seen me through more than one rough spot with bal-anced perspective and unconditional love as I struggle with the professional and personal matters of sexual and clergy abuse.

Thanks to Zoya Slive, Seymour Slive, Richard Hoffman, Steve Klarer and Ellen Highfield, Mike Lew and Thom Harrigan, exceptional colleagues and friends in "Soup Group" in Cambridge. Thanks for the fierce and passionate exchange about life and the profession, your commitment to social justice and political action, and fabulous soup.

Special thanks for the pleasure and privilege of working with my dearest friends on the *MaleSurvivor* International Weekends of Recovery Team (*malesurvivor.org*): Howard Fradkin, Jim Struve, Joanna Colrain, Lee Beckstead, Lynn MacDonell, John Crowe, Ernesto Mujica, Bill Burmeister, Sandi Forti, Don Laufersweilier, Hilde Jacyk, Paul Linden,—and especially Dale English—thanks for the rants, the jokes, the dance, and the hard, hard work. I will treasure you all of my life.

In 2007, Dale English and I ran a workshop for survivors of religious and ritual abuse in Salt Lake City called the *Wolf in God's Clothing: A Workshop for Survivors of Religious Abuse*. To those who participated in that phenomenal weekend, thank you. You know who you are. I will never forget what you shared and what you fearlessly live every day.

Thanks to all the men in *MaleSurvivor* who live and thrive in stormy nights and new days. And thank you to my clients past and present: your courage and tenacity teach and inspire me every day that I am privileged to sit with you in your recovery work.

Thanks to the following who have personally given me hope that it is possible to live both a religious *and* a spiritual life and who contributed their time and wisdom to this project: Suzanne Toolan SM, William Stoeger SJ, Paul Dupuis, Frank Reitter SM, Frank Cluny SJ, Bill Kondrath, Pravajika Gitaprana, and especially Peter Gelfer OH, who was so helpful with resources and input.

Thank you to Pravajika Vrajaprana in Santa Barbara for every reference, every single erudite or sacrilegious conversation, for poetry, licorice, toothpaste, and bad jokes.

Special thanks to Swami Tyagananda in Boston: I cannot express what it means to have your friendship and to grapple with you about everything from radical politics to spiritual awareness. Thank you for never wincing when confronted with the difficult subjects and for always holding the highest bar in your personal and spiritual life.

Thank you to Swami Asheshananda, my guru, who always asked the most of me, gave the most to me, and never crossed the line.

My family is truly the most precious gift in my life.

Thanks to my sister, Rita Humphreys, for seeing me when I did not see myself.

Thank you to my sister-in-law, Reverend Elizabeth O'Dea in Salt Lake City, for your loving support and vision, and for making it possible to offer *Wolf in God's Clothing* in Salt Lake City. You provided your church as a safe space for those who no longer had one.

Thank you to my son, Naren, and my daughter-in-law, Jessica. You both keep me close to the music and help me listen. And special thanks, Naren, for patient technical assistance when I was desperately in need of computer first aid.

Thank you to my daughter Sarada: for pushing me to do my art and to live my life to the fullest. You helped me remember why I was writing this book in difficult moments, inspired me to ask the hard questions and to bear the difficult answers.

To my daughter Dhira: it is difficult to give words to how deeply you have been my teacher in the loving poem of your life. Thank you for all the ways that you attuned yourself to both this project and to me as I struggled to give words to subjects both difficult and hopeful. It is because of your rigorous reading, your spectacular and nuanced editing of the manuscript, and your indomitable spirit, that I had no choice but to write a better book.

Last, thank you to Doug, my husband and soul companion. Thank you for everything spoken and unspoken. You have had to live with me as I struggled through this book, and you alone know what it took to write it. It is my joy to watch you live your spiritual practice and your love every single day of your life.

There are many others both alive and deceased that I did not or could not mention who have contributed to this book. If you have not been cited by name, please accept my deepest gratitude.

CHAPTER 1

———— ✠ ————

Introduction: The Nightmare of "Light"

All night I could not sleep
because of the moonlight on my bed.
I kept on hearing a voice calling
Out of Nowhere
Nothing answered
Yes.

                                                    Zi Ye

I am born and bred in the water of religion. It never occurs to me that there is anything else. Like salt in the ocean, I drift in this sea without question and without resistance. It is the wonder of a child's sweet prayer and a girdle of safety. It is all I know.

My Sicilian family is a mass of contradictions, noisy and secretive, hard working and disorganized, religious and raucous. It is a house full of run-on sentences, interruptions, frustrated and naturally lazy artistic talent, furtive silences, fear-filled preoccupations. My family is open and welcoming. Our closest friends are Jewish Holocaust survivors. They celebrate bar mitzvahs and first holy communions equally.

I am the youngest child; my siblings are a decade older than I am and gone from the household by the time I am seven. So, from an early age, I develop a predisposition for quiet, because I spend so much time by myself. In this place, I correspond without the words of prayer.

I am always singing, because I feel something like a constant presence. I sing in the bathtub, I sing outside—often without the words of song, just notes and sounds. Because there is no way to speak of the experiences inside that move me, I read and reread the lives of the saints in a little booklet that the Sisters have given me. I am drawn to the women martyrs, especially those who die to protect their purity.

Parochial school teaches me the standard dogma, yet, oddly, at home, they laugh at the saints, and at my piety in particular. It is confusing to be encouraged and ridiculed for devotion. As I grow older, my family obsesses over virginity. It is the crown jewel of a Sicilian bride. But, in the house, there is both rigid modesty and sexual humor at the children's expense. From early on, I am instructed to be hypervigilant about boys, about strange men on the street, yet at home am blindly exposed to a long list of sexual predators who are family friends and relatives. Something has happened to me with one of them, but I am too small and too overcome to hold it in my memory. I am told that sex is terrible, but I am also told it is the most wonderful thing I can ever do with my body. My mother cuts my hair. "Don't be vain. . . . Don't look like that. . . . Never give in. . . . Wait." I am growing, my body is changing, but I often cower into shame. The family does not see or understand.

Yet I do love my life, the richness of my family's love, and the music I make. There are always plenty of books in the house, so I read everything I can find. But things are becoming more complicated. There are many colors between black and white. I have new forays into exuberance as I discover myself as a girl but am also chastised for asking the innumerable questions that life poses. I learn that there are minefields everywhere: in relationships, outside the church, in the body, in and outside my own mind.

Danger is always present. It has the potential to suck one in at a moment's notice. Sin is almost a concrete operational entity. In my Catholic Church, supplication is the order of the hour. There are rumblings and mumblings that sacrifice has more to it, or less, but none of it makes real sense. The secrets, mystery words, selected silences confuse and disorient. I study my catechism. But, when I challenge the pope's infallibility, the teacher tries to choke me. Although the authorities come to know about this, there is no report. I am almost expelled from school.

Sometimes I look beyond the dove stuck in space that overlooks the Mother of *God* with papery skin and an amputated heart fluttering on the outside of her fragile blue breast. Being human seems to have the potential to contaminate me, if I soil myself with indiscriminate self-touching or neglect of the rituals. No wayward thinking, no talking back—*stop asking questions*.

I am guilty of the questions themselves—guilty of seeing, guilty of knowing and the unknowing, for disobeying, for speaking, for feeling.

The only recourse is to be *good*.

Better to look at things from a distance: read the lives of martyrs and mystics without really understanding sacrifice or spiritual experience. Up close, they banish Francis of Assisi from his own community, preferring the tidily subdued Thomas Aquinas or devout renditions of Therese of Lisieux. Don't bother with St. Augustine's shadow or Teresa of Avila's questions. Don't scratch the patina off the paintings. Shadows are everywhere. Joy is suspect.

I read about St. Maria Goretti, the patron saint of virginity, who has been attacked at the age of twelve by a young farmhand named Alessandro Serenelli. He tries to rape the pious girl while she fights back, screaming that it is a sin and that he will go to hell. He chokes, then stabs her 14 times in a blind rage. Maria lives for two days after forgiving Alessandro on her deathbed; she dies holding a crucifix and a medal of Our Lady. The story is embedded into my body-soul—a juxtaposition of purity and Sicilian sensuality, budding innocence and pubescent seduction. Family and Church have instilled a cultivated naiveté and uninformed piety along with implicit sexual preoccupation. It is a lethal combination.

When I am 18, I create an ecumenical coffeehouse for students in my church. I work closely with the young charismatic priest in the parish. He builds me up and breaks me down over time, gradually seducing me into a sexual relationship. Considering how I have been raised, I know only how to comply. But, even here, I fail to give him what he demands because of the fear of losing my virginity. The relationship further complicates my sexual confusion and destroys my sense of integrity. I am bound up and shut down because there is so much to hide, even from myself. But it has rarely worked to question perception, anyway. Most of the time, what I feel is too degrading to address. I dissociate experience from belief, body from thought.

Shame and its bewildering set of emotions consume and disorient me. It is excruciating because there are no words, people, or places for respite; solitude becomes the very source of emptiness and self-loathing. But, even so, it does not quell the inner promptings. I do not stop singing.

I take all of this with me when I transfer to a Jesuit college far from home. It is 1967, and only a few blocks away in Haight-Ashbury, others are marching against the war, for Caesar Chavez, and with Dr. King. But, deep in the wells of Catholicism, there is another subculture and another war, with its own ongoing conflict between spirit and history.

Vatican II has broken wide open, bursting the corsets of tradition in alarming new ways. Nuns are wearing short veils and miniskirts. Priests celebrate Mass with Oreo cookies and grape juice. But all of this tumultuous change brings my old questions to the forefront. Also, just living in a city exposes me to life outside. I witness everything: the poverty, the politics of the street, diversity, bigotry. My closest friendships span the cultural divide and challenge the personas of charity and open-mindedness with real issues of race, privilege, and culture. I begin to experiment with my emotions, especially anger. My spiritual bubble is bursting around the realities of the oppression and injustice I encounter every single day with the children I tutor, the friends I make and lose, even the men I date, who are clearly not white or Catholic or American. I am still terrified about confronting the issues of my sexuality or pushing the envelope too far when it comes to experimenting with relationships or substances where I could lose control. *Control* is still key, because otherwise I cannot trust where I will go. Nevertheless, I know I am alive because the membrane of fear has at least been ruptured; I experiment in my own thinking.

There is still a great hunger, for what I cannot say, because there are no descriptors. I cross into some tenuous religious adolescence and find a Jesuit priest to be my spiritual director; he seems trustworthy and real. I learn another new language for experience and begin a kind of spiritual practice beyond churchgoing. It is both a relief and a stressor, because I am challenged to question with more penetrating acuity. I begin to pay closer attention to other inner rumblings. I give more time to listening to the inside, even if my mind is full of cross-talk.

This develops into more serious spiritual exploration, which culminates in the decision to enter a religious community of nuns who seem to embody a reverence for interior life, as well as service to the poor. They appear to be forward thinking, yet outwardly conservative. They wear a modified habit, which appeals to my sense of stability and containment. Their emphasis seems to be on community, which promises to fill a longing for connection. I meet women from all age groups who are living an intentional spiritual life. There is richness in the legacy of contemplation in a world of action. There is also a profound kinship with music, and I engage in the vibrant creativity of writing and performing with voice and instrument. I hope it will sustain me in confusing circumstances.

But, from the first day I enter, there is a double bind of apparent openness and shame-making suppression; it is not always clear where the demarcations lie. I am encouraged to learn current theology, mystical literature, and biblical scholarship; but must beware of outward critical thinking in the community corridors, especially if it conflicts with the charismatic novice mistress.

In the religious formation training, the focus is on the relationship with the divine. The novice mistress is obviously one of Christ's favorite brides. She is articulate, beautiful, and quite formidable. She gives meditation instructions that seem to lift one to an apparent level of exclusive connection with the Almighty. Occasionally, a bit of her orgasmic mystical fervor filters down to the rest of the nuns under the sister's direction. It becomes apparent however, that in order to succeed in the novitiate, it will be important to carefully mirror her thoughts and mindset. Soon, it also becomes clear that I have too many opinions.

In the academic arena with my theology professors, though there is liberation from the oppression of dogma, my psyche runs amok because of what I am learning. There is inquiry, and debate—a guarded dialogue takes place. But I cannot bring this back to the community. Community means togetherness. Full membership requires accommodation and deference—no analysis, no questions.

It is important not to distinguish myself in the membership and to be seen as in line with its qualities and regimen. There is a silent pecking order of who is acceptable and who is inadequate and particular criteria for those deemed fit for religious life. Those who do not measure up are shut out. The novice mistress questions my inability to conform and therefore my mental stability as a religious.

Comply in the name of community. Disappear in the name of community.

There is a silent pedagogy here regarding spiritual authority: those in power are never wrong; they alone have a direct line to God. They hold the moral high ground, even if it directly opposes one's own personal conscience. Blind obedience creates the mask of humility but not the ability to view oneself deeply or realistically. Subservience generates superiority. I begin to notice that deference to the authorities moves someone up the religious ladder; it also creates fear of losing place—or face. But this mock humility has nothing to do with a healthy perception of limitations or gifts.

Pride is the covert shadow of the meek.

What will it take to fit into the girdle of convent life? I must be compliant and manage my questions. I should contain my difficulties with the community's opulence. For instance, it is difficult to justify the vow of poverty when the sisters live so far beyond the means of most of the people they serve. But it does not work to question religious authority, as a nun once explained to me:

> Who do you think you are? Who are you to dictate to the community about the practices of a religious order? Obedience trumps your personal vision of poverty. You are proud. Your behavior is provocative. You talk too much. You are too intense. You have questionable friendships with people outside. You habit is too short, too raggedy, not representative of a good nun. You should be ashamed.

I am indeed.

I become confused about the differing messages I receive about religious life, the vows, and community culture. It is impossible to decipher the complicated unspoken rules in the community about chastity. The practice of celibacy here is a concoction of homoerotic romanticism and protocol. I encounter piety as a ruse for sexuality. Homosexual activity and seduction are practiced with decorum and denial. (If it is not sex with a man, it is not sex.) While being groomed by an older nun who is in love with me, I am accused of having a "particular friendship" (which is code for *homosexual liaison*) because I pray alone with a nun from an African community who is also struggling in a new country to understand this convent culture of doublespeak and double binds.

One night, one of the other novices has a psychotic break and tries to throw me off the balcony. But I never ask for help for the novice or myself. It is not safe to speak of this or any of these other troubling circumstances. I do not trust that the community will help this novice and fear that it will punish her, instead. As for me, my association with *outsiders* in the convent has already compromised my position in the community. I pull into my confusion so deeply that I block the incident entirely from my mind. Many years later I will return to the same set of stairs and remember the tussle of that long night when I talked the novice down from suicide.

I wear a habit and a veil, a perfect metaphor for the cloak of sanctity over skinless circular shame; it burrows deeper and deeper inside as I endlessly monitor my outside. I am quick to take full responsibility for any negative interaction or exchange and often set myself up for failure.

My reaction to living in the convent has been a combination of beauty, music, and an intense experience of mystical life, even as it creates denial, withdrawal, rage, perfectionism, and exhibitionism. There is a profound dis-ease in my soul. I am disconnected and overwhelmed both from my outside world and within myself.

I prepare to take vows. A psychologist, who has been my adviser in college, is serendipitously hired by the community to interview the aspirants. He is alarmed to see what has become of me in the time I have been in the convent. It does not take him long to find just how compromised I am. I am overweight, shut down, depressed, and fearful. What he cannot quite decipher is that my soul is as frozen with self-doubt and demoralizing shame as my emotions. He raises his concerns, not reckoning how the novice mistress will react or how the community will handle the information.

The novice mistress immediately declares me mentally ill and insists that I take a leave of absence. She is relieved to see me go but disconcerted because my exit causes some agitation among the members. I leave the convent in shame.

The community refers me to an old Hungarian psychoanalyst who assesses my emotional stability. "Dahling, you are neurotic, of course. But you are certainly not crazy," she says. "This illness of yours is environmental, not mental." She explains over time that, because the system created such confusion and conflicting messages, I was bound to fail.

The diagnosis creates nothing less than a dilemma of grace.

The years ahead will be full of questions, exploration, falling in and out of old paradigms and new possibilities. I will both discover safety in relationships and love and repeat old, sick patterns. I will marry a man outside my religious tradition who resonates with my own longing and interior life. I will encounter new spiritual worlds, to find the same deep mystical language and experience a stronger sense of presence. I will find a teacher who demands a sharpening of spiritual awareness. He will hold my trust—and keep his boundaries.

I will also discover that religious communities may be different in philosophies or paradigms but human behavior is pretty consistent. I will remember what is safe and what is not, but only after other violations that I have been too dissociated to note have affected my own child.

For many years, the psychological journey to recover myself will be consistently hit or miss. I will find that the psychotherapeutic process is as limited as organized religion has been in recovering my soul.

As for my spiritual struggle, there will be many surprises and fierce marvelous grace.

Then, I have a dream. . . .

I am a stump on a bed. I have no limbs. My nerves unravel like string around me. I am mute, drooling, and incontinent—my body encased in a plastic skin of numbness. I smell my own decay. There are family and friends around me, but they do not seem capable of understanding how to help me. They speak of me as if I am invisible.

I am dead to them.

I lose sight: blind beyond black. My eyes forget what it was to see.

Then, in the moment—and, later, in the small shards of memory of this dream—I am filled with stillness.

Nothing from nowhere answers nothing.

But there It is.

Inexplicable freedom.

Yes.

A dark and unutterable heaven.

The decision to write this book came from a casual and what I thought to be a rhetorical question about something that had possessed me for decades. My remarks were usually made off the cuff lest someone actually notice how disturbing the subject really was to me.

The question was: with all the books, documentaries, discussions, and arguments, why had no one spoken of the impact of religious abuse on the soul? Why did it seem that people who suffered some form of violation in *God*'s name struggled not simply in their psyche but beyond that—to the core of themselves? How do people recover what is most essential to who they are, within whatever one calls the *soul*?

"Good question. Why don't you write about it?"

For those who have lived through such a hell, the long road to recovery can be a series of missteps, odd friendship choices and living arrangements, marriages, divorces, children wiser than ourselves, much loss, loyalties to tragic causes, particular or disastrous professional decisions. There may be some good therapy, some very bad therapy, more religion, no religion.

What happens inside is more difficult to talk about. It is as private and profound and endlessly surprising as the invisible Whatever that doesn't let up, despite how little or much attention we give to It.

We look at the impact of religion for good and for ill. Surely, it nurtures and organizes communities around celebration, contemplation, and concern. It opens wondrous gateways, comforts those in pain, and provides safety and hope to the vulnerable. It stimulates the highest forms of art, music, and literature and is often the touchstone for the deepest elements of human experience.

But sometimes religion, or at least those who represent it, does great harm even as it serves. Religion in its less divine aspects has created war, genocide, racial and sexual oppression, subjugation of women and children, physical and sexual violation, and ritual abuse.

Religious abuse is what people suffer when leaders of their faith communities or others punish, humiliate, or otherwise exploit them in the name of God. For many, it can devastate their sense of self and their principles. It can alter their experience of the world, their bodies, their sexual orientation, their relationships, their sense of meaning. Sometimes there is no place for a God of love or a love of what was once divine.

Recovering anything sacred after a betrayal from religion graphs a voyage of possibility and inquiry that may seem unimaginable to some of us. There is a scar in the soul that is easily bruised again. Even the term—God—can be a minefield of conflicting feelings, memories, and images.

How does one trust gravity once the ground disappears?

Truth is a pathless land, says Krishnamurti. It does not chart a narrow course. It covers a planet of possibilities and many points of view.

In this book, the reality of religious abuse and recovery is witnessed through physical, emotional, and spiritual lenses and in the words of those who have experienced it firsthand.

In the second chapter, we explore the course of psychological and spiritual development and the impact of trauma throughout the life cycle. We witness the potential of the human soul from birth to death, how it is sometimes thwarted, and when, even at the end of life, it can be transformed.

In chapter 3, we focus on the institution of religion; we see how dogma and religious teaching can be corrupted by insularity and power in ways that defile the original message. We distinguish the differences between the family of blood and the family of religion—and the tension of similarities. We explore the power of what is unspoken: in the culture of family, race, sexual politics, and identity. We note the cost of religious abuse in the areas of sexuality, for women and children, in race and class. We examine the potency of shame in all its manifestations.

Chapter 4 challenges priests, rabbis, ministers, lamas, swamis, roshis, and imams to consider the needs of the people they serve with more complexity. We note the effects of religious leadership that do both psychological and spiritual harm to those who put their trust in the individuals who represent a religious tradition. We address the sacred task of spiritual direction in the dynamic between pastor and his or her congregation, guru and disciples, spiritual teacher and aspirants. We assess how such relationships can become compromised and abuse excused, justified, or kept secret. We hear from the interviewees themselves about what would return trust to the process of spiritual direction and pastoral care.

In chapter 5, we examine the value and meaning of sacrifice and how it is sometimes misinterpreted or misrepresented in a way that is harmful and even lethal, especially in the light of current events. We bear witness to the physical and psychological cost of suffering like this from the testimonies of those interviewed and hear from them how the meaning of sacrifice can be restored.

Chapter 6 overviews sexuality and its sacred place, the value and the violations of celibacy in religious life, the pernicious issue of clergy and guru sexual abuse. We discuss the definition of pedophilia, distinguish the specific differences of perpetrators from those they abuse. We carefully assess the sacred and intimate relationship of spiritual director or guru and disciple and why it is so difficult for survivors to find resolution after a sexual violation. We look at the most difficult of perpetrations in the form of ritual abuse. We assess the signs of spiritual trauma in response to violation, the issue of shame, what happens when the community is silent or punitive to survivors, and what is necessary for healing the soul of an individual and a community in the end.

Last, in chapters 7 and 8, we consider the path of restoration and the dark heaven of recovery that is possible for reclamation of spirit. We question how or if religious institutions can make meaningful restitution for the violations done under their watch, what options work best for recovery. We address the complicated and important task of forgiveness for a survivor, when, if, why, and how it is possible. We explore the process of psychotherapy, when it works and why it often fails to heal. With all of this, we grapple with the dilemma of longing that remains.

From the words of the interviewees, we look at what inner restoration means, what it takes to reclaim the sacred and rewire the spirit. It is they who bring this book to life. The author's perspective and witness, despite all attempts to be nonjudgmental and cross-cultural, are North American and exist within a Western cultural landscape. Yet, my hope is that what is witnessed and written can resonate with the reader's own spiritual path and individual story.

As the author, I am immeasurably grateful to each of the people I was able to interview. They have been or presently identify as atheist, Muslim, Buddhist, Hindu, hybrids of Mormon and Reconstructionist Judaism, Orthodox Jewish, Unitarian Universalist, Protestant-Buddhist, Native American, and Catholic—and a member of an unnamed community that the interviewee does not wish to reveal. They are many races. Their stories took place in California, Arizona, Utah, Illinois, Indiana, Michigan, Massachusetts, Virginia, Pennsylvania, New York, and New Jersey in the United States, as well as in Germany, Italy, Nepal, India, Israel, and Palestine.

What they speak of is not a simple matter. But, without their personal input, this would be just another academic treatment of a profoundly complex subject. It is the words of those who were interviewed that give bones and blood to this book. For consistency and the sake of confidentiality, each interviewee chose a pseudonym for himself or herself that will be used in the text. Some of the stories were altered to preserve anonymity. The interviewees had complete control over their own material and signed off on every exchange that is in print. It is hoped that the author's words are a testament to their resolute courage and the immense spirit that informed each interchange.

Like all of us, the interviewees are works in progress. Not one of them has completed his or her life purpose, and at the time of this printing they are all still alive. For a number of them, it is a subject for debate whether death will even finish their saga. These individuals exude resilience in the face of anguish that penetrates deeper than the effects of the physical, psychological, or sexual cruelty they may have suffered. There is *something* behind or beyond the mind that bears an inexorable but sweet hunger and a tenacious spirit.

This book is about that hunger and that fierce grace, which I define as profound resonance with kindness and compassion. This grace is relentless. It frees, but neither freely nor easily. It can be as simple as breath, when breathing is simple because your lungs actually work. Fierce grace enables the spiritual lungs air enough to breathe when there is no wind and the ground disappears.

Change is a gradual thing, punctuated by occasional markers of acceleration like wonder, death, or trauma. The movement within is below the shame, the lack of self-esteem, or the painful self-sabotage. It may be slower still.

But it is said that when we really hear and are truly heard, something changes not only in our minds but also in our bodies. So we bear witness. We have no illusions about what can be fixed. Yet, when the stories are told, something may change in our own bodies, our own voices. When words are spoken or faces clearly seen, it can sear us with silence or with *ah-hah*. And, perhaps, something happens in our souls.

And, like the old newspaperman, we might insist that we have ceased to believe in the unknowable. But, he would tell us, it will be sitting here nevertheless, calmly licking its chops.[1]

CHAPTER 2

———— ✖ ————

Trouble in the House of *God*: Trauma and the Life Cycle

Where there is dismemberment in the beginning, there is remembrance in the end. The fulfillment of the cosmic game is the discovery of what was covered and the recollection of what was scattered.

—Alan Watts, *Two Hands of God*

To simply be alive is a remarkable thing. Nothing is static, from the skin down to the soul, for we are changing from the inception of life until the last breath we take. Our inevitable birthright is to be human, but there are endless possibilities and loopholes in the process.

While we humans are physically and neurologically complicated we are even more convoluted than our synapses and muscle groupings. There is much to consider in human development—not only in the body or psychological and emotional growth—but in the confluence of these aspects, and their varying rates of development within each individual. There also appears to be an inexplicable *something* that moves deep within our consciousness, which concerns us here. And, in the schema of life, it is this core of the self that we must address, from the beginning of life until its end.

THE QUESTION OF CONNECTION

Culture and religion are often as much a part of us and of our development as our own skin, which is constantly changing on a cellular level. At first, they may be all we know beyond our relatives: our universe. Rituals, traditions, and cultural habits are the flora and fauna of interconnectedness that surround our everyday life. Some families make the most of the tools, customs, and symbols of their ancestors; others construct new altars through television or computers.

Religious life and culture live in the landscape of race, cosmology and in the particular current events or catastrophes of sexuality and gender politics, poverty and war, genocide or holocausts, slavery, and famine. Throughout the life cycle, such trauma impacts a person, a family, a race, a religious culture. All of these realities belie trivialization here and cannot be adequately addressed in these pages although they affect each individual story.

Physical or psychological trauma, whether it happens to individuals or in a community, affects some aspect of human growth to a lesser or a greater degree, and, depending on the context, can simply paralyze growth altogether. The force of the trauma is not just in the body or even the brain but also in the core of a person, where it can arrest the natural progression of the spirit.

Even at the beginning of life, the impact of distress, shock, or physical or psychological injury can determine the course of our inner development from that moment on.

So, as we consider religious life and how it is affected by violations and betrayals, intrusions and neglect, we can recognize the powerful interplay that begins quite literally at conception.

Even in the womb before birth, our brains are growing at an expediential rate—the body, the budding intellect, and the raw reactions—even sexuality. These ways of growing develop at their own pace. They are not always in sync with one another.

In the beginning, we are utterly, infinitely open. We are aware not of ourselves but of the person reflecting back. This person is the formulating ego, the "you" that gazes at the "me." First, the mother, then the rest of the world, is looking back. Then the conscious self and its evolving ego are accumulated as we live with others. And, even if there is little to connect with, this ego of ours is still there, mirroring the space around us.

The formation of "self" begins with immense physicality, building on our reflexes and habits, imitation, differentiation. We are a plethora of needs. We need to eat, to defecate, to breathe, to be touched. Our skin is a radio transmitter of sensation, psychically attuned to the environment and to the ones who care for us. Initially, we have no defenses. We take in whatever comes our way.

Time and place are *here*, *now*, and *this*. We begin to use language and develop imagination based on the connections we make; we soon learn what we can trust. But the self and its ego are all that matter in this appraisal.

As the months go by, we find more complex ways to interpret our relationships. Our needs are determined by different criteria of safety, based not so much on the body as on the ecosystem of other's affection or neglect, availability or indifference, kindness or aggression.

We become a reaction machine, imitating and experimenting. It is not possible to fathom the moral consequences of our actions as yet, so our sense of good is based on what helps and our sense of bad in what hurts. Our thinking is sensate, our judgment egocentric and one-dimensional. Life around us is determining whether we feel confinement or freedom. There is also the omni-presence of the society around us, which dictates the nature and meaning of our world.

A child's best inner resource is what is most susceptible to betrayal: his in-nocent receptivity. There is an almost indescribable state of openness. Noth-ing quite surpasses the fragile exuberance of it—at life's initial ascent—when boundless possibilities, energy, and beauty begin to flower.

It may be said that this openness itself creates a sense of presence some might name *God*. Perhaps, in our families and cultures, we have other clas-sifications or transcendent titles for this presence. Words like *spirit* or *soul* may be seen as almost physical containers; perhaps *angels have wings* or a *God lives with them in a heaven*—which has a location with an address—as does hell. *God* (or whatever we call this divine presence) is indefinable but named any-way. We quickly endow *It* with qualities and characteristics that are familiar to us, taking our cues from those closest to us, or the boundless liveliness of nature itself.

> I was in utter awe. I would look to the skies and smile. I'd feel a warm smile coming back down to me directly from *God*. I knew he really could see me looking up at where he lived, up there in the clouds. Heaven—a place so beau-tiful you can't even begin to imagine how great. I prayed regularly, at least mornings when I awoke and then before bed. I prayed the regular prayers like we were taught, but I also prayed in open verse: a conversation between me and *God*. I would pause, wait for him to hear me, and respond. While I never heard his actual voice, I just knew he listened and felt an answer during the moments of silence. I was so happy. I felt really close to *God*. We would talk together in my head, off and on during the day—sometimes out loud when I was sure no one could hear because they wouldn't understand. *God* was my "buddy," always there, always present, by my side. (William)

Yet some of us experience a less than available divine being, especially if our own families somehow fail or neglect us.

> Incapable of pleasing parents who were emotionally as distant as heaven, the child reached out to a mysterious God who asked only that I love Him and His son who gave his life so that I could be free from the selfishness of sin. This life after all was meaningless. It was but a stepping stone to earn eternal life with Him in His kingdom of heaven. My role models were the saints who gave their lives for their faith in this Triune God. There were answers to every question, except for the ones that required faith that this God would never give you more than you could handle. (Chris)

Perhaps we conclude that *God* is a bit like a critical parent and that his love depends on what pleases or displeases him. Maybe he is a magical all-knower like Santa Claus or the boogieman. Maybe in the culture we live,

God is a she instead—she may have four arms and a sword, a garland of skulls or a basket of blessings. Wherever we are and whatever we name the divine, the pictures, stories, or rituals become part of the dense mysterious universe inside our minds.

We do not question.

The stories we hear are the only stories.

The pictures of hearts or wings, the flames or swords, the devils or demons are real to us.

This is who *God* is.

> The *God* of my childhood was benevolent and all-powerful, all-knowing, and had every conceivable ability. He was to me more of a malevolent "watcher" and "punisher," and we were to just assume that what he did was good, though I found myself thinking of him as cruel. At times it was hard for me to believe that he was real. (Jacob)

The benevolent and the malevolent aspects of God can be confusing or terrifying. We may have no way to differentiate the fairy tale from our own experience of truth.

THE QUESTION OF DILIGENCE (AND CONNECTION)

Around the age of seven (the Catholic Baltimore Catechism refers to this as the "age of reason"), there is a shift from magic to concrete formulations. It is our own age of technology, a time to make tangible sense of things. The world seems black or white, good or bad, right or wrong, one way or no way. It is a time when sexuality and sexual appetites appear to go underground. It is at this latency stage that we may begin to listen to the stories differently. Even when given mythic status we may still accept them at face value. We take on life and relationships differently, as well. We might become more self-protective; we wish to be competent and seen as capable, especially in the eyes of the others. We hope to please *God*, especially if he or she inhabits a more personal place in our emerging inner lives.

> I loved going to church. It was in Latin back then, but I would hum along and say the few words I knew, still not knowing their meanings. But it didn't matter; it was for *God*, after all. Lent was great. We went to church every day, and then there were Stations of the Cross, then traveling to neighboring churches to pray. *God* knew me, and I knew him. All was good. I believed "He is, was, and always will be," as I was taught. He was all-knowing, all-powerful, knew all and could see all, he knew before we sinned and if we told the priest the truth in confession. I was a sinner like everyone else, but after confessions *God* would love me again, and the next day I would go to communion. That was then. . . . (William)

There may be plenty of conversations with *God*. Although by this time, there can also be an emerging sense of what is expected by everybody else.

This may be the only way to wash, to eat.

This may be the only way to pray.

This is surely the only way to dress.

Don't look there.

Don't do *that*.

Don't touch.

Don't ask.

Don't speak.

As a little girl I remember distinctly talking with God in my head. This was most often during times of despair and fear. I know I did believe that I had my own personal connection to God, and I wanted very much to feel this connection solidly within my soul. Yet I doubted it often and had to struggle to relax into a place of comfort and safety with God. After all, I "sinned" so often. (Kate)

For a child, the small girdles of safety and solidity, curiosity or the sense of God's presence is dependent on the world outside for its freedom. If God's love is based on reward or punishment for *our* behavior, are we unworthy of this love when something goes awry? If we are responsible in some way for everything, isn't it our fault if wrong happens to us?

Maybe we are *too* exuberant, spontaneous or willful.

Maybe we screw up too much. . . .

This is the birth of shame, although it can happen earlier than the age of seven: when a child first comes to believe herself defective. If we see ourselves as contemptible, and unlovable, we believe we have not simply made mistakes; we *are* a mistake.

Shame can become an identity. It can shrivel our true self for a contracted one, a self that must accommodate the image of the critical reflector. We must adhere to the expected protocol or face ourselves as worthless and failed.

So we fashion ourselves to fit into a likeness of the one that accepts or rejects us on the basis of what we do, not who we are.

This is what a family looks like.

This is who the Chosen are.

This is what a girl should do.

This is what a boy must be.

This is what God says is good.

This is *who* God says is good.

Even as we grow older, our child ego never disappears. The sheath of a false self may stubbornly cover whatever we are. Long before any blatant violation, we can get stuck in a shame-based hologram of pain and fear. The all-pervading reality of this shame is the backdrop for abuse. It can create the setup and perpetuate the eventual fallout of trauma. This is often why we must later escape ourselves in any way we can. In the child mind, we know only what we have been taught about ourselves from others' words or actions with us. If our true self has been ruptured, we have no filters to counteract this experience and could be destined to perpetuate it throughout our adulthood. We only know how to defend or pretend.[1]

> Let's go back to a six-year-old who's in the first grade of a Catholic parochial school, and a sister from the Order of Our Lady of the Seven Sorrows. (I can't fathom why they chose names like that for nuns.) I remember we were getting ready for our first communion. They put in your head that you had to tell God what you did wrong before you could receive him into your whole being through this wafer of bread that supposedly is his body and his blood. (I can't fathom what a six-year-old does with that except believe it.) She held up this picture that is forever emblazoned into my memory, of the picture of hell, with their little white winged cherubs, pink skin. Their skin is turning black because they are being burned by the flames of hell. She proceeded to tell us this was what was going to happen to us if we committed a mortal sin, which is a complete break from the love of God. . . .You could end up in the flames of hell like this. That instilled a level of fear that in retrospect was just as severe as any other thing that could cause post-traumatic stress in a person. (Chris)

If there is a sexual violation, especially by someone who represents *God*, our shame and confusion grow as our bodies disconnect from our souls. We may have been told that *God* and his representatives are all-good and all-loving, but our experience is now otherwise. Our own sense of being good or bad depends on the whim of those who have the power; yet, ironically, our state of being and what is happening to us appear to be our responsibility, as well. We are too little to separate from the ones we love, depend on—or fear. We may wonder: has *God* failed to save us from the harm He let happen because of what we were forced or seduced to do? There is a break in our stream of consciousness. It distorts the memory and our sense of self. The child's ego digs in its heels in an attempt to hold on to who we are, but it is clinging to a distortion.

> You'd swear he's got his own little perverted scripture book and followed it chapter and verse, and on occasion he would take his semen and anoint me with it—say more Latin crap, a little cross on my forehead, and lips and hair, and over my heart. He sent me to the bathroom after the first time and made me wash my mouth out with soap. It was a vile thing I'd just done, so I should go back and pray for forgiveness to God. I'd say, "But I just did what you asked!" And he said, "Don't breathe a word of this to anybody—your mother, your father, your brothers, your sisters. I'm connected to *God*, I'm *God*'s man on earth, and if you say a word of this to anybody—do you want your mom gone?" I said,

"*No!*" And my 10-year-old mind couldn't process it: damned if you do, damned if you don't, even telling me he was the only one that loved me at this point in time—my mother and father—they wouldn't love me, *God* certainly didn't love me because I wasn't pleasing God yet. I had many more counseling sessions to go through. (William)

If we experience this kind of violation, we must choose between what we have been told to value and what is actually taking place. The tension rises with each phase of development. We may have to shut off some of our life force out just to manage our thoughts, our curiosity and questions, our opinions, our joy. We may be withholding information and secrets even from ourselves. It can take decades *before* the sheaves of memory break through the defenses into our awareness—if they ever can. We often store our pain creatively and unconsciously, until our bodies tell their own stories.

> I didn't have any memories of it until I was an adult, well into my forties . . . It started to come back on a massage table while I was getting a massage. And I remember, he started massaging on my lower back, and it just was like these images came flashing back at me. And I was just like, "No, don't touch me, no!" And he said, "What's going on?" "I'm not sure but this just doesn't feel comfortable." (Will Michaels)

Trauma can change everything for a child who is supposed to be busy with other things, like curiosity, friendships, and play. Yet, it is also important to recognize the power of resilience. A loving relative, therapist, or teacher, or a protective clergyperson can keep us afloat or create a channel where we can survive. Sometimes nature itself soothes a troubled nervous system and provides us some deeper connection with our spirits.

Nevertheless, this is a time when we can begin to deconstruct some of the myths we have heard, even if we do it rather clumsily. If we are safe enough, we will start to question the information and tell some stories of our own.

THE QUESTION OF SEX (AND CONNECTION AND DILIGENCE)

Adolescence. A time of many awakenings. Our bodies begin to unfold with physical and sexual quickening. We leave a part of childhood behind to find a new version of a self that works, that is ours. We may begin to carve out what is most important and perhaps to challenge what we once believed. We may resonate with new input, even originate some of our own unique outlook on the world around us. Unless we have already experienced profound disruptions, the possibilities seem endless. Adolescence is most often a period where *we* matter in our relationships, even the divine ones. We may want to interact with a *God* that really sees us, at a time when we are struggling to decipher who we are. Often we are trying to make sense of things by declaring how we are different. We might pull away from the family. Our identity may be more dependent on allegiances with our friends, our music, our religion. If things are not going right, we might become fixated more on a substance or a piece of technology than a human relationship.

Yet our philosophical reflections and our evolving spirit can be quite tender. Even a random interaction with family or Church, which once seemed to provide our stability, can alter our course.

> I was confirmed when I was 13 years old, and around that time I became aware of the difference between the Lutheran and the Catholic perceptions of Communion. By this I mean that the body and the blood of Christ *represents* or *becomes*, respectively. One day I crossed the boundary of the Lutheran perception, and, while taking Communion, I thought that the sacrament had transformed or *became*. Much to my surprise and for the first time in my life, I felt the presence of God before me, a sense of awe never before felt. When my parents and I returned to our seats, I failed to sit down. My mother, in an angry whisper, said, "What is the matter with you? You look like you have seen a ghost. Sit down!" It caused me such pain that I never took Communion again. I never told my parents. I rarely went to church with my parents after that and became an agnostic. Years later, I came to the understanding that my mother had a great deal of control over me and had somehow convinced me that it was wrong to feel or *experience* God. (Eleanor)

Because of the power of the family or culture and the strong need for kinship, sometimes newer connections can still regenerate what has been present all along—our fear of abandonment.

> I felt so guilty my whole life for having questions. You know you're supposed to be able to put your questions on the shelf, if they interfere with your faith. (Shimon)

Maybe it is not safe to speak of our dilemmas to anybody, even to God.
This is the *only* book.
This is the *only* holy place.
This is the *only* way to talk about it . . . .

We may sacrifice individuality, our sense of humor, or our spontaneity in order to fit in. We may have to split our real self from the costumes it must wear out of a sense of solidarity. Besides, the tension of shame or fear of exposure often takes its toll. The mind of the group can make us agree to things that might be otherwise unthinkable. Sometimes we are unconsciously cut off from our own moral compass, either by repeating an unsavory action that was once done to us or in our silent passivity about some similar violation on someone else.

It may be that, because of our culture and family, we feel we have no choices. We may have to pretend in order to survive, even though we are compromised by our compliance. But the tension of shame or the fear of exposure often takes its toll.

> So probably from 13 until 19, that Mormon part of my identity was so strong. Then the gay part of me, or the sexual part, started growing stronger. Because it was so against the Church . . . with the Mormon dream of what I should be—I had to put it someplace. So I really started living a divided life: I would outwardly represent something I thought was positive to people, but inwardly I would be constantly aware of how I was attracted to guys, and shouldn't be attracted, torn between the guilt and the pleasure, the wanting men but wanting to be good . . . . I remember the elder gave me a pamphlet called "To the One." . . . It was literally for "the *one* person in this congregation who is homosexual, these are my words to you," which sounded so reassuring and caring but said, "It would be better that you tie a millstone around your neck and throw [yourself] in the water than be a homosexual." (Adam)

Though the cliché glosses over the reality, sometimes even acute suffering can build whatever one defines as soul. In the midst of our distress, we may discover a kind of diligence in the deep well of presence, and some subtle and profound interior rumblings that can change our vision and our heart. In fact, sometimes the pain we experience is the subtext to another kind of awakening and the beginning of a more complicated, nuanced inner life. Many of us report that the pain of adolescence is what originally generated a new direction toward a more intentional life.

But none of these various processes of development grow consistently in any human being. Each life and its responses are different from anyone else's. We may grow physically and even emotionally—but not always "spiritually."

On the other hand, even an active and apparently advanced interior life is sometimes housed in a person who has been developmentally arrested at adolescence. This kind of arrest makes it feasible that an otherwise highly intelligent and evolved person could exploit somebody else. It is confusing for those of us who assume that the growth of the soul is in sync with all other stages of emotional development, especially if an abuser is entrusted with our spiritual welfare.

Perpetrators are often victims of childhood physical or sexual violation themselves. They are in a loop of reenactment born out of their own shame and revenge. Gershen Kaufman writes: "The scene of forcible violation is a reenactment, a transformation of a scene of equal powerlessness and humiliation experienced by the perpetrator at the hands of a different tormentor."[2]

The desire to possess what the other has or to possess the other altogether is primitive and probably unconscious. But those in power occasionally act as if their survival justifies siphoning the elixir of life from the vulnerable. It is especially tricky if the perpetrator is in a position of authority and apparently manifests charisma, wisdom, or holiness. It is something that we will return to again and again as we explore the complicated spider web of abuse.

THE QUESTION OF LOVE (AND CONNECTION, DILIGENCE, AND SEX)

Adulthood: the physical and psychological processes should be in some kind of alignment, and the individual appears ready to assume a responsive, if not responsible, place in community. Yet the signifiers of maturity are often ambiguous, especially in the spiritual realm.

As adults, we leave "home." This can be both a physical transition and an emotional undertaking. Ideally, we are in a position to experience a deeper connection with our own bodies, psyches, sexuality, and souls. We often seek and achieve true intimacy with another. As we progress through the decades, we incorporate what we have learned thus far with what is real to us in the moment.

In the reflection of our beliefs and values, we differentiate a deeper sense of self. We may encounter some tension in our individuality as we relate as adults to family or personal philosophy or religion and as we make our own meanings of things. It can be a time of intense critical rumination as we debunk more conceptions or systems of thought that we had left unexamined until now. We may take on a more complex interpretation of life that is reflected in our relationships, our judgments, and even our sense of humor.

As we think about the world outside and the world within, the truth may not be as black or as white as we once believed. In fact "truth" may be an acquired taste. At each phase of development, there are more and more subcategories to interpret and complete. If we are not yet finished with some of the emotional tasks from adolescence or even childhood, we can get stuck in a two-dimensional framework that informs or deforms our world views and relationships—and, of course, our inner life.

The adult process of understanding the connections that bundle this experience with a *God* or some ultimate meaning become more multifarious. It can wildly vary in life cycles, systems of thought, generations, and culture. Perhaps we find we need more structure to hold our thoughts together as a consequence of how we were raised or what we suffered. But the opposite may also be true for us. We may have to dispose of the old structure altogether and seek freedom in an entirely different approach to the divine or to the self.

I am [no longer] a practicing Catholic. I don't have any connection to or interest in the Catholic Church. I consider myself a spiritual person, but not connected to any religious dogma. I think in a way it's ridiculous to suggest that all of creation, all of life in its amazing and varied form, came to be because some inorganic chemicals met in a singles bar a couple billion years ago. That to me is as ridiculous as claiming that you can speak for God because he came to you and told you that he wanted me to give you two hundred dollars for a new temple. I guess my philosophy is the golden rule: no more, no less. If that's in place, all is possible; if it's lacking, then nothing is possible. (Joseph)

It is significant to note how earlier trauma plays out in the life cycle as we reach this point in our inner lives. Those who were once strictly religious but have experienced some form of abuse in their church or sect may dissolve their ties with religion altogether. Others, because of a powerful experience like narrowly missing death or finding sobriety after a life of chaos, may find their own meaning in a newfound structure of belief.

Sometimes, when devout people are exposed to new environments away from the familiar, their inner rules change. There may be situations that require new skill sets, which can be empowering or liberating. Even with the inevitable travels and travails, experiences like this can sprout an awakening that sets a new direction for an inner life no matter when it happens in a life cycle. When there is this kind of interior growth, the emphasis on rules and regulations can give way to a deeper internal code of behavior and practice.

Sometimes individuals discover another experience or journey within that has a completely different framework than what they would have ever imagined. It can happen with a book or a meeting, a trip away from one's own culture, or perhaps with a profoundly disturbing or inspiring incident.

It is difficult to describe with words what happens to those who have a powerful spiritual or mystical experience. Their inner journeys can lead them to a greater depth of knowledge and understanding of their universe—or self-delusion. Nevertheless, authentic mystical experience does not necessarily belong to a religion, although every religion has its mystics. It can happen suddenly and only once—or, after long years of intentional practice, be a constant steady state of being. It can be a direction, an impulse toward transcendence, a condition of unknowing—but quite the opposite of ignorance. Hazrat Inayat Khan, a Sufi, says it cannot be studied or put into words. "The beauty which the knower knows and the lover appreciates, the mystic worships."[3]

What often manifests in art or music or in the wellsprings of language for us may also give evidence of something less concrete: a new quieting prayer, a budding meditative state, perhaps the trembling wondrous experience of silence. While it may or may not have anything to do with an organized belief system, it can be a profoundly interior experience. The images and paradoxes of the past may also break into the present, which can enrich or complicate an inner conversation. Our first excursions of the spirit create a tender openness in the soul, which is akin to an earlier fragile innocence. It makes our contacts with spirituality even more poignant and initially more vulnerable.

I had a couple of spiritual experiences after that appointment. One of them, two of them were pretty profound; I attributed those experiences to that meeting with him. What else could I do? Because I've never had anything like that happen before in my life. In any event, those made me have extreme faith in this person. . . . This man was real. He was a real holy man. What else was I to think? (Eleanor)

It is at such a time that, even as fully formed adults, we are susceptible to abuses by those in power—like clergy, mentors, spiritual directors, or gurus. Because the good and bad elements of religion are often mixed up together, betrayal at this time still confuses perception. If we have been abused before and the violation now happens under the auspices of healing the spirit, there can be profound damage, even to the circuitry in the brain. The impact on our inner life can be as devastating as childhood trauma.

How is it that those who do the harm could seem so profoundly stunted that they desecrate the deepest part of themselves by harming ones placed in their spiritual care? How can they so drastically compartmentalize the ideals they espouse from what they do to others? The incongruities between their philosophies and their actions are often so confounding that it is easier for a community to blame their victims than to metabolize the truth about their spiritual leaders or members. It often falls on the ability of the community to bear an unbearable truth: that even those who represent the highest good are at times capable of evil. Such a realization in itself is possible only if people in the community have the developmental capacity to grasp the twin possibilities of both holiness and harmful actions by their spiritual leaders and the stomach to do something about it.

Communities sometimes adopt a group-mind that differs developmentally from what prevails when their members are operating alone. The strength and maturity of a group can help to elevate individual members to think more expansively. But the opposite is true, as well, as a narrow dogma can influence a community's relationship to race, gender, sexual identity, tolerance of other traditions—and recognition of possible abuse in-house. The ability of the leadership to instill empowerment and freedom into spiritual life may have a lot to do with whether a religious community can tolerate flexibility and withstand controversy or scandal. Either way, individuals have an ethical responsibility to think and to investigate for themselves.

THE QUESTION OF INTEGRITY (AND CONNECTION, DILIGENCE, SEX AND LOVE)

Somewhere around midlife, there may be a crisis of sorts for us, as well as a critical juncture in our development. The losses of youth, the accumulation of power or accomplishment, professional advancements, our immobilities, or the life passages of our own children affect us on many fronts. This may be a time when many of us are in a position to give back some of what we have gleaned from life, free of the restrictions that bound us at earlier times. It may be at this stage in life that we focus on new ways to expand our individual concerns to a larger venue. We may experience a renewed capacity for imagination, reinvigorated by what we have learned thus far. Our ego may not be so captivated with itself. In fact, at times we may be able to almost disappear from having to play center stage, not only in front of others but also inside of our own mind.

After a lifetime of practice some of us reach a state when we have moments of pure immersion and concentration in what we do. We may experience both a high degree of awareness and a loss of self consciousness. This *flow*[4] is mastery at a high level. One who has achieved such a state also seems young in spirit and quite open to innovation and new ideas. Often there are no words to describe such a state of being, except being fully "alive."

One hopes that the passage of time could conclude with both the fruition of significance and outer success. Yet sometimes life's journeys do not bring such evolution. They may instead engender stagnation, greed, overextension, or cynicism. If our ego has not developed beyond its identifiers, we are stuck in self-conservation because we cannot imagine how we can *be* anything else. This is when vanity or hubris show up as almost pathetic or desperate attempts to cling to the past. Instead of expansiveness, we can become jealous or contemptuous of younger, more elastic souls. Our fears make us suspicious of joy. At any moment, the truth may reveal itself and the sterility of our real inner state be unmasked. The challenge instead is to feel our fear—the fear of aging, of losing our minds or our looks, of death—and fully live. Pushing such an envelope can free up much of the energy that has been trapped by our concerns.

At the later stages of our development there is the potential for real wisdom and integrity, acceptance of life as it is, deep compassion, and an expansiveness of perspective. A violation or calamity at this stage may not necessarily shake us. Even those of us who have experienced a holocaust or the brutalities of war or genocide have the potential to extrapolate meaning and significance in the midst of horror. We may be able to interpret suffering with a divine perspective, or perhaps our understanding will have a less definable (less personal, if you will) sense of the ground of existence. The old norms may cease to apply. We may learn to be authentic or as authentic as we can possibly be. Sometimes it is because we have lost so much that we see no reason to hold to the old paradigms. We might find resolution with what is gone or what is in the process of dying—or we may not . . .

Good things come out of bad things. One thing I've had to say about my life: if this hadn't happened, I don't know that I'd be as strong as I am, because I think I'm pretty strong. It's so interesting, as a child brought up Lutheran, I was very religious as a child. I was going to be a missionary. I think you develop a kind of concept of *God*. Then I became an atheist and then fell into my spiritual path, and knew exactly what *God* was. And then—it's like . . . stumbling away. (Eleanor)

Disillusionment can come, but everything does not necessarily fall apart. As in all stages of life, there are many possibilities.

THE QUESTION OF LIFE (AND CONNECTION, DILIGENCE, SEX, LOVE, AND INTEGRITY)

The prospect of older age and the events that precede the end of life provide the true test of all previous developmental tasks, especially those that have not been met. It can be a Catch-22, especially when or if we long so deeply for what we once had and are still bound by old life scripts.

> I try prayer. I don't know, I'm supposed to get comfort and healing and so forth. But I don't know. It scares me, too. I'm 56 years old; I have less time in front of me than in back of me. . . . I don't want to die, knowing—I still feel this indelible spot on my soul—It shows up. I can't erase it, you know? I'm just not good enough on some level . . . the Catholic thing rearing its ugly head again. (William)

It is at such a time that old habits, past traumas, and unfinished business come to roost. If we have nothing but old inner markers to hold to, we may be fearful or bitter about what seems to be the loss of our faith or other philosophical girdles that held us in place. Some of us approach death as we may have lived, clinging to our identity, helplessness, or regret. We might culminate our existence with the same fear, anger, or secrets that we lived with all this time. Many of us do not release life or loved ones so easily. We may have disappointments and regrets about our lives. But even our disillusionment can serve us; it can break us open. After a life of betrayals or spiritual loss, there is still the potential for other possibilities. At this stage, we could actually choose how to evolve.

We may be willing to let go of our health and vitality, and even our cognitive abilities with some acceptance and peace and perhaps anticipate what comes next with openness.

We may have an opportunity to come to terms with our own lives and prepare for the adventure ahead called death, however difficult it is to imagine.

> The idea that there's a big-ass calendar with one day that's got a red circle around it—and that we're not here anymore—that the world will get up and people will still deliver newspapers and eat tofu and screw and borrow money from each other and clip their toe nails—and we're not here—we can't process that! (Joseph)

But we die. There is no getting around it. It can be as liberating or as fearsome as we wish to make it.

However it ends, people from ancient spiritual traditions corroborate what the scientific community reports about the time of death: that individuals enter a sphere hard to define but significant to witness. In many ways, this transition can resemble a reverse sequence of conception as each system in the body and brain consecutively closes down.

Those who have had near-death experiences say that at this point, one often remembers every incident and thought he or she ever experienced in exquisite detail. There may be a struggle to hold on in the face of the unknown. But, at the bridge between life and death, even in the midst of extreme torture and violence, a rush of endorphins is released into the system that blocks out pain.

Researchers also report that individuals who have survived a clinical death have a greater zest for life; their concern about material possessions is diminished, they have more confidence and a real sense of the purpose about the rest of their lives. They often become more spiritually enthusiastic and have a greater sense of tolerance and compassion. They also may have a reduced fear of death because of what they have experienced.

Witnesses describe those individuals as exhibiting a quality of peace or perceptible bliss, appearing to possess an intensified self-awareness, a profound and indescribable peace and calmness just before death. Many who had no particular belief system speak of an unmistakable benevolent presence as they move back and forth between death and life. The dying might report a kind of comprehensive knowledge and light. This light appears to be visual, but it is combined with a sense of boundless love. It is difficult to describe with words without resorting to old belief paradigms that have little to do with personal experience.[5]

For persons who have had a lifetime of intense interior practice, the transition from a state of deep meditation into death may appear to be an almost seamless movement. It is not always easy to distinguish when life actually ends.

Our journey of life is a process affected by so very many variables. Throughout our cycles, we have had opportunities for development and occasions of impediment. But it is our birthright to grow physically, mentally *and* spiritually, in freedom and safety, no matter when or how it unfolds.

For some of us, it seems that we still cling to air instead of words. But the heart is a relentless engine of longing. It remembers something from longer than ago: when sound was unimaginably still, when space was unimaginably safe, when something was unimaginably there. The soul makes its journey, even amid devastating violence or confounding evil. The soul makes its way, perhaps despite us.

We have been born, we have lived, and we die with immense possibilities for the soul. Even with the compromises of mind and spirit that trauma can bring, there is also the surprising ability to respond to life with compassion and kindness until the last moment of existence.

It is this very capacity of fierce grace that will see us through as we look at the dark side of religion, and the soul's tenacity and resilience in the face of it.

RECOMMENDED READINGS

Fourteenth Dalai Lama, Jerome Engel, Jayne Gackenbach, Ph.D., Joan Halifax, Ph.D., Joyce McDougall, D. Ed., Charles Taylor, Ph.D. and Francisco Varela Ph.D. *Sleeping, Dreaming, and Dying, An Exploration of Consciousness*. Boston: Wisdom Publications, 1997.

Fowler, James W. *Stages of Faith: The Psychology of Human Development*. San Francisco: Harper, 1981.

Hoffman, Richard. "The Hatred of Innocence," *Boston Globe*, November 1998.

Levine, Stephen, and Ondrea Levine. *Who Dies? An Investigation of Conscious Living and Conscious Dying*. New York: Anchor Books, 1982.

CHAPTER 3

—— ✠ ——

Hell's Prayer Room: When Religion Is the Abuser

Someone who doesn't make flowers makes thorns. If you're not building rooms where wisdom can be openly spoken, you're building a prison.

—Shams of Tabriz

This is your blood
This is your body
This is your muscle
These are your cells
This is your heart
And, this is your heart
Here is your hat
Here is your veil
This is your bread, your meat, the milk, the sweet
These are your candles
Your water
Your smoke
Here is your table,
This must be your music
Your mantra, your mala
This is Medina. . .
Here is the book
There is the Prophet
This is Our Savior
Our Guru, our Teacher
Our Father, Our Mother
The Mother of Bliss
The Mother of Sorrow
The Mother of *God*
The Mother of Satan

This is the wall
Here is the ground
This is the door
That is the gate
Here is the road
And surely the way
This is the end. . .
And truly the kingdom
Of Heaven
Of Mecca
The city of Mandi
Palani
Palmyra
The holy Al-Najaf
The mountain of Sinai
The Temple of Salt Lake
The riot of Stonewall
This is your home
This is your home
No, this is your home . . .
Oh, dearly Beloved
Dearly Departed
Dearly Anointed
Dearly Appointed
Better be blessed
Better be saved
Better be ware
Better be damned
Better be gone
Better be still

—Mikele Rauch

OPENING THE DOOR

The first vision by a prophet (or *divine being*) births a transformation from the ordinary plane of living to something *wholly other*. Those who witness a prophet of this magnitude probably experience their own inner revolution and see the possibility of transformation in themselves. They may spend their entire lives keeping in sight or under the direction of that visionary. Sometimes these visions plant the seed of a religious movement.

The beginning of such a movement is neither intellectual nor linear, although later it will likely be dissected, deconstructed, and demythologized. The ones who come next will begin the process of cataloging the information and creating a methodology around what those at the beginning experienced directly. The next generations are the ones to build buildings, make rituals, write scriptures, and create laws to celebrate or commemorate the original vision.

Only a few fully achieve the vision, yet every religion bases its life on set standards inspired by that first inspiration regarding all manner of human life: what a person eats, one's sexuality, family life, and social responsibilities; and how one engages intellectual and spiritual curiosity. Religion characterizes a way of life and often prepares a person for death. It can create communities and divide them. Sometimes religion and the experience of what theologian Rudolf Otto called the *wholly other* can generate great art and music—and occasionally these are the very things that are later suspect to the keepers of the faith. The artists and musicians may bring vibrancy to religious life and at times a more accessible sense of the divine. But art and music can also create inner revolutions in people that the religious leadership cannot always control. Throughout religious history, there has often been a tension between the artists and the hierarchy. While they may need each other, they do not necessarily trust each other with the soul of the community.

Sometimes religion provides a replica of spiritual experience without any true connection to the experience, where the simulation becomes more "real" than the truth. Jean Baudrillard describes this as *simulacrum*, a phenomenon demonstrated when reality and meaning are replaced with symbols and signs and human experience becomes a simulation of reality rather than reality itself. Baudrillard notes the stages of such a simulation: first there is a reflection of a profound reality; it then masks the profound reality; eventually even masking the absence of a profound reality; but it has no relationship with a profound reality at all and becomes only a representation of it.[1] If religion masks or perverts the original vision, or if it simply covers over the absence of it, the external manifestation becomes more "real" than the internal authenticity it represents.

ENTERING THE HOUSE

Religion is set up to give a structure to something seemingly impossible to define: the deep and sometimes overwhelming experience of the ultimate meaning of existence. This generates cosmology and institutions that create practices, rituals, dogmas, codes, prayers, processes of behavior, and suppositions about the importance of intentional life. Mythologies serve to give significance to religious history, and those who practice religion hold the stories and sacred texts in literal or figurative degrees.

For many, religion is the family of the family. It is the skin over the blood and sinew of ancestry. Religious affiliations provide kinship that replicate the familial connection, no matter where members live. Religious life may even set the cultural tone for private life and dictate personal matters more than one's own family. But the nature of the individual family also indicates more specifically how religion is practiced and whether or not there is integrity in that practice. In some families and for some individuals, the religious culture can override personal "response-ability" and even conscience, creating a dilemma when it comes to one's own principles and morality. Quandaries about race, social justice, sexual orientation, children's rights, the role of women, and spiritual practice may complicate allegiances.

While churches or temples are often the main center of community life, dictating family relations, social interactions, economic considerations, and moral regulations, what happens outside the boundaries of community or back at home behind the door may not always align with what occurs inside the church building. Currently, because of the Internet and international media, the world seems to be in conflict with traditional religious culture. It is happening in almost every part of the globe where people have access to computers and televisions; everybody is watching each other. Even in the most remote villages around the globe there are groups of men and women, boys and girls, who gather around a gleaming blue light coming off some small screen in a shop or who line up to use a computer in an Internet cafe. Although there is an economic and generational gap about how the Internet gets used, access to information and conversations take place among people all over the planet, opening the potential for possibilities in religious life and education (including indoctrination) that would have been incomprehensible in even in the last part of the twentieth century.

At times like these, it is possible to be a secular member of a religion without having direct contact with a particular practice or community, except for holidays or life events like weddings or funerals, or to be a religious zealot without having any exposure or interest in an inner life. One's spiritual affiliation may be quite unrelated to any religious realm or location at all. But the influence of religious culture can play its part on the psyche, nevertheless, despite where, how much, or how little it is practiced.

> We look at religion as the ultimate paradigm if you like, a way of living that carries within it fundamental truths that nobody can challenge. When you talk about morality; and other similar issues, even the source of many forms of legislations, constitutions, goes back to religion. I mean, religion basically contributed to it. It's only recently that we started talking about human rights, women's rights, and alike. The United Nations basically drafted new charters to regulate human conduct and set boundaries that limit governments from abusing their own citizens and regulate relations between nations. But, if you think about it, other than those recent developments in ideas, most of our traditions, values, and customs that relate to marriage, to children, to community, the source of them all seems to go back to religion, and it is the same in every society. (Rasan)

BEHIND THE DOOR

Whether one's connection with religion is secular or religious, there are often specified relationships between religious members and family units. Those within the religious community may enjoy special privileges of care and intimacy within the family because their associations represent the most sacred and the safest relationship of all.

If the individuals who represent the religious community engage in a violation with another member, especially a child, the devastation can be as confounding and as detrimental as any that could happen inside a family. The effect of this kind of abuse is deep because the source of the betrayal is so close, as close as kin. Further, the family and the community around it are often blind to what is happening right in front of their eyes, or, worse, may protect the perpetrator at the expense of the survivor.

It may seem unthinkable to a community that one who represents the highest good could be capable of an infraction like this, but it *is* possible. Such violations make a mockery of sacred space and sacred trust.

For a child like William, it would have been inconceivable in his religious culture or in his own family to question what was about to happen to him—and therefore it was inconceivable for him.

> I don't know the mind of a predator—how it works is something I can't fully comprehend. But he just started by complimenting me and my penmanship and how well I did and how well I answered the questions and wrote on the tests or whatever and then proceeded to walk out with me to the school bus, start chatting about nothing in particular. Then he put his hand on my shoulders; we walked out to the school bus. (William)

He remembers the priest grooming him for the sexual abuse with the bitter understanding of his own mother's unconscious complicity.

> He said that he'd like to come over to my house some time. I still had no idea what was going on; I did think it a little odd the extra attention I was getting, but I couldn't put two and two together. Then in the afternoon, Mom said he called and he's on his way over, and the Irish Catholic woman that she was— she was just so excited he was coming over. And he sat in the kitchen with her and myself and said I would be an excellent candidate to become a priest by the way I expressed myself. He had permission by my Mom to basically have free reign with me. (William)

Children do not usually have the choice or power to do anything about how religious abuses affect them. They mostly know only how to comply with what is most familiar to them.

OUTSIDE THE HOUSE

Sometimes communities participate in the covert abuse of their members by not having the courage to voice what they see either because of blind ignorance, or because their own discomfort with the truth provides the morally vile excuse to deny it.

In William's Irish Catholic culture, it was inconceivable that a betrayal would ever take place at the hands of *God's* representative. Even when people on the outside saw something was wrong, nobody made the effort to do anything about it.

> We were just stopped at a stop light when I was sitting next to him, and he basically French kissed me and my eyes would dart and I'd see other drivers drive by. I'd see them turn and I'd see their eyes connect with my eyes and they immediately looked away. I'm thinking, "Oh my goodness!" You know? And then the little part of me says, "Why won't somebody stop, blow their horn, something?" (William)

The violation is double when those who should know and be responsible deny what is right before their eyes.

> So at what level did people feel something might be going on, or were they completely oblivious? There was one nun in particular who actually made a lot of the arrangements for me to go back and forth. And . . . it's curious to me that she wouldn't actually wonder if something was going on, um, or if her own relationship to the hierarchy or to her orders disallowed her to ask questions. (Victor)

Often, when there are discrepancies in religious tradition that ostensibly promote social justice and basic human rights, victims of abuse face not only humiliation for themselves but repercussions for their families, while the community often bears and abdicates its own responsibility to see or to do anything about these discrepancies.

> I was gang-raped by three people I knew, and I couldn't say anything, because in my culture, your family is dishonored if you lose your virginity. So I kept quiet, and the rapes continued. The next time, I was pulled off a commuter train, and no one lifted a finger to help me. Everybody turned their head away. They were all looking out the window. (Samila Bellil)[2]

Naturally, there are cultural and personal contexts that color any transaction. Certain customs or practices that seem to be abusive to the outside may be woven into the fabric of the community tradition, so it may be hard to identify them as abuse.

Female circumcision, for instance, is a particular Muslim custom that ignites strong feeling in many Western advocates for women and children, especially as there is no reference to it in the Qur'an or in medical theory. Yet, the argument against it becomes more intricate depending on the country and the manner in which it is done. As Western awareness of female genital cutting has grown, anthropologists, policymakers, and health officials warn against blindly judging those who practice it, saying that progress is best made by working with local leaders and opinion makers to gradually shift the public discussion of female circumcision from what it is believed to bestow upon a girl and toward what it takes away.[3]

What does not get much notice is the growing support for modernizing Islamic jurisprudence and the revival of *ijtihad*, which was once a vibrant Islamic tradition of independent thinking and reasoning about sacred texts. There are also many differences among women within political and religious Islam. Christina Hoff Summers writes eloquently that many Muslim women may not agree about whether to wear the veil or whether their mosques should be divided by sex, but "what unites them is commitment to the universal dignity of women." They are opposed to forced marriages, honor killings, genital cutting, child marriage, and wife beating and are dedicated to the educational, economic, legal, and political advancement of women.[4]

It is important to note here that cultural sensitivity, personal philosophies about sexual freedom, or identity politics do not adequately cover the contexts of gender, race, or class in the world or even in one country. Within each framework, none are equal in gravity. Summers gives a compelling example of the irresponsibility of some Western feminists who equate their struggles and those of the women in repressive misogynist cultures without distinguishing their differences. Comparing the rapes of American girls in suburban stadium parking lots with acid burning or genital mutilation is unfair for example. No woman should experience these in any culture or religion. But to make these situations equal in scale or gravity is a reckless misuse of scholarship and doesn't help either cause. Luckily, Muslim women are not waiting for Western feminists to sort this out. Devoutly religious women are quietly organizing to resist. Summers notes that "the feminism that is quietly surging in the Muslim world is quite different from its contemporary counterpart in the United States. Islamic feminism is faith-based, family-centered, and well-disposed towards men."[5]

But who or how one is oppressed or abused may continue to be a difficult call to make from the outside. Values and tradition are circumstantial by country and religious ethos and should be observed that way, except when it comes to children and their right to safety, protection from violence, freedom from sexual and physical servitude, and the concerns of every person regarding full respect and human dignity. As the planet becomes "smaller," the questions around oppression and individual human rights of women and children will become increasingly more complex. Cultural mores will often collide as people from differing contexts enter each other's spheres. Even in the Internet age, as human beings are exposed to the others outside their culture, tradition, or religion without enough information or meaningful contact, many may react by becoming insular and tribal instead of more inclusive and open.

For adults, personal choices also profoundly affect their rights in their families and culture, prompting some to choose to leave their ethnic or religious fold. Irit, for example, is an Israeli Jew who married Rasan, a Palestinian Muslim. Unconditional love and the solidarity of her family had been her birthright—until her marriage.

Then everything changed.

> Just three days before my sister died, she saw my father and told him that I was going to get married. She asked him to forgive me. He didn't. When my sister passed away three days after, my family sat for the Jewish shiv'a. My father said, "I'm actually sitting shiv'a for my two daughters." He was the only one who was saying that and actually went along with it for the rest of his life. Basically, I was banned from my family for the twenty-some years. (Irit)

The organization of religion relative to race and location may define not only a particular family but also nationality and national identity. Irit experienced both the privilege and the pain of her heritage. In many other places in the world, her Judaism would set her apart as a minority, yet, because of her marital choice, she now lives in Palestine. She knows the ironic paradox of being both a minority and a dominant power.

> I would have never known what it's like to be oppressed; I would never know what it's like to be Palestinian, to be a minority. To be on the other side, you never know it until you are there, until you go in and out. For me there was a way and a time that if I felt—it was too much. I had an escape way. I could go to the nearest Jewish town, speak with my accent and be *me* again, while they [her children] didn't have that escape. So I learned how they feel—but not really—because I had an escape. (Irit)

She now describes the woeful dichotomy of her advantage as an Israeli Jew in Israel, as it relates to traveling with her own daughter.

> They put the sticker on my daughter's suitcase saying she's dangerous and put a different sticker on mine saying I'm less dangerous. They have decided who between us belongs and who does not. It's me and my daughter that they are separating now. I got mad. I took off my shoes, because they were asking for daughter's shoes, and I said, "Don't you think *these* can be dangerous?" I stuck my shoes in his face, because he was taking my daughter's shoes. But he didn't take mine. "No," he said. "You are okay." So when they made the decision between me and my daughter, it hurt me. This is the paradox, the big advantage. (Irit)

How and what people learn beyond their religious culture can also go against them. Critical thinking, authentic questioning, or originality in spiritual inquiry may get squelched in the name of solidarity. If there are specific rules about *God*—who is first, who is chosen, who is family, and who is outside the fold—what happens when there is *no* space for dialogue or doubt and no variation allowed for life scripts, rituals, or prayer?

Religion falters when it closes off so much that it allows no range of view-point or expression of ideas, when its life and spirit are replaced by a grim adherence to shame-making formalities. When there is an excessive adherence to the letter of the law, the vibrancy of love and care can get riddled with scrupulosity, especially when precepts oddly eclipse the spirit of the original tenets. It is even difficult for some rule keepers who experience little spiritual exuberance of their own to tolerate those who live more jubilant, generous lives, even if the joyful are observant of the dictates of their religion.

Victor reminisces about the Catholic nun who had been his teacher at the time and recalls a disappointing exchange later in his life.

> So she asked me what I was doing then. . . . I talked about my work with the AIDS Action Committee, social action work, how I worked with child welfare. Her face was hardening and dropping at the same time. And she was folding up her yearbook and her papers that she had brought with her, and she said, "Well, aren't you just full of yourself?" I'm probably around my early thirties, and this is the response I'm getting. . . . I did take all those lessons early on and turned them into something good. And the message I got from her is that I'm just full of myself. (Victor)

Such an exchange has nothing to do with Victor being full of anything but his own fulfillment, which was a palpable and perhaps infuriating realization for the nun who may have been struggling with her own depleted spiritual state.

In some religious systems, it is more about social and familial connections than about beliefs or even experience when it comes to affiliation with the faith. Although the ideology can be the reason for the association, one's fear of abandonment by the community can be as great a deterrent as the difficulty of breaking the principles one espouses.

For a woman like Naomi, the Church had been her primary sustenance and connection since birth. She had been prepared to sacrifice everything for her community. It was inconceivable that she could be separated from it even when that community failed her husband and herself. When her husband, Shimon, had a crisis of conscience, and was deciding whether to stop attending church, Naomi's personal war between allegiance and principle created such a dilemma of fear that she had to reevaluate her place in the spiritual family:

> I was terrified about our salvation, and I was also terrified of our temporal life. What if Shimon gave up and stopped going to church? What would everyone think of us? Now I know that many people do think things because I was one of them, and I thought that I was nicer about it than a lot of people. I could still see they were good people and believed God would be kind, but I still thought that they weren't focusing on what mattered most or had sins to clear up, that kind of thing. I didn't want my family to be looked at that way. I didn't want my husband to be the one left sitting at baby blessings and outside the temple at weddings. (Naomi)

Shimon's own relationship with his community was both a lifeline and a strangling rope. The legacy of his Jewish heritage almost seemed to be in his very DNA, despite the pressure from the religion he was raised in (the Church of Jesus Christ of Latter-day Saints) to disregard it. He is currently a Reconstructionist Jew, having resigned from the LDS Church.

The story of Shimon's father's own religious conversion was one of death and loss, betrayal and love. Shimon's father and his mentally ill sister were secular Jewish orphans but had been turned away from their synagogue during high holy days at an hour of great need. The LDS Church took them in. While Shimon's own story is connected to his father's dramatic history of betrayal by the synagogue and, later, by the LDS Church, as well, it is enough for us to note that, from an early age, Shimon was raised with the dichotomy of being in two worlds:

> I grew up with a sense of confusion here in Utah. My father had this intensely Jewish identity but we were Mormon. . . . One of the dilemmas I faced is that I learned Jewish thinking from my father. This involved asking a lot of questions, critical thinking skills, and debating skills. As I reflect back on it, this really didn't fit into Mormon culture very well . . . My first word was, "Why?" You know, I remember as a kid when I wanted to know something, I said "Why?" and they would answer, and I'd ask them "Why?" about that. I thought if you could push that far enough, someone would give you an answer that meant something. But usually—no—they just got mad at you. (Shimon)

Shimon grew up with the tension between his two religious worlds—his analytical Jewish side, which was suspect, and the philosophically conservative Mormon part, which was both tenuous and fearful. In this irresolvable situation, he had to choose between compromising accommodation or permanent consequences.

> My family grew up with this paranoia after my father's betrayal by the Church, that at any moment, if you misstep, bad things could happen to you. . . . It's not just that you would be shunned, I mean . . . they would take your salvation. They were going to take your reasons for existing. I think even that would not have been so bad except that with [our] situation, unlike some, there wasn't even any hope. You couldn't repent, because you hadn't done anything wrong whatsoever to influence the outcome, which was very frightening if you're talking about eternal consequences. (Shimon)

The price of self-determination may be costly, especially with a religious community that cannot bend. Shimon, a heterosexual man, found himself in an ethical dilemma when, as a psychotherapist working with gay clients, he had to confront the Church's position on homosexuality.

> I think possibly because of my own journey, I have a real sense of empathy for what homosexuals in our Church must go through—this complete inability

to fit in, ever. And the knowledge that at any moment who you truly are, if anyone knew that—I was horrified by this dilemma and realized this isn't something that ever goes away for a lot of people, and it's not like they can choose to be different! (Shimon)

He wondered how he would be able to do ethical therapy with gays and lesbians when he disagreed with the LDS teaching that homosexuality is a psychological disease and should be "cured." He simply could not justify such a position.

This is religious teaching that would harm people who actually are most in need of healing, because they've suffered, not that it's wrong, but that they've been suffering in silence, and unable to talk to anyone. (Shimon)

It was Shimon's deliberation process that led him, in the end, to take on the rule of church authority. Shimon had been reading books about other religions and asking questions about *God* that were forbidden in his own community.

I can't force that on them, I have to tell them I don't think I can help them, I'm wondering if that's what I need to do as a therapist, so I started reading about it, and the more I read about it, the more it's clear. I can see that the Church doesn't know anything about this. (Shimon)

Shimon's mind was a relentless engine of inquiry despite the coercion of the Church, and even when his conclusions made him a heretic in his religious culture.

And this time, I said to myself, "That is stupid, if ideas are that dangerous, then *God* did something wrong. I am going to find out what this idea is that I just glimpsed a vision of, because if I don't follow my mind and look at the idea, how can I be an honest person?" (Shimon)

To question and test information is the lifeblood of spiritual inquiry. The methodology and the results are based not only on traditional scientific method but on a vigorous process of discernment, which is an inner search for truth. And, for Shimon, his personal truth was in conflict with his Church. Ultimately, his own analytical process produced the painful but important next step.

And all the sudden, I found that my entire view of what *God* was and how *God* interacted with me was different. It was terrifying because I didn't know what to do with it. The scriptures work but the institution doesn't work. I can do it with their books, but I can't do it with their Church, and this was a terrible dilemma for me. (Shimon)

Between the Church and his truth, Simon opted for truth. It was a lonely choice.

SHUTTING THE DOOR

Sometimes religious communities cordon off their collective souls to simplify the confusion and behavior that is at odds with their teachings. It is difficult for individuals in these groups to decide how to push against the standard. They may fall prey to habits of inertia and convention, which are often even more potent because they are unconscious. The community's silent policies of engagement may have nothing to do with the spirit of the religion.

If individuals are children or are already psychologically compromised, some of the rules and regulations can override anything else and create a vicious cycle of compulsivity. The push-pull of approval and rejection can drive other self-destructive habits and obsessive thinking and behaviors. If the individual is a child who is already concerned about offending God, it can present a fearsome dilemma.

> I would be afraid of going to sleep at night, night after night, out of fear that I would have done something wrong during the day, I would die during my sleep, and I would end up in the flames of hell. It isn't that I didn't sleep, obviously I did, but it's the fear of dying, and wondering whether or not I was okay with this God. (Chris)

There was a double bind about doing anything wrong, or almost doing anything at all.

> This created what the Church would call becoming *scrupulous*, which they said was a sin itself; worrying too much was something that I shouldn't be doing. So I become *scrupulous*, which again in retrospect are the roots of obsessive-compulsive features, which I've had all my life. I can clearly see now that it all came from the Church's teachings and the instilling of that level of terror about living and about just going to sleep at night. (Chris)

Children and adolescents who are psychologically or economically impoverished may also become prime candidates for militant religious movements that make it palatable to target, hate—or kill the *other*. When young people learn to disgrace, mutilate, or torture others for the sake of religion, they dehumanize themselves and the ones they harm. Dr. Umar Faruq Abd-Allah, scholar-in-residence at the Nawawi Foundation, a nonprofit educational foundation dedicated to the promotion of relevant and meaningful Muslim teachings, calls this kind of stance a form of *spiritual autism* in religion, in which a person in the community can become detached from his or her own essential personhood and see others as things instead of humans. There is a kind of religious patriotism that divides *us* from *them*, a frequent use of the epithet "evil" for whomever the *other* is, and perhaps a sense that one's own religious suffering is unique and without parallel. It shows up with the compulsive adherence to the rules and rituals and in immense resistance or confusion if there is a change in protocol. Actions of violence or retribution that would be intolerable for an individual become virtuous to the group. The unthinkable is then justified.

Religion fails when its truth is so selective that those out of alignment with its uniform codes of conduct are shunned, punished, or killed. The future for its adherents becomes fearsome, especially if there is a deviation from the prescribed observances. Rewards and punishments depend on how individuals follow the rules, *unless* they themselves are in a position of authority. If the leaders operate under their own set of rules, this behavioral discrepancy creates a crisis of morality not only for them but also for every person in that community. If the only way to be part of such a system is for members to adhere to what they have been told, even if it goes against their integrity, the community loses its interior compass.

CLOSING THE GATE

Religious (and political) attitudes of intolerance and narrowness—even militarism in some organizations—that often trump the original values of their founders, these standards are not always intellectual or spiritual stances: these reactionary characteristics are far more sociological than anything else. A religious tradition may have an extremist subgroup that unconsciously has more in common with its religious "enemies" than with its own philosophy. Such factions in each religious tradition are more similar to one another in their reactivity to theological modernism and intellectual inquiry and often seem to share these general characteristics:

- The church, temple, or synagogue is the central, perhaps the only activity or focus in the family.
- Acceptance into the particular religious community is based on extremely specific criteria, which have few or no variations.
- There is a closed-door mentality regarding what is allowed and available from information or new material from the outside: this stance is often solidified and protected by an authoritarian power structure.
- Science, research, and dialogue are seen as dangerous.
- Personal judgment in certain communities is not to be trusted unless there is a central (usually) male figure in the family or community.
- Evil and weakness appear to come from a failure to comply with the precepts of authority. The evil and weakness are then projected on those outside the system. Interactions with those "outsiders" is discouraged or even punished, unless the community members are evangelizing.
- Love is conditional; the only way to merit *God's* or the community's acceptance is to follow the party line or be in that particular sect.
- Sex, sexual orientation, and gender roles are often rigidly defined.
- Humor is not to be trusted.

ople operate in fear, which becomes more prevalent than freedom or joy.[6]

- Truth becomes absolute and unchanging.
- There is little tolerance for ambiguity.
- There *are* no exceptions.

These tenets describe the characteristics of a religious *fundamentalism*, when there is a total commitment and belief in the infallibility of a particular scripture, as well as strict compliance with religious authority: fear, insularity, exclusivity, and rigid physical observance of the law are the mode of operation.

> I think there are certain religious communities that are invested in seeing themselves as unique and at the same time oppressed. For that, they can inflict punishment on others and see their acts as justified. Their historical suffering blocks their ability to see their own ill-doing. (Irit)

A community like this often operates in permanent post-traumatic stress: it is locked in a response of terror and paralysis about possibilities that threaten its very existence. There is a sense that what is *outside* the community is harmful. Such a community recognizes itself only as victim. In this way, there is little opportunity to take responsibility for the oppression of others. The community knows only how to continue this cycle of oppression into either the next generation or whomever is the *other* to them.

When there is only *one* acceptable way to go about the business of life, God becomes both distant and anthropomorphic. Those with this point of view use the worst of their own personal characteristics as descriptors of their God. God loves or hates because they love or hate. They hijack the original tenet of the vision and adopt a legalistic and paranoid rendition of their own projections instead. It can become difficult for members to endure the stringent desiccation of their spirit for long without succumbing to more mean-spirited manifestations of their shadow, all in the name of God.

Naomi struggled mightily to reconcile her personal principles with what she had been told to believe throughout her life. The story of her own spiritual evolution mirrored her husband's crisis of conscience. Naomi's dilemma produced a cataclysm in her own mind because her decision to follow her own sense of right and wrong eventually resulted in expulsion from her community.

> I remember our own family conversations about less active people where we loved them but knew *we* were the enlightened ones. I wanted to stay and fix the Church until I found myself so broken this was not an option. (Naomi)

Naomi had to struggle just to make sense of her decisions, what they meant for her relationships with her family and with the only community she had ever known:

The Church claims to have all authority concerning the eternal relationship with all of you, and I fear they hold all the temporal authority, too. I remember seeing my old young women's president at the symphony. I knew she could not be wearing her [Mormon] garments under her dress and realized she must not be active anymore. I felt physically sick. I fear evoking that feeling in people I care about because I know it can happen. I worry, if people stay in the Church, how can they ever accept me? The things I internalized from lessons cry loudly that they will not. (Naomi)

There is a brittle fragility to holding on to such undeviating adherence to a power structure or a particular doctrine. Secret fetishes, sadism, pornography, sexual and physical abuse, masochism, self-injury, or suicide often become the underbelly of such rigidity. Those who dictate one thing in public may actually practice another in private. This particular mind-bind exists in the darkness of undercover despicable actions. The shadows seem to show up when people hide their demons from the rest of the community or simply close down in depression, hopelessness, or isolation.

Ideals and, consequently, rules do change over the years because of war, prejudice, or simple exposure to other people. But communities can take their historical sense of being chosen, being oppressed, being singled out, or being the demon—and act it out generation after generation.

Irit speaks of how this plays out for herself and others.

If you live in a small community like a ghetto, anyone else is considered an outsider, and when you exit that closed community, your act is certainly seen as betrayal. Over time and after many generations, this turns into a pattern, which becomes a historical force that starts to affect the psychology of the political behavior of people in their daily life at the present. When I go back, I've tried to observe Israelis on the airplane, at the airport. Often I have this feeling of discomfort around them. I don't really feel comfortable going anywhere else. (Irit)

Comfort may be confused with safety, but it is not necessarily the case. When religions reject any openness to the possibilities of diversity, they can lose their perspective and possibly contract into narrow-mindedness or even militant bigotry. It is an unfortunate complication of insularity.

OUTSIDE THE GATE

Beware of the emotions that are hosts to violence, for they lead to sorrow

—Mary Strong

There are religions that ardently insist that they are "equal but different," yet have an underlying agenda about power and who has access to it. That power frequently rests with the one with the *penis*—unless he is openly gay.

Male preeminence remains the central paradigm in most church institutions and religious systems. The symbols of heterosexual male dominance are manifest in family structures, in the hierarchy, even in art and architecture. Even so, homosexuality may be the open secret of many religions' closeted clergy; for in every religious tradition with a literalist bias, the "closet" usually is closed. There are always exceptions, of course. A religion that either condemns homosexuality or denies that it exists within their communities faces enormous challenges to be authentic, compassionate—and transparent.

When the requirement for traditional perfection is to be part of a nuclear family with a *female* wife, a *masculine* husband, and dependent children, and when the only way to be a credible member of a spiritual community is to be straight, the conflict inside can be unbearable.

> Being gay in [the Mormon] culture is beyond hell. I wanted to be cured so badly. The family is the center of Mormonism; it is the sacred, potent unit. It is a great failure that family can only be the family almost by the Ozzie and Harriet definition, and anything outside that is not family at all. (Trevor Southley)[7]

Because prejudice within the community has created such a lattice of shame around sexuality, there is pressure for gay men and women to hide who they are from others, even members of their own families. Often, they must hide even from themselves.

Adam, a young gay psychologist, grew up in a strongly religious world, utterly isolated in his struggle to please a heterosexual *God*.

> It's like I am so odd and unique and perverted and wrong, an abomination, and what is freakin' wrong with me that I'm the only one that feels these things? And I've got to get rid of it to be able to be loved by God. It really started becoming this thing of, in order to have God's love or acceptance or to get the goods, which are the Celestial Kingdom and Godhood, as Mormons believe, I had to get rid of my homosexuality. And that was really the core piece of—it's a battle—it's either God wins or my sexuality wins. . . . And how am I supposed to kill God? (Adam)

Adam was in conversion or reparative therapy, which is for "strugglers" who want to overcome homosexuality. It not only succeeded in shaming him but also infected his spirituality.

> My experiences of it [reparative therapy] reinforced the idea [that] *gay* is bad; my sexuality, gay sexuality is bad; I have to be heterosexual. Just this reinforcement of these theories seemed to fit my experience and made sense to other people and gave me hope that I could be heterosexual if I just tried enough. If I wasn't becoming heterosexual, there was something wrong with me. If I wasn't changing, then it meant that I was too tempted, I was too weak. It was this constant reinforcement that if I'm still masturbating or if I'm still having sex or wanting

to have sex, it's because I'm weak to Satan. Satan really plays a role in all of this, which I'm so sick of. (Currently I'm just so sick of the idea of Satan, I just think it's a fairy tale; but he was a very strong person in my life.) Satan and I were buddies, it seemed. He was my shadow literally. Either I was fighting him or I was succumbing to him. My *weakness* to him, my inability to ignore him or to defeat him, kept me from God. [This] solidified my separation from God. (Adam)

Secrets and boundary violations are also the shadows of some of the most sanctimonious preacher, strident politician, and raucous hecklers. When homosexuality is demonized, a shadow of homoeroticism can show up in the art and the obsessions of that religious culture. Sexual acting out and sexual abuse abound within religious communities, even as gay men and women are often targeted and persecuted by the religious authorities who are in their own particular closets.

And then people get scapegoated. That the Church, you know, will distract people from the things that they want to be talking about and get them inflamed about other things:; homosexuality, women's ordination, abortion, you know, all the things that I say; if you really trust God you let God figure out if that's a problem or not. (Victor)

When abuses and grievances occur, especially violations against children, religions often incorrectly assume or scapegoat homosexuality as the perversion, when the perversion actually has to do with a sexual disorder that manifests in all sexual orientations: pedophilia.

Wrongly believing pedophilia as an exclusively male homosexual behavior, has become an excuse for rampant homophobia. But it is an abnormal pathological interest in children or adolescents that involves obsessions about children, humiliation, torture, or sexual abuse of children, and it is a psychological disorder among straight and gay people alike. Religious pedophiles may be young or old, male or female, and are often those entrusted with educating or maintaining the health and well-being of young persons.

But pedophilia is not the only way children are exploited. Religion has veiled its own shadows in its complicated relationship to *others* of a race or class different from that of the dominant group. When there is dire poverty, neglect, war, or violence, it is easy to see how children can be pawns in the hands of unscrupulous religious. Children without education or who need food or security, for instance, are vulnerable to military or revolutionary recruitment. Children may be forced into the front lines or into minefields; be brutally enslaved, raped, or abused; or be recruited for suicide missions. In the name of God, they are sometimes forced to commit atrocities even against their own families. Initially, the pressure may be covert: it can be a compelling mix of custom, indoctrination, manipulation, and fear. Eventually it may seem like the only way for the vulnerable to save themselves.

There is a problem when religious sermons and instruction are counterintuitive and contradictory. When the *God* who loves seems to hate or when thoughts and actions regarding the body are both revolting and blessed, there is a kind of cognitive dissonance that stretches the limits of reason. Often, this shows up in how a community deals with sexuality.

> There were two things that they taught us growing up in Lubbock. The first is that we are awful, sinful, miserable creatures who are going straight to hell and *God* loves us. The other was that sex was dirty, nasty, immoral, and disgusting but it was so special you should save it only for the one you love. And people wonder why we grew up crazy.[8]

Chris, a young man moving into adolescence, had to grapple with the complications of his particular religious education, a French Canadian family culture, and his emerging sexual awakening.

> All of the sudden you're 12 years old, you're hitting puberty, and now the religion is teaching you that this area is mortal. This area is what you don't fool with. You're not to look at your own body, touch your own body, acknowledge the feelings in your own body. All of these things that had anything to do with sex were evil, mortally sinful. And the thinking that came across to me from scripture was that if your right hand caused you to sin, then you cut it off and you throw it away, because it's better for you to enter the kingdom with one hand than to spend eternity in hell. So, though I never cut my genitals off my body, I began the process of cutting myself off from myself as a sexual person emotionally and psychologically. The adolescent in me knows only too well the terror of sexual feelings and trying to stop thinking about them. Try to take a shower without touching your body, washing your body, how to stop yourself from spontaneously ejaculating—just stop it, stop it, stop it! (Chris)

Throughout history religious groups have also unconsciously made people with physical difference of skin color or those with abnormalities into objects of pity, shame, or buffoonery and rationalized exploitation with a half-truth from doctrine or scripture. Pity is not the same thing as compassion. To tacitly condone ridiculing the disabled by silence or patronizing them is neither innocent nor innocuous. Why is it fair game, for instance, to tell disabled jokes in religious circles, although mocking *God* could result in someone being censored?[9]

Christina Martin is a British standup comedian who has been censored because of her "religious material." But, she says, it is hard to picture a context where mocking disability should ever be hilarious: "Unfortunately, increasingly, that is the case: I tend to hear an average of three or four per gig, which is a lot when you consider that disabled people hurt nobody, suffer more than most, and arguably deserve empathy and respect rather than abject mockery.

And that is merely what these jokes constitute—mockery. In failing to censor this type of thing they fail to protect the people who arguably need it most. In censoring me, they halt a relevant debate in order to protect a super being and his fan club. Who would have thought that the all-powerful *God* and his millions of followers needed more protection than disabled people?"[10]

On every continent, indigenous religions and cultures are also persecuted or marginalized in the name of *God*. Bigotry can be as blatant as the policies of the Ku Klux Klan and militant extremists, or it can be embedded in sophisticated evangelization protocol or political correctness.

For the past 200 years, children of Native American, First Nation, and Aboriginal communities, have experienced rampant physical and sexual abuse in religious boarding schools. The Bureau of Indian Affairs and government bodies historically have removed these children from their families and tribes and placed them in religious schools where they have been whipped or raped and forced to eat lye soup or to kneel on boards. "There is a lot of historical trauma people carry with them," says Ron Sully, director of an alcohol treatment center on the Yankton reservation. "Just about everyone coming through here is carrying it, but they don't know it. They attribute it to something else. All that trauma from the boarding schools—the sexual violence, the family violence—is contributing to alcohol abuse."[11]

Often, religious bigotry does not manifest itself through blatant or brutal abuse. In some cases, what is unsaid often has more power than what is spoken. Joseph's experience as an African American in a Catholic school run by Irish nuns was at first impossible to define as an exhibition of racism or classism. What was happening to him as a child was not exactly apparent to those who participated in it, even his own parents, who sent him off with the goal of receiving a better education.

> I went to a missionary school. I think that the act of being a missionary in many situations is an inherently violent act, violent in that you have assigned yourself the right to displace some person's culture or religious and spiritual life and to replace that with your own. Now, if you're the kind of missionary who goes to some country and spends your time simply exemplifying what your religion believes or preaches, you spend your time helping to dig wells and build schools and help sick people, and organize a community garden. And, after a while, there's some quality you exude that makes people curious. That's when the conversation about your spiritual foundation and practice needs to start. But to go announce that the people here need to stop practicing whatever they practice and practice your religion, I think, is an act of violence. (Joseph)

Racism (or fundamentalism, separatism, sexism, even feminism) is most insidious in its unconscious elements. Religious institutions can veil their racist agenda in education when they proselytize, in a country other than their own or in parish ministries, among the poor and the disenfranchised. People of color may be *saved* out of their native rituals or culture by those in the dominant race who have their own ethnocentric viewpoint about how to worship or how to live. This perspective trickles down into the community with unconscious messages of what is right and what is best, often with subliminal racial undertones.

Religion fails when it insists that the cultural clothing be as important as the spiritual message, as Joseph experienced in his "religious" upbringing as an Irish Catholic. In the parochial school in Indianapolis, the nuns taught religion to an all-black student population through the only cultural lens they knew.

> The fact is that I never heard the word Africa one time in eight years. The idea that there was something to bring to this setting with these children from across the world that wasn't what they were taught back in Kerry—it never occurred to them, never occurred to them. (Joseph)

In Joseph's school, there was no question about the quality of his education or even his treatment by the nuns. Rather, the steady drip of oblivious prejudice undermined the entire experience.

> I was in a school setting where there was zero interest in, or even awareness of, what spiritual, religious traditions my ancestors might have practiced. When I tell some people I went to parochial school, they're bracing for stories of physical and sexual abuse. I have to disappoint those people because I don't have any, even though the act of being a missionary is, in one sense, inherently violent. My teachers were not angels; they certainly had their shortcomings and bad moments, but I'm convinced that they essentially cared about the kids. They cared about educating us—and by the lord Harry—you sure got an education at a parochial school. There were no blatant violations of my person. It was not that there were moments of physical or even psychological abuse as such. It was the cluelessness. (Joseph)

It is important here to notice how natural it is to pass judgment about the bigotry of *others*. As we noticed when we looked at Islamic feminism or Jewish oppression, it is all too easy to be defensive or strident about a personal perspective because there is little information or an unconscious bias about those who are *not us*. Even political correctness can be a veiled "*ism*." People are often listening and evaluating from their cultural viewpoints and values. This is troubling when it comes down to any missionary approach to race, gender relations, sexual orientation, or disability within another community, even if the intent is earnest. It may be difficult to evaluate or expose prejudice within religious systems, but there is no excuse for violations of basic human rights.

Those in a *diaspora*[12] of any kind who long for a connection to their roots must confront other challenges for themselves and their families. For Irit and Rasan, an Israeli Jewish and a Palestinian Muslim, there is still the question of finding a community that will authentically support their American children when their own religions and cultural roots are so divided. The reality of being in a society where both their ethnic and religious identities are truly intact takes mere academics out of the living-and-dying equation of race, religion, and culture.

> What bothers me is that I want each one of them to find a group, whatever that group is, I don't really care. If [our daughter] would find a community of people—I told her, "You know, our problem is we're not complete in any circle. We are not one hundred percent of any kind." In a way, after so many years of living in America, we have become like many Americans, share the same values as the average American. We feel the change in our way of life when we go back home to see our extended families. We're no longer the people we used to be. (Irit)

While the aspects of a religious identity often frame its outer reality, they do not necessarily have much to do with numinous[13] life. The externals of religion or even theology are often confused with internal experience, yet it is also possible that these do not even intersect.

> As a child, I did not have a personal relationship with *God*. I was exceedingly interested in religion, however. Religious issues seemed more important than establishing a "relationship" with *God*. I'm quite sure that it was in second grade that I plagued the teacher with questions like "If *God* [Jesus] is love, how can he send all the people in the world who have never heard of him to hell?" (Eleanor)

Reason intersecting with indoctrination, the inner dialogue conflicting with the outer monologue—it can become quite confusing.

BEYOND THE GATE

Survival or the recovery of one's own spirituality may involve a break from the religious organization or its theology altogether. For Victor, his former religious affiliation with Catholicism has lost its credibility, not only because he no longer agrees with the exclusivity of the Church but also because of what happened to him there.

> I find organized religion dangerous. I understand people's need for community enough to be able to say, if this is where you find comfort and solace and meaning or friendship or whatever, that's great. I have no problem with that. When

ositioning your soap box and talking about your beliefs being the
nd somebody else's belief being the wrong ones or your way of life
ht one and somebody else's life being the wrong one, you lose me,
't go there. And I can't go there in large part because some of the
,.-- who were saying those things were turning around in my life and doing
something else all together. (Victor)

Delicia had devoted her entire professional career to Catholic service and
was working to help survivors and parishioners in her diocese come to grips
with the betrayals of the clergy. The impact of the abuses and the collusion
of the legal process, commercial enterprise, and medical and psychological
services in keeping secrets or perpetuating the system eventually took their
toll.

> I became very acutely aware that the evil that was perpetrated on the individu-
> als or, in some cases, clergy, or many individuals, was not just the sin between
> two people; it had enormous impact on the community, and not only the com-
> munity within the Church but also the community at large. . . . It was not
> only the Church but society or the community at large, that participated in
> the violations because I don't know how many times executives from insur-
> ance companies sit down on a table and pay out money when it was the same
> person over and over again without speaking of that something different had to
> be done, or the judges that sealed cases or the doctors who covered up things
> or the police officers who looked the other way when reports came in. I really
> think that the community helped conceal it for longer than it should've been
> concealed. (Delicia)

A FORK IN THE ROAD

This is, then, how religion harms those it should protect: by failing to tell
the truth and by encouraging the community to participate in the failure.
The truth does not necessarily produce relief for us, but truth is what religion
supposedly holds dear. And, in the case of any kind of religious abuse, hiding
the truth will produce toxic, incapacitating shame—in the victim, in the
perpetrator, and in a community that does not require accountability. For a
victim of any kind of religious violation, this shame does not emerge from a
balanced recognition of his limitations. Since one is often too vulnerable to
realize that the shame does not belong to him, he may bear the weight of the
perpetrator's violation *and* his shame.

Shame is the sadder underbelly of the perpetrator's pride. It deceives the
one who is harmed by perpetuating the lie even when the lie is about himself.
Pride and self-interest may drive the perpetrator, but it is really shame that
brings him to the deplorable place of an abuser. It is what motivates him to
reenact what may have been done to him and thwarts his capacity to connect
sufficiently to his victim to recognize the harm he inflicts.

For a perpetrator, these abusive connections distort the emotional bridge between himself and others, as well as the boundary. Respect for these distinctions is the foundation of what it means to be in relationship in family, culture, or religion itself. Yet, if one has been taught to morph himself into a particular image in order to exist in such a relationship, he will always fall short of the expectations of the sick system. And if the community's response is only a conditional acceptance, it will be only more confusing. A negative conditional connection may not always look like anger or retribution. Instead, a relationship that is only marginally accepting can be cloaked in pity, coercion, or even a provisional love. A withering glance or a leering gaze from someone who is admired or revered can be as unbearable as physical, sexual, or verbal abuse. The impact is demoralizing because the receiver is then the victim of the other's propaganda, agenda, or desire. That is why those who experience this kind of treatment often create a false exterior or a set of coping behaviors for survival. Shame is overriding any meaningful connection even with oneself because the *self fails itself*.

Shame is a sickness in the soul. It is often difficult to address because the degradation is often at the human core. It differs dramatically from the healthy experience of shame, when someone recognizes his own limitations and faults. Toxic shame is often the outcome not of a person's own actions, but because of what has been done to him. It is the misconception that what has happened to him has permanently and irrecoverably polluted his own fundamental nature, removing the possibility for recovery or even responsibility. It often negates any outside avenue of support because the self feels so far from its center that it cannot even touch it. When one has been badly betrayed, especially with sexual or emotional violation, it is hard to imagine how to make a safe and meaningful connection to anything.

Those who have experienced such betrayal will do what they can to evade feeling such shame, but it is self-generating. For shame is a cannibal; it will eat the self by attacking from the inside. And to reiterate, shame and its shadow-twin, *shamelessness*, can consume others, as well. These characteristics show up in debilitating guilt mixed with intense rage, revictimization, the fear of being known. The shameless deny any wrongdoing and go about their business with grandiosity or perfectionism, by exerting punitive control over others.

There is another aspect to shame that exhibits something harder to name and even more difficult to demonize—malignant self-sacrifice. This particular side of shame comes neither from healthy self-confidence nor from realistic humility. Those who actively strive to always be seen as less than they are may actually have a kind of closet narcissism in which individuals see or create themselves as indispensable in their caregiving and need to be recognized not for their contributions alone but for their goodness. They may experience themselves as indispensable and have a fierce attachment to their identity as minister, spiritual leader, or self-sacrificer. They might unconsciously put themselves and their parishioners or loved ones in a double bind of power and guilt, all the while claiming to be the worst, the least, the last. Their need to control the politics of giving creates an inability to see where they fail to care. And, a fear of criticism or of being found deficient creates an inability to be reflective.

Whether persons have an overinflated sense of self or are intent on constant self-diminishment, whether they must be seen as the very best or as the worst and least, they simply cannot get out of their own way. They are stymied and stuck inside shamed and damaged egos. All of this is a manifestation of debilitating shame.

One who feels this toxic shame will do anything not to feel it, even shameful things. She will hide. She will compromise. She will become very busy trying to outrun it. But it reverberates into a downward tightening spiral, reflected repeatedly in compulsive action, addiction, or codependence.

Shame runs the show all around.

It creates an institutional separatism that has nothing to do with the principles of religious life.

To gay, lesbian, bisexual, and transgender individuals, shame is another contribution of an invention renamed "family values."

> I really tried. I was told I could be straight and heterosexual, and this was the way to do it. It was the solution to my religious problems, that I could get rid of the homosexuality, that I could cure myself and be heterosexual. And from 20 to 27, I went from this extreme of trying to be straight. I used the principles that I was told could make me straight; but then I kept going back to men. I really did have very extreme identities: I was really with the Mormons, or I was really with a gay—and my idea of gay meant I was a big whore and I did lots of drugs, and then I would redeem myself and then go back to being Mormon, and at the same time it was in conflict with my professional identity as well. . . . I was very lost in knowing who I truly was or could be. (Adam)

Shame and its sister, fear, beget silence.

Silent shame is the muzzle for women who are brutalized, defamed, or defiled in the name of *God's* law. That shame is passed from generation to generation, protecting fathers, brothers, and sons of women from the responsibility of treating all women with dignity and equality. Even the women themselves, knowing nothing but such shame, rarely speak out on behalf of those they would otherwise protect. At worst, they inculcate the hatred that was shown to them and continue the cycle with other women, other children, and their own daughters.

> In 2005, a young Muslim woman was raped in a French school. Of course, everybody knew, but they're so afraid of these young men that they prefer to close

their eyes. When the verdicts came down in this case, the courthouse turned into a madhouse. Eighteen teenagers were convicted of raping a 15-year-old girl over a two-month period. But what really shocked France was how the mothers of those boys reacted. "You call this justice, seven years in prison for some oral sex," says one mother. "It's the girl who should be behind bars." (Sharon Lipkin)[14]

Silence of the fold can beget cruelty toward all those who are outside the reigning religious affiliation. Sometimes this silence is responsible for bigotry, oppression, or even murder, colluding to make the *other* an inhuman object, instead of a human soul.

I was perplexed for many years about how the black community took Christianity, took the white man's religion and so passionately, when the religion was being foisted on them by their white slave owners. But . . . the promise of suffering in this life for an eternal reward . . . is a great way to keep people down. . . . It was for a lot of . . . black people an absolute psychological necessity, because of all that stuff that the minister says when he comes down to the tent on Saturday nights, if that's not true, well, the thought of it not being true is simply too hideous to consider. (Joseph)

The silence of shame is the second rape for the sexual abuse survivor. It blesses ignorance and forces one's eyes wide shut. When bystanders both see and negate what is right in front of them, it only increases shame for the victim because his plight seems either his responsibility alone or crazily hidden in plain sight. Shame creates a cesspool of compromise for witnesses who reason or justify their failure to respond.

The thing that pisses me off the most is the fact that nobody around, picked up on any of the clues, nobody around questioned anything . . . people were blinded by their faith. Nobody was tuned in to me enough to notice it; I literally moved it in the back of my closet, big walk-in closet, that was my little world, the back of my closet, you know? I felt I was invisible. (William)

From the roots of shame, other actions within the religious community disconnect and obscure the community from reality: self-righteousness, dogmatism, isolation, or exclusivity. Fearing what others think often thwarts principled action.

Yet it is the *non*-actions that speak louder than any words. . . .

Finally, there is an understory of shame that is reenacted again and again: how a person in power, who has held another's tender and most vulnerable spirit, could betray her in the context of caregiving or deny responsibility for harm—just when, like a bird with trembling wing, frail and splendid, she was ready to take flight.

And, just part of me thinks that if he ever acknowledged in any way what he had done, I would've been in a lot better shape—you know—spiritually. (Diana)

How could any Church or community ignore what happened, shun or pathologize; how could anyone be failed again by being cursed for something they have no control over, without hope or resolution?

It's not just shunned, I mean—they're going to take your salvation. They're going to take your reasons for existing. I think even that wouldn't have been so bad except that with this situation unlike some, there wasn't even any hope that you couldn't repent, because you hadn't done anything wrong whatsoever to influence the outcome, which was very frightening—eternal consequences. (Shimon)

To be left with the mask of religion, a thirsty, shell-shocked heart, or nothing at all. . .

Yet, even in *nothing*, there may be a relentless thirst that becomes a presence in itself. This particular experience, though it can be difficult, is not only a jagged edge of darkness—it may also be the balm. It often resonates with love (not pity), which has no name or sound, yet reverberates with many names, many qualities. It may create a restlessness that deeply connects to music, beauty, or nature, or intimately responds to suffering in all its forms.

As curious beings, in the midst of all that we experience, we can create imperatives and experience a quandary that arises out of the resonance with what is before us. We crave freedom. In the words of Annie Dillard, "it is our water and weather. It is the world's nourishment, generously given; its soil and sap." We cannot exist without it or without the necessary questions that freedom generates: Why? Why not? Who am I? Who are You? What if? Whatever for?

Some of us may actually do better with the questions than with definitive answers. It may be in this kind of open-endedness that the spirit comes alive.[15] What we discover may not be comforting, at least at first. What comes at the other end of this open-ended inquiry? Perhaps, something that words barely touch, where recovery may begin to take place.

And, religion may have nothing to do with it.

RECOMMENDED READINGS

Armstrong, Karen. *Islam: The 4000 Year Quest of Judaism, Christianity, and Islam* (New York: Ballantine Books, 1993).
Kimball, Charles. *When Religion Becomes Evil* (New York: HarperCollins, 2002).

Patel, Eboo. *Acts of Faith: The Story of an American Muslim, the Struggle for the Soul of a Generation* (Boston: Beacon Press, 2007).

RECOMMENDED FILMS

Constantine's Sword, James Carroll, 2008.
Downpour Resurfacing, Frances Nikara with Robert Hall, 2008.
In Good Conscience, Barbara Rick, 2005.

CHAPTER 4

— ✠ —

Spiritual Leadership and the Trance of Religious Power

An appalling and horrible thing has come to pass in this land. The prophets prophesy falsely, and the priests rule at the back. And my people love to have it so.

—Jeremiah 5:31

Do not meet abuse with abuse.
Do not wait in ambush.
Do not strike at weaknesses.
Do not lay the dzo's burden on an ox's back.
Do not praise with hidden motives.
Do not bring a god down to the level of a demon.
Do not misuse the remedy.
Do not take advantage of suffering. . . .

—"The Seven Point Mind Training Root Text"
Chekawa Yeshe Dorje[1]

Those who are spiritual leaders bear the burdens and the gift of our spiritual welfare. It is tenuous, precious, and sacred. As pastors, masters, imams, gurus, rebbes, teachers, sisters—they are sacred friends. But these friendships can also be dangerous.

In every religious tradition, the clergy are supposed to work tirelessly to guide others on their spiritual journeys. Many live what they espouse in honesty and humility and have profound interior lives that reflect empathy, wisdom—and, one hopes, integrity. Some of them manifest a palpable spiritual power. Their connection to the community varies with their mystical or ecclesial viewpoint, even within their own traditions. They teach. They speak publicly. They represent a standard of living by their own example and by how they run their organizations. They attend to the rituals, the money, the schedule—and people. But their primary responsibility is to safeguard the inner life and spirit of those entrusted to them. It is a condition of character that has nothing to do with talent or star power. It doesn't even rely on what anybody thinks about them.

But spirituality and its shadow side go hand in hand. The dark end of spirituality is insidious if it is unconscious or, worse, when it is consciously hidden. If those who lead do not understand this, they, as well as their communities, are in serious trouble. And the people who suffer the most will *not* be them.

DO NOT MEET ABUSE WITH ABUSE . . .

For Chris, the sacred ideals of service and spirituality were trumped by the sacrilege of his sexual abuse by a priest. The mask of spirituality was ripped away to reveal this darker reality.

> The child loved the mystery, the stories: Jesus teaching the elders in the Temple at twelve, already knowing that he must be about His father's business, later feeding the masses, healing the sick, raising the dead, forgiving the sinner, banishing money changers from the temple, dying to make all things right between His father and man. The glory of God was brought into being every day through the consecration of bread and wine as it had been done for centuries. The host was transformed into the body of Christ. I prayed to it like a living being for years as an altar boy and prospective seminarian. I bowed to Him, loved Him with service and prayed to Him that I could accept that His will, not mine, be done in every part of my life. This mysterious being was more real to me than human beings. God was perfection and His son preached that we strive to be as perfect as His heavenly father is perfect. It's all I ever wanted: to be "alter Christus," another Christ and a priest. But I failed. If only I could have stopped growing at age 10. I could have been just what God wanted. A simple child with blind unquestioning faith. But then came puberty and the desecration of the temple. (Chris)

The shadows of spirituality are not always obvious. The religious life of service is often complicated by less apparent dangers. While spiritual leaders feel the effect of triumph and trauma, lives and losses, the good and the evil in their congregations, they are not always in a position to be observant or responsible. Those who care for others' spiritual lives are often in treacherous physical or psychological circumstances themselves. Their ministry might exhaust them, even if what they witness and what they do personally inspires them. Ideally, they are wiser, grateful, more connected to life and, one hopes, to their spirits because of their position. It accounts for endless hours of work with people who may or may not be able to be saved or restored and why many tolerate such difficult conditions, often with little support. Responding to people's real and perhaps messy lives creates a sense of meaning and vibrancy that is rewarding—but precarious.

Sometimes, leaders choose to face the trauma or distress in their own ministry because they are enlivened by their experiences. It may be more palatable than returning to the "safety" or mundane existence of their own lives at home and may be why it is sometimes hard for them to remember to stop or rest, or why they may have so much resistance to taking better care of themselves.

Religious environments like these can create compassion fatigue. The emotional residue of witnessing the pain of others day after day can create a compelling overstory that distracts ministers from their own problems. They may bear sympathetic witness to unimaginable agony, but they can become addicted to it, depleting themselves emotionally and spiritually even as they are fed by the experience of others. It creates a kind of *psychothenia,* a phenomenon where one gets so oversaturated with input that the capacity for metabolizing any experience diminishes even as the thirst for stimulation increases. It is like a person who drinks salt water to quench his thirst: as one becomes more dependent on participating in the tragedy or the comedy of other's lives, the more dehydrated and drained he himself becomes. Ministers and spiritual leaders sometimes do not want to leave the "battlefield" of ministry. Those consumed by their vocation, like people caught up in war, can deform themselves by subverting passion, mission, and loyalty with an ego attachment to duty.

> It hits your soul, and one of the things it's looking at, and this is just a question or something, the existential impact on folks who are working in toxic situations. And it will be different for each person, but I don't think we have come up with some guideposts of how people process that is going to be different. Psychologically, people process it, but I don't know if there are any guideposts on how to do this on a spiritual level. (Delicia)

The work of the pastor can be radically dangerous, addictive in its purposefulness, and perhaps, as Christopher Lasch says, "a refuge from the terrors of one's own inner life."[2]

Compassion fatigue can also create a moral exhaustion, when ethical failings and cynicism of the pastoral caregiver override another's boundaries or needs. The unbearable suffering of others can become not only accepted but perhaps even condoned. If a leader is overworked or undersupported, he can forget what it was that brought him to the work—and why it is he continues to do it—much to the detriment of the ones in his care.

DO NOT WAIT IN AMBUSH

Pastors are supposed to comfort the afflicted and occasionally afflict the comfortable with their spiritual message or by living lives of integrity and service. It is the responsibility of ministry to move others to be more than they are. But being a public inspirer is seductive, *especially* if one is good at it. Many become mesmerized by their own power to captivate the crowd. It is difficult to name this in themselves because any motive other than their selfless service would be shameful to admit.

Spiritual leaders may enchant their followers—and possibly themselves—with the unique atmosphere of intimacy and trust they build. The congregation often abandons itself to their grace. In their presence, followers might experience such a diminished sense of self that they relinquish much of their own critical thinking. Religious persons can become entranced by their own charisma, especially if they are recognized as spiritual authorities or holy people. Yet, when the leaders encourage this kind of compliance or hero worship, it no longer feeds a spiritual caregiving and instead nourishes an insidious type of egotism. Grandiosity poses as sainthood. If they demand loyalty without earning it through authentic action or accountability to their congregations, religious leaders will morally stunt themselves and compromise the ones who trust them.

With the darker side of leadership come moral lapses. Sometimes, when something is amiss, the community and those closest to the top exhibit a recognizable anxiety. Drug, alcohol, and sexual addiction, covered up by rigid outward behaviors, can spread through the community. Those in leadership may take their congregations with them through the emotional ups and downs of their own whims or whimsy, obsessions or rage, while some in the community will react by swinging on this teeter-totter with fear and relief, replicating their own difficult pasts. If the leader forces others to collude with him to hide his personal problems, it can reproduce a sick family system. The disease hidden by the head of the "house" will then often show up in one of the "children."

When the one in charge has secrets or addictions, there will always be those in the membership who will cover up for him or deny what may be in plain sight. Here, the actions (or inaction) of the community speak even louder than the silence of the leader behind closed doors.

DO NOT STRIKE AT WEAKNESS

The behavior of the clergy, because of their public position, is not simply their individual or private business. What they do with their members and how they do it are more potent because of *who* they are. And if they use anyone for their own purposes, the repercussions will appear in *other's* spiritual lives, a cruel consequence of religious abuse.

This especially shows up in the complicated area of sex. Michael Downing was in a Zen Buddhist community where roshis had a practice of sexual relationships with women students. He speaks about the fallout in his community when harm done by leaders was diminished or dismissed.

If you sit down with the women and the men who were hysterically sobbing about their relationships with their male teachers—you realize that serious harm was done to these people. And you have to work backward from there. There is only one precept: do not harm. When people do not have a clear idea of harm—they accuse others of being Puritans.[3]

The budding spiritual life of a young woman was almost destroyed by the sexual relationship with her religious teacher. The ramifications were psychologically devastating. But, over time, the spiritual impact was even greater.

And part of the time I would try to just blot it out. But it started to affect my meditation. The ironic thing is that before he did that, I had one of those experiences where something was clicking into place and a lovely dream, and some kind of real sense of a constant Presence. I thought I was getting that affirmation that there really is something to all of this because it felt like some transformation inside of me. And then that happened. So partly I think what I wanted to do was get back to that place emotionally and in terms of my constant recollectedness and all that had been there before his attempts. So I tried to meditate a lot, and maybe for about a year it seemed like I was holding out. But then, the second year, I just started crying a lot, and I couldn't make it stop. (Diana)

It may be difficult for religious leaders to separate the intoxication of sexual violation from spiritual contact when it comes to power. But if this happens, the soul of the survivor, not simply the body or mind, takes the greatest hit.

DO NOT LAY THE DZO'S BURDEN ON AN OX'S BACK

It may be tempting for a community to want to manage the public face of things, as well as their private politics, especially if there is suspicion that something scandalous is going on. But, if the leadership allows this, hypocrisy will destroy any attempt to protect, creating a bewildering double bind of guilt and duty for the community.

Ideally, the truth will reveal the limitations of leadership just as well as its stature or brilliance. But often the opinions of the leader are considered to be beyond reproach or dispute; members of the congregation are afraid to question because there are ramifications if they do, squelching any opportunity for critical thinking. If the community has transformed its leaders into the only all-knowing icons, dissent is unthinkable. Though the process can be quite intoxicating for ministers, it shuts down the conscience of the community.

Shame makes people keep secrets. And, if leaders blame the victims (or blame the devil), it is *their* shame that the community protects. Yet once they force people into this situation, they betray the community.

In medicine or psychotherapy, there exists a forbidden zone where the fragile membrane of trust and dependency removes the possibility of equality in power, making the other unable to withhold consent. In pastoral care, there is an even more powerful relationship of intimacy and trust, much like that of parent and child, because spiritual caregivers lead people into the most personal territory of the soul. These relationships in this regard are not secular arrangements. In some circles, the formal word for these kinds of obligations would be called *covenant*: they are sacred acts. Those who lead have a commitment to the deepest well-being of the faithful. It is the core of the spiritual contract, not simply the status quo.

Will Michaels, a Unitarian Universalist minister, was calm and matter of fact as he related the story of his childhood abuse by a Catholic priest, until he started to talk about his personal covenant to protect the children in his church. Then he began to cry.

> We're trying to put policies in place at this particular church that enhances the safety of our children. "Why do we have to do that? Why do we have to make these policies; isn't it a sad state of affairs in today's world?" And I said, "Absolutely, it's a very sad state of affairs, but we have to do it. We absolutely have to do it. No adult can be left alone with children without two adults in the room or two children; you know that's just what you have to do. That's just the sign of the times, unfortunately; and it's just not going to happen while I'm minister of this church. It's just not going to happen!" (Will Michaels)

Violence, neglect, and sexual misuse of children and adolescents are epidemic in every religion across the world.[4] In the name of religion, both boys and girls have been used as sexual toys; girls, as well as boys, have been shamed, maimed, or even murdered by their families; children, not just grown men, are given the means to kill or commit suicide for *God*. It is up to the spiritual leaders to protect their community, even when their own religious hierarchy says otherwise. If they fail to do this, they will only add to the heavy load of pain so many bear and fail to keep the covenant of sacred trust.

When those who lead betray their people with further secrets, lies, and cover-ups, they defile the soul of the community and further debase their own.

> How is it that they can desecrate the deepest part of themselves and of the ones placed in their spiritual care? How can they so drastically compartmentalize the ideals they embody from what they do to others? They don't wake up one day and all of a sudden little kids start looking good; they know it the whole time. And they don't say anything. And maybe they think *God* or prayer would get them through it. But they wanted and abused kids, and they knew—they knew it was wrong. (Francis, priest and clergy abuse survivor)

Nuns and women spiritual leaders are not exempt from the shadows of abuse. Sometimes the violations by a female clergy person are difficult to name because they may be more covert and because women often initially sent a more nurturing side. In schools, convents, and spiritual communities, the early indicators of abuse are often subtle, even to those who perpetrate the abuse themselves. Sometimes discipline goes too far. Women have often been guilty of physical abuse or of deeply demoralizing those in their care with shame and self-doubt.

> Suddenly she said, "Stop. Put down your pencils. Someone in here is cheating, and I think she knows who she is." Oh my God. . . . So then I went with her to some room. As I think back, I know there was this cut-off, splitting thing that must have happened to my psyche. She tore me up verbally and said that I didn't deserve to be there, that my parents were paying good money to send me there, I was ungrateful and I was selfish—and just total shame—I don't really remember actually what happened after that. (Kate)

If the leadership is patriarchal in structure, it is up to the women who work in religious life to consider not only where their rights or their voices fit as women, but the rights of female children as well as other women. This is very difficult because the double standard of power and accountability between men and women is often deep within the culture of the religion. Women are often taught to hate themselves and to pass their hatred on to daughters, to sisters, and to one another. Sometimes the female leadership teaches and participates in the culture of misogyny by supporting a dominant side of male authority and encouraging women's self-contempt and disempowerment.

When religious female leaders enact this kind of leadership and allow a male authority figure do harm to their sisters in a community, they fail not only those harmed, but themselves.

> The thing that distressed me, angered me almost more than anything about what happened was the convent culture, the context that existed there that allowed everyone to almost willingly remain ignorant of what this man was doing. And that—that almost is the worst part of it for me. And then, it continued. (Diana)

DO NOT PRAISE WITH HIDDEN MOTIVES

If people in spiritual leadership enter a monastic or religious community as adolescents, not only may they be trained for positions of leadership without having had the opportunity to engage in normal diverse relationships within or outside their families they can become developmentally stunted. Such situations in leadership can severely arrest emotional growth and feed a situational narcissism even as it gives the leader credit for more maturity than he may possess. A spiritual leader may be unclear about his own boundaries because certain limits like this have never been explained to him. Perhaps he has never been given concrete guidelines about how to relate to or lead others; often, such leaders have had no real support or modeling to actually teach them how to live their own spiritual lives.

No one would understand this better than a member of the clergy who is a survivor of some kind of religious abuse himself. Survivors in the ministry have had to struggle with themselves in ways others barely understand. This is often reflected in the fierce passion they bring to their pastoral work, especially when it comes to the protection of children. It is a characteristic that Francis brings to his work as a missionary. Because he was abused, he says he has a different view of his Church than do other priests.

> I appreciate the danger in the church and the capacity for danger—and for real harm. I'd have to turn in my collar if I was to sit there, [with] somebody who's really been hurt by the church, and I would spout some pious party line, or deny it, or ignore it! (Francis)

Of course, clergy must pay special attention to their own countertransference[5] and the unconscious elements of their personal stories that may get in the way of the work they do. But this countertransference can also be a remarkably intuitive tool for the assessment of trauma and for helping one be attuned to the particular signals and spiritual issues of other religious abuse survivors.

There are always those in every spiritual tradition who truly live the ideal. Though an individual may have a rigorous and profound spiritual practice and intend to hold ambition, lust, or power in check until the very end of his life, the ultimate responsibility is *always* with him. It is up to *him* to uphold the physical and moral limit in the exchange no matter what someone else does or whether or not someone even understands why he himself must maintain those limits. His hats, his ring, his collars, veil, or robes cannot excuse his accountability even if he is "pressured" to commit a questionable act. Clerical identity never provides a license to harm or to blame the victim for the act of harm, nor should religion ever provide an excuse for not protecting the victims.

> I'd hide under the big porch, I'd hide near the chimney, on the roof behind the garage. My mother knew my hiding places and would come get me when it was time for my counseling sessions, saying "you know . . . it's hard to become a priest and this is my calling, you either have to go upstairs with him or go in the car with him, whatever he deems necessary on this day." (William)

DO NOT MISUSE THE REMEDY

Power can be difficult to navigate with balance, especially for those who are vulnerable. Community members may also allow their leaders to get away with abusive acts because they don't have the resources, maturity, or technology to make them stop. Victims and the community therefore may have even subjected themselves to unthinkable acts because of their love for the leader.

For a young nun in a religious community, the spiritual master was the hub in a wheel of admiration. What he did to her was all the more confusing because there was no room inside her mind or within the community for him to be anything other than perfect.

> The strange thing is that I was so caught up in the environment of adoration that others (and myself) bestowed on him that I never allowed myself to see him for what he was. In my very soul, of course, I knew that the sexual abuse that was occurring had to be wrong, but I didn't know what to do about it or how to understand it, nor did I know how to tell him to stop. He forgot that he was ordinary. I think, basically, we are all ordinary, no matter what our profession or path in life. It is grace, a gift either from *God* or guru that makes us realize that we are part of the All-pervading. Once we think we are spiritually special or extraordinary, we are destined to fall. Depending on how high and how much power has been granted, so the greater the distance we must fall. (Eleanor)

The spiritual leader is supposed to be there as witness to the sacred journey and as a sacred friend. The relationship is supposed be based on mutuality and respect. But, for any teacher, even one with palpable spiritual stature, the dark side of hubris and pride can still take hold at any point, at the expense of the community. If celebrity is "a mask that eats into the face,"[6] the *mask* of holiness burrows even further into one's true face. A spiritual teacher may often have the acclaim of a rock star; she can occasionally be a victim of her own success and the projections of others. It becomes even more problematic than rock star status because the mask of sanctity can hide or retard authentic spiritual accomplishment. If this is the case, she is no longer *a* teacher in her mind but *the* teacher. She might have seen herself as the focal point of her spiritual community, not as its servant. The intoxication of power, coupled with massive projection on the part of her followers, only feeds the shadow of greatness. Even if the spiritual guide possesses remarkable abilities, her psychic or paranormal powers do not automatically equate with real spiritual development, nor does her intellectual acuity and insight replace genuine humility or self-awareness. So it is all the more dangerous for a leader if she begins to believe her own remarkable press.

Beyond any difficult relationship, misunderstanding, or power struggle between the leader and the community, a dangerous shadow is created by veneration. Followers may adore their leader, especially if the devout come from families that were either extremely rigid or out of control or if they were shown no love at all. The spiritual leader appears to offer something that should have been a birthright to everyone. But one's charisma may feed the very thing she encourages others to watch out for: a sense of entitlement, using people for one's own needs instead of serving them. Adulation like this numbs the spiritual sense and cuts the leader off from her ethical compass.

Even with a high degree of sanctity or mystical awareness, the leader will never be free from the shadow side of the ego. It is always a temptation to believe one's own publicity and to consider oneself entitled to exact special privileges from followers, often sexual or monetary.

The other end of sanctity is hubris.

The people in churches, mosques, or temples may love their leaders—they might even put them in a special chair and worship them. They may go to great lengths, even to their own detriment, to believe that their leaders would never betray them—but, in the end, leaders are still human beings and, like everybody else, have the power to do great things *and* to commit evil acts.

DO NOT BRING A GOD DOWN TO THE LEVEL OF A DEMON

One of the least understood relationships in the West is the relationship between the spiritual guide in the capacity of guru or teacher and his student or disciple. Those who commit to this kind of relationship, an Eastern model, often sign onto another cultural norm far different from their own. We will consider this relationship not only in its original Eastern cultural context but also from a North American perspective.

In some traditions, the delineation of power and stature between *master* (or *guru*) and *disciple* is a tradition of spiritual practice that holds a special place and relies on the discipline of a dedicated intense inner life based on contemplation under the tutelage and direction of a spiritual mentor. This relationship elicits a special boundary because of the profound nature of the intimacy between teacher and aspirant.

The word *guru* literally means "one who dispels darkness." Ideally, he can awaken the divine in a student and help integrate these experiences. Even if the guru or teacher has experienced enlightenment or has had a glimpse of the very nature of reality, he is still human. So, in his humanness, he should not encourage his "disciples" to give up complete control of their minds or lives to anyone, even to him.[7]

In Eastern tradition, the relationship between the guru or teacher and the disciple is based on respect, commitment, and devotion. It can be as potent a connection as that between a mother and her child. This level of intimacy is both profound and dangerous. Westerners who have had neglect or abuse in their own lives are often only too happy to surrender their hearts to a teacher. Unfortunately, sometimes they also suspend judgment or good sense.

Paul Brunton says it best: "In the end he [the disciple or follower of the spiritual path] must free himself inwardly from all things and, finally, both from whatever teacher he has and from the quest itself. Then, only can he stand alone within and one with God."[8]

In the guru-disciple connection, there is often a life-changing exchange, a bond of love and trust that is unspeakable. What happens may truly be unlike iny other human interaction. Yet blind acceptance or wild devotion doesn't help foster spiritual growth, and the follower is not necessarily in a position to discriminate. But if the guru buys into the persona of divine perfection where ethical standards and morality do not apply, he desecrates everything he represents.

The spiritual teacher is supposed to communicate spiritual knowledge, not his individual personality. The disciple is encouraged to give up attachment to her own desires and her sense of ego identification. But there are many ways this kind of surrender is misunderstood and misused, especially if sacred teaching is corrupted for personal desire.

> He was really, really manipulative. I remember very clearly that he implied to me that I was attached to my body, and to my concept of my own independent self. It was because of these attachments that I would not sleep with him—and that attachments are bad. (Beth)

In Western psychology, there is a great deal of emphasis on the development of the *ego*, the human sense of self, distinct from the world and other selves. In the Abrahamic traditions, the idea of ego can be seen as the exaggerated sense of self and as something to be avoided. But, in Eastern religions, there is a distinction between the unripe ego as the focal point of the personality and a ripe ego, which is defined as a more mature inner self not so dependent on individual recognition or accolades. The ripe, mature ego is not only grounded in itself at the very core of existence but capable of detaching from a sense of self-importance. "Giving up the ego," then, is a term that gets lost in translation, especially when one tries to view a Western concept from an Eastern perspective.

There is real value to sacrifice, austerity, and the withdrawal of one's attachment to pride, which decreases clinging to the sense of *me*. Considering how often this is misunderstood, these values must be cultivated and taught with wisdom. Whether or not a leader's cultural framework is different from that of his followers, there is never an excuse for demanding sexual, physical, or psychological exchanges from disciples under the ruse of seeking separation from an *attachment* to self. The relationship as guru or spiritual master should never confuse his disciples' sense of self with misnamed selflessness; nor can a teacher cut someone off from her dignity or human rights in order to "teach" a lesson, no matter how he justifies it.

Although there is no independent standard of right or wrong or a consistent culturally relative standard of ethics, thinking persons have an inner standard of personal boundaries that they must honor within themselves. In the context of sexuality particularly, it is more than dangerous when those boundaries are crossed, especially if the teacher insists they are "impediments" to some kind of breakthrough.

I was in this fairly isolated environment, with a person from a totally different culture from me. I had this idea that there is such a thing as cultural relativity and I just needed to be open. He was not interested in teaching me about Buddhism—I would ask him questions about Buddhism, just basic things about suffering or about truth, or questions about what meditation is supposed to be like—He just would not want to answer the questions. It became very clear that what he wanted was to sleep with me. (Beth)

A budding spirituality or devotion can never be compromised by the spiritual teacher's personal needs or by the justification that what the teacher and the follower do together will always be for the good of the student. Individuals may forfeit significant parts of themselves to do what the teacher wants in a mindful positive manner, but to relinquish values for the personal benefit of the teacher is not only confusing but decimating to emotional and spiritual well-being.

Sometimes the teacher himself may believe that his appetite for power is above the norms and limits of others. He mistakenly sees *his* actions as holy or consecrated, forgetting that others are not simply objects with which to meet his personal physical or emotional needs. He may even justify what he does as something necessary for *his* spiritual development, rationalizing his engagement in a sexual or psychologically harmful encounter with a member of the community as being an important experience for *him* to learn about. This particular kind of contact also severely devastates the teacher-disciple bond.

DO NOT TAKE ADVANTAGE OF SUFFERING

Spiritual leaders may transmit wisdom or spiritual attainment. They may have achieved Samadhi, moksha, or satori or received enlightenment. But, especially *because* they have reached a heightened state of awareness, leaders should never promote their own considerable talents for personal gain or to inflict pain on others.

If someone comes to a religious community after she has left another one, it is because she longs for God, or meaning, or community. Most likely, she is in some pain. She wants to deepen her practice and to find a way or a connection to something bigger than she is. She needs to be on this journey in safety; she does not need to script another betrayal.

Someone who is emotionally compromised must be given spiritual direction with even greater wisdom and skill. Sometimes the emotional problems or situations of students are beyond the expertise of the teacher and cannot be fixed simply with meditation techniques. The student may need psychological or medical help before he is ready for the rigors of intense spiritual practice. In fact, spiritual exercises for someone who is severely unstable can be quite harmful, especially if he is engaging in a rigorous program of physical austerity and meditation. If a vulnerable person like this takes on more than he can metabolize, he is susceptible to mental collapse.

Some people who pursue a committed religious life demonstrate a high degree of compulsive service or self-destructive rigor in their practice. It is often quite common for spiritual communities to attract such followers. Sometimes, in their fierce attachment to their teachers, they will sacrifice anything or anyone to be in the "inner circle." They may even engage in excessive power struggles in the group politic, to the detriment of others and even themselves. Or they may lose the ability to think for themselves and become utterly dependent on the leader to dictate the most minute details of their day-to-day existence. Excessive piety can mask psychological instability. Dealing with such instability only on a spiritual level, without taking into account a person's emotional state, can be dangerous for the person—and even for the spiritual caregiver.

If a leader does not trust himself to give spiritual direction for whatever reason, he should be honest enough to say he cannot work with the person, no matter how hard it is for her to understand. It is not always her business to know why he set the limits he may have to set. But it is *his* business to protect her spirit, no matter what she asks for. And, although the spiritual journey is ultimately the student's personal responsibility, the teacher's position of power cannot be ignored.

It is the custom in some religions to salute a member of the clergy or a spiritual teacher in some way as a sign of respect—to bow in respect to teachers, to kiss their rings, or to take the dust of their feet. A teacher's speech, lineage, past actions, or reputation, however, cannot generate such respect automatically. Persons in spiritual leadership must prove their mettle. They must welcome dissent. Their integrity and spirituality are products of their own inner journey and practice, and they should be encouraged to open the doors and the windows of their lives and be as transparent and clear as the light they intend for others. They must invite their students to develop discrimination, the ability to encounter a problem and consider a course of action to determine whether it resonates with their own truth and integrity. It is a capacity that is learned and developed over time in the course of inner development. Spiritual teachers are supposed to give others the tools to learn how to do this. Their sacred task is not only to offer nourishment but also to teach their students to nourish themselves.

In so doing, the spiritual teacher must find colleagues and spiritual mentors of his own to keep him honest and give spiritual support and real feedback when he himself is vulnerable. If he isolates himself from peers, he will depend on his followers to need him. Their projections, their burdens, or their adulation will exhaust or corrupt him.

We long for honesty, tolerance, gentleness, joy, defenselessness, generosity, patience, faithfulness, and open-mindedness, not fear, secrecy—or shame.

We need to know that those who care for our souls will not claim a spiritual stature that they do not possess. We want our leaders to remind us that power does not belong to anyone alone. Spiritual leaders must not use trust to psychically manipulate or exploit. Their faults should not be reinterpreted as opportunities for followers to overcome ego attachments or to prove loyalty, especially if what they do compromises human rights, ethics, or personal integrity.

We have a right to demand zero tolerance for sexual, psychological, or physical abuse. Those in leadership cannot retreat from listening to difficult truths, even if it means chaos or pain for the clerical community or the people they serve. That means that they cannot shoot the messenger or shun the victims. They must be challenged to listen with compassion to those who have suffered, even if it is difficult to hear what is said, and to encourage the community to do so, as well. And, whatever happens, the spiritual community must never be made to justify violations, especially of a spiritual leader.[9]

As adults, we must ask questions and discern what the correct path is for us. Children cannot necessarily make such assessments, and therefore we have a responsibility as a community to be hypervigilant about keeping them safe from coercion or harm. Nobody is free to pursue the course of her spiritual development if she is forced into it. Then she simply complies out of fear instead of proceeding because she has been empowered to do so. Lao Tzu says that "leadership based on love and respect is better than leadership based on fear and coercion. But leadership is best when the people say, 'We have done this ourselves.'"[10] The job of a religious leader is to facilitate freedom. He does not need to create more bondage.

People depend on authenticity more than charisma and do not need a hypocrite to lead them to an interior life. They look to the leader to be kind but do not need him to use platitudes to explain away the terrible events that happen in their lives. They depend on him to speak the brutal truth but should not experience debilitating shame in the face of it. They count on him *not* to flinch from or feed off their suffering. They hope he can admit his mistakes and apologize for them. They need to trust that he will *never* cross physical or sexual boundaries. They hope he never plays with facts to get what he wants or to sound better to himself or others. They ask the leader to model self-vigilance, not self-absorption.

Many want to be able to follow the example of a spiritual teacher in having a rigorous interior practice. And, whether they know it or not, they need for him to remember that he must stay awake until his last conscious moment. Because, of all people, the teacher is not off the hook until he is dead. If a spiritual leader shakes his head as he reads this and thinks that this would never pertain to him—if he believes this could never *be* him—he needs to look in the mirror.

There are no exceptions for accountability. *All* of us are responsible—to our communities and to ourselves.

RECOMMENDED READINGS

Ihla F Nation. "Face to Face, Confronting the Guru Disciple Relationship," *Gnosis*, http://www.leavingsiddhayoga.net/gnosis.htm.

Kain, John. *A Rare and Precious Thing: The Possibilities and Pitfalls of Working with a Spiritual Teacher* (New York: Bell Tower, 2006).

Kramer, Joel and Diana Alstad. *The Guru Papers: Masks of Authoritarian Power* (Berkeley, CA: Frog, 1993).

Wilson Schaef, Anne and Diane Fassel. *The Addictive Organization, Why We Overwork, Cover Up, Pick up the Pieces, Please the Boss, and Perpetuate Sick Organizations* (New York: Harperone, 1990).

CHAPTER 5

— ✠ —

The Blood of Angels: Psychological and Physical Abuse in the Name of *God*

The pig and the chicken were on their way to breakfast, trying to decide what to have. When chicken said, "Let's have ham and eggs," the pig then replied, "That's fine for you. It's a small donation on your part, but it's a total sacrifice for me."

—Anonymous

I gave you my blood
I gave you the body
You have stolen my function,
my gumption, my instinct,
It squandered my muscle
It dried up my cells
and tore up my heart
my heart, my heart
I brandished a hat
I hid in the veil
I carried the candles
the water
the smoke
I poured out the water, the oil, the salt
I ate all the bread, all the meat, all the sweet
I ate up your dirt, your semen, your shame
You were fed. You were full.
There was more. There was all.
"Give me more. Give me all" . . .
I was still. I was spent
I was sick. I was dead.

—Mikele Rauch

Every religion asks something in return for the promises it offers. Religious people are called to give of themselves, separating wants from needs, and to offer what they have for the good of themselves and others. They are assured that they can achieve a state of being or a realm that is exalted, but they must sacrifice something that they would otherwise not forfeit. The task at hand is to discuss the meaning and validity of sacrifice in order to give it its due respect and to distinguish when religion incurs abuses through the sacrifice it imposes. Yet, this exploration is complicated by a Western psychological perspective that often errs on the side of the need-based ego instead of a mature and self-actualized ego that is not dependent on constant affirmation from the outside. To give freely without investment in acknowledgment or payback is considered the highest form of love and service. This classic religious definition of sacrifice initially gives little nuance to what it means to relinquish one's own essentials for the sake of the greater good, yet it is a misunderstood and profoundly important part of conscientious intentional existence and religious life.

Sacrifice (from the Latin *sacer facere*—to make sacred) is a gift of a life—a way of a life. It gives meaning to suffering and the pain of others and offers a way to address the forces of evil. Sacrifice can be physical, mental, political, economic—or spiritual. When it comes to religion, it entails giving what is valuable in us to the blessed task at hand. It implies selflessness and, with that, the indefinable quality called *love*, another often overused and misinterpreted word in religious communities.

Love is sacrosanct, often divine. It is an offering. Sometimes, this offering is hidden from view. But, for some, the gift is not always freely given, nor is it even understood. In fact, certain sacrifice labeled as demonstrating love or charity can result in the destruction of one's mental stability, emotional balance, or integrity.

I GAVE YOU MY BLOOD—I GAVE YOU MY BODY

Kate was a precocious child in a large, anxious family. She describes the shaming physical abuse that seemed to follow many episodes of psychological abuse. Her exchange with a nun in the parochial school speaks for itself.

> I had a lot of spunk. I wish I would have known that more at the time. I wish I would have been able to feel good about that, because it just got wrapped in terror and fear. In the fifth grade there was a nun we called Chugalug because she was very fat, ugly, moved slow, and just seemed so miserable. I was at the chalkboard doing some math, and she came up to the board—probably correcting. She got to mine, and it was wrong—whatever she said to me was really humiliating—in front of the class. She turned to walk away, and I stuck my tongue out at her, so of course the whole class started laughing, and she turned around and came back and just grabbed my face and just slapped me across the

face. So then I was more humiliated and red-faced. She turned around again, and I stuck my tongue out again at her. She came back and again slapped me, even harder. (Kate)

At first glance, it appears Kate was simply willful and disrespectful. But, underneath, she was trying to keep her own sense of self despite being humiliated.

In penmanship, and the nuns always had to have it just right. They would pick it up take it to the trashcan, and just rip it, and say "that's not good enough." They must have projected everything out onto us: all of their pain, all of their repressed parts of self that they couldn't have and couldn't own. I think I was certainly a target because, at that age, I was not very good at shutting everything down and people pleasing. (Kate)

She looks at the situation now with some appreciation for the child that she was, forced to sacrifice her pride and spirit.

I fought back. I was aware of the humiliation but knew that I couldn't articulate any of it myself. I left the class feeling like my friends were saying, "Cool!" But inside I still felt like crap. Because it was just a façade—me trying to defend or protect myself. (Kate)

Kate's sacrifice was not optional. Adults may have more choices, but sometimes the purpose is lost in the corruption of service by authority.

YOU HAVE STOLEN MY FUNCTION, MY GUMPTION, MY INSTINCT . . .

Patrice entered a spiritual community's training program with the intention of sacrificing and serving. She had hopes of becoming a spiritual teacher. Unfortunately for her, a combination of events resculpted her reality and made it impossible for her to continue her practice. In her community, there was a specific, almost ritualistic adherence to prescribed words and actions. The physical rigor and the intense pressure to master an extremely complex spiritual practice in a short time created a psychological quandary. She was forced to make a choice between her own way of thinking and her teacher's way. Her sense of self, her talents, and her individuality were compromised because of her treatment from both the leadership and the community; she experienced an emotional and spiritual breakdown but received little support or understanding of her situation from the leadership.

But the part that was really difficult for me was that there was a make-it-or break-it attitude around the teacher's training, and everyone was afraid that they weren't going to make it. We were subjected to this very rigorous, what some people would call like a spiritual boot-camp kind of process—day after day of the same: up at five and in bed by one or later. To top it all off, there was a strict adherence to the exact words that were supposed to be used. The teacher wanted to introduce a whole new way of teaching the class. I felt used because she told me, in front of the group, that it was going to be my job to write the manual. But first I was going to have to get rid of that "psychology." (Patrice)

The power of authority and the community is strong, even in groups where the sacrifice or the abuse of sacrifice is less dramatic. Indeed, many religious communities *are* one's family more than blood, but the relationships and care within them are sometimes just as conditional or as tumultuous as those negotiated with blood relatives.

When I could perform for the group, everyone loved me. When I was not performing in a way that they felt was beneficial to them, I was discarded, and that's really how it felt. (Patrice)

Not all "mind" control is inherently malevolent; it is the manner in which it is used and whether, in the course of the educative process, options are actually available. Education is a form of mind control that implies that the student has the power and the makes the decision about whether to learn. The locus of control should always remain within the individual. In indoctrination, the person who is being "trained" does not have independent power to accept or reject the ideology.[1]

Keeping one's own mind under coercive circumstances sometimes comes at great emotional and moral cost for oneself and others. What Shimon sacrificed for his personal integrity was most agonizing for the ones who loved him most.

I thought the worst of Shimon when he could not believe. I even wondered why *God* had told me to marry him if it was going to work out like this. I was so scared of what people would think of us. I was afraid of their pity as much as their ridicule. And then, one day, the church was not a place I could feel safe, either, and so these fears are even more personal. I did terrible things to Shimon because I thought it was what the church would have me do. So I fear others might be capable of the same thing. (Naomi)

Naomi made the resolution to follow her own conscience and to support Shimon. With this decision came the realization of all she would also be giving up. In a letter to her family, she wrote:

I love all of you. Those who can stay in the church should know that there is a big piece of me that envies you. I envy your experiences. I never wanted another path. I believe I could speak for [our family] in saying that self-preservation has led us to where we are now. All of us are trying to survive and heal. It is extremely painful to think of not participating in very special sacred occasions with you. It is so sad there are not words for it. I feel like this is the path I must take for my sanity and the preservation of my family. I fear that others will think I made this decision lightly or without regard for the things that matter most. It is because I can see no other way to hold together the things that matter most that I make this very painful decision. (Naomi)

For Naomi, as for many women, the personal spiritual journey is always interrelated with those in her family or community. For them, being a woman *is* the ultimate sacrifice.

YOU SQUANDERED MY MUSCLE, IT DRIED UP MY CELLS . . .

In the history of each of the five major religions,[2] there have been formulas interpreted by men, rituals usually created by men, scriptures written by men, laws dictated by men, and yet a demand for sacrifice from the community that included and even relied on women and children. Religion is a personal and institutional reality for women, but it has also been a source of their further subjugation to men. Many scriptures and prophetic writings have been misconstrued to create a dominant and permanent male power structure. Most of the time, God is represented as a man.

Women are often out of the loop in religious hierarchies. Few of them hold any overt authority in the structures of religion (although they may have great influence behind the scenes). Even though three of the major religious systems (Christianity, Buddhism, and Hinduism) have a strong feminine lineage of spiritual giants, they seldom have substantial female leadership in their hierarchies except in convents and occasional ministries. In many of these systems, women are instead asked or forced to maintain the peace in their homes or churches, even if they or their daughters are silenced, sexually misused, physically violated, beaten, or mutilated. In the name of God, they sometimes lose control of their own sexual lives, reproductive power, and self-determination, and if they refuse to comply, they may be punished, banished, or even killed. Occasionally it is religion that is in the image of society's most regressive components, especially when there have been centuries of male domination. Today, women's struggles in all five world religions are leading to greater self-determination; women are making progress and receiving attention—but the sacrifice is great. Women are often seen as demonic, temptresses, less than human, objects of sorrow, chattel, or simply invisible.

The fear of women is enmeshed in many religious cultures. Women may be seen as a dangerous combination of idealized subject and sexual object, making them easier to abuse because they are not seen as equal humans. In conscious or unconscious ways, women are viewed as *others* capable of threatening men with their intellectual thoughts or enticing men with their sexuality, while often being kept on the outside. This is perhaps the most plausible rationale for the widespread sexual and religious abuse of women in Christianity, Islam, Judaism, Buddhism, and Hinduism. Their suffering is often discounted, their voices ignored. For this reason, women in every major religion struggle with debilitating depression and drug abuse in secret.[3]

Beth, an American Buddhist, had gone to study in another country with a *tulku*, someone who had been identified as being born with advanced capacities for enlightenment. *Tulkus* are taken away from their mothers and families and raised in the all-male environment of a monastery which can sometimes stunt their emotional development. This particular young man had found a way to use Beth for his own purposes without taking responsibility for his sexual violations, while confusing the boundaries of personal space and spirituality.

> He was always like, "No, no, no, I am not your guru." He was very clear about that, which makes me realize how totally manipulative he was. Because on the one, he was keeping his *karma* clean by saying, "I'm not your guru; this is just whatever it is, you need to go somewhere else for your guru and therefore whatever relationship we have, I'm not responsible to you the way I'm responsible to a student." (Beth)

Women like Beth are not necessarily or simply victims. Yet, the participation in the process of their own subordination can compromise their intentions and their spiritual lives. Many have been shaped by religious leadership to internalize the idea of their own inferiority. Once they are robbed of their own strength or spirit, subjugation is the natural progression.

> I felt like I got to this point where I kind of cracked and I did a total about face. I just couldn't reconcile my gut feelings that what this guy was doing was not right, everyone else's seeming indifference to his behavior, and my own desire to learn about Buddhism. So from thinking instinctively, "No, this is not right! I shouldn't have to give up this, my body, to learn about Buddhism," I just flipped and started thinking, "Okay, so this is great and this guy totally knows what he's talking about and I'm really lucky to be here. I'm going to learn everything from him. He is amazing, he is enlightened." I just did this total mental flip, and all of a sudden I had no place in my conscious thought for all of the questions and doubts and objections I had been having. I think I just shoved them all as far away as possible, telling myself, "Nope, can't pay attention to those doubts! Can't pay attention to those gut instincts! There's no place for them." (Beth)

This situation is a variation of what is known as the Stockholm Syndrome.[4] When an abuser shows his victim some minor kindness or, in this case, some spiritual attention, especially in a situation where the victim has no way out and even when it benefits the abuser, the victim sees that kindness as a positive trait. Often a small token of caring can produce extreme loyalty, even love for the abuser. When there seems to be no way out of a morally compromising exchange with a spiritual leader, a person may look for a small indication that the situation will improve or change. Often in such situations, the abused will defend the abuser and justify the violation as either part of the spiritual training or as a sign of special spiritual privilege.

Ironically it was Beth's love for her spiritual path that also led her to give in to the immense pressure of her situation. The combination of psychological and physical factors, her isolation from anything familiar, and her desperation led her to a position of immense vulnerability.

> I have always been a feminist. When I think back to that time and think about how I accepted that situation, part of me feels embarrassed. How did I not just call this man on his complete and total bullshit!? What was I thinking? And the only thing that I can think is that I loved Buddhism and spirituality more than I loved feminism. I was willing to think that there were truths in Buddhism that were deeper than those in feminism. I also I think I had culture shock. I was in this foreign country, in this fairly isolated environment, with a person from a totally different culture from me. I also had this idea that there is such a thing as *cultural relativity*[5] and that I just needed to be open. I think I was just really off balance. (Beth)

Throughout history, women have been placed in a position where they had to sacrifice even what was most valuable to them for the sake of others. Carol Flinders is both a spiritual writer and a feminist. She remarks that the final triumph of patriarchy over women is the codependent personality. "Codependence" is defined as self-sacrifice at the expense of one's own integrity, where there is a need to nurture what is out of control and a sense of self that is profoundly underdeveloped.[6]

It is important to clarify that the term "codependency" means an aberration and a misinterpretation of love. The codependency literature has often been misinterpreted; it has created a set of harmful beliefs about self-esteem and self-care at the expense of others. In fact, the codependent personality often demonstrates another aspect of closet narcissism. The person's need to control the politics of giving creates an inability to see where she fails to care. And extreme fear of criticism or of being found deficient creates an inability to be reflective. In fact, the codependent person may mistake her self-care and self-vigilance for self-indulgence because they require that she rest, or eat, or take time away from the work she is dependent upon. In the end, codependency has more to do with the giver than with the receiver.

Carol Flinders argues that women have learned to subdue the forces of their own extraordinary thinking powers, their desires, and their souls with the misbegotten notion that, in asserting them, they will betray or override their husbands, fathers, pastors, or sons. "It doesn't need to be policed, this extraordinary machine, for it has achieved the perfect balance between force and finesse. The ancient threats, of ears cut off and pitch poured on the head, of beatings and hangings and burnings, are never voiced because they do not have to be." The codependent personality, Flinders goes on to say, "is the final triumph of patriarchy."[7]

AND TORE UP MY HEART, MY HEART, MY HEART . . .

As we have seen, the consequences of personal sacrifice are so profound that they can often result in lifelong isolation from family and community.

Irit and Rasan have lived their rich lives and raised their incredible children with little contact from Irit's family—the penalty for their decision to love and marry. Irit remembers her father's last days with sadness.

> He was dying. When I went to see him in the hospital, I was with him all day. It was five years I hadn't been there. This trip—I had planned just to see him. After five days, he saw that I had been with him all day. He couldn't speak, but I saw he appreciated my effort. I said to him, "My kids would like to meet you and see you." For me it was important for him to know that I have kids. It was important that he knew their names before he died and that he would take with him that piece of information. So I told him their names, and he asked, "Where are they?" I said, "In the U.S." Actually, this was our last conversation. This was the first and the last. . . . It was very hard for him to know that his daughter was marrying a Muslim. For him it was the end of the world. I was cut off. For him, it was disastrous, and I learned to forgive him. This is how he grew up and that was his world; he didn't know better. For him, it's something that is a sin. (Irit)

Families can still grow; they can learn and give again. But there is no way to make up for what has been lost over time because of the choices people have made, even if they are the most authentic choices for them.

> My mother is in a nursing home. I have sisters and cousins, and we have a very close family, and I really enjoy that. I realize now that the family was part of me that I missed in all these years. I had to choose, and I made a choice—and I paid the price. I mean, I'm not regretting it; I think it was a good choice for me. (Irit)

Even so, after all that has been sacrificed, at times we are left with a sense of betrayal and diminishment from our spiritual home.

> My family seems to be of no importance at all. If I had written a heartfelt letter to any organization I had given thousands of dollars to, my money alone would have made me worth their time. In my church, nothing about me makes me worth anything. (Naomi)

Shimon and Naomi have had to leave their community and move to another city to begin their new life. Their grief is mixed with resolve and even gratitude. But it is a wrenching process.

> I struggle to forgive. I have lost so much. I have lost the activity of my husband with whom I used to attend the temple and play in the orchestra. More than that, I have lost the simple joy I felt in believing that all of us were important in the Church, even me. (Naomi)

There are other sacrifices people choose that they hope will move them from loss to gaining a kind of personal or spiritual advancement. Almost every religion has a form of spiritual discipline that is enacted as a form of withdrawal from the senses of the body or from the intimacy of relationships—abstention from alcohol or indulgences is seen as a way to enhance individual strength, meditation, or character. These practices may include solitude, simplicity in living, fasting, sexual abstinence, and prayer. There are profound cultural differences regarding austerities that make it impossible for us to judge the qualities and extent of such sacrifices in each community. But, no matter where or how they take place, without an integrated and balanced mind, these various forms of penance can be dangerous.

Personal austerity is not meant to desecrate or compromise the body or soul. Fasting and early-morning meditations or prayers can be important practices to deepen spiritual practice. Self-denial is meant to deepen the focus. Yet, sometimes, the psychological and basic physical requirements of individuals are neglected or consciously forfeited for religious reasons. Physical and psychological stress are not necessarily detrimental in the context of sacrifice but become suspect when austerities are selectively imposed by the powerful upon those without power or emotional balance. It may be neither therapeutic nor inspirational, especially when the one asked or forced to practice penance emerges weakened and out of balance. This particular "sacrifice" can degenerate into emotional or mental illness.

In Patrice's situation, the consequences of her treatment temporarily broke her body and mind. It had nothing to do with her spirituality.

> Someone should've recognized the signs that I was malnourished and sleep deprived Instead of sensing I needed attention, I was told to just be quiet, that no one could help me right now, everyone was busy. It is disturbing that there were people there who could have helped. There were doctors there. Anyone could have gone to ask a doctor to check on me, but no one did. I was even told by someone that there were doctors here, and I asked, "Could someone have a look at me?" No doctors came, but one person suggested a bowl of rice with a little bit of herbs thrown in. That was my "cure." I was starting to starve. I had the sensibility to know that this was not a safe environment and that I could go into a kind of mental malaise by not sleeping and eating. I needed some kind of intervention. (Patrice)

In some religious systems, there is a distorted relationship between self-effacement and holiness. The ripe, functioning ego that is necessary for an intuitive and conscious mind is relinquished for a mistaken notion of humility. The process becomes a form of degradation, which is an essential component of a broken psyche. This kind of self-abasement does not create real humility, which is based on a sense of clarity about what is authentic and real inside. In fact, it generates the opposite effect in a needy, self-involved ego. Under this kind of mortification, humiliation destroys the sense of self by pointing to physical and mental weaknesses and past "fallen" behaviors. One's unique talents or qualities are often reviled or misused. Though the goal of such a practice is for the individual to lose an arrogant pride, what happens is often the opposite; mortification and shame capitalize on the mind-boggling concept of our being both "chosen" above others and condemned, building up a false and unreliable self, which is the ironic outcome of shame.

Patrice, for instance, was degraded and manipulated by her teacher and in the community, which compromised any real sense of self.

> I was being told that I wasn't getting it right, and I was being verbally punished in front of a group of my peers every day. It was as if I was the one the teacher felt she could berate each session, just enough so that everyone else would snap to attention. The teacher had also taken me aside and told me that I had the potential to be a great teacher but that I must follow her verbatim or I would fail. My intention for becoming a teacher was to help numbers of people to live better lives. I admit my ego wanted to be recognized as a good teacher—but not at this cost. (Patrice)

I POURED OUT THE WATER, THE OIL, THE SALT . . .

In order to prepare someone for radical change, especially deep inner transformation, her reality must be transformed, even shaken. Yet, when someone is isolated from the outside or from her own community to evoke a behavioral change, her frame of reference can quickly shift in a disorienting way. In a closed religious world, sensory overload or deprivation can produce extreme confusion, which in turn creates a crazy-making double-bind reality. Under these conditions, memory does *not* serve. Instead, it can become fuzzy and broken, which makes clear recollection of events impossible.

> I was disoriented, but I was not able to sleep after the third week. I was talked about, and never spoken to [except] "Stay here. Sit still. Be quiet." I was put in a house that was empty during the day. I was told not to leave. Was I locked in? I don't know. I didn't try the door. (Patrice)

Performing extreme acts of atonement for the world and oneself can be dangerous if they are not based in an authentic interior practice and supported by a healthy spiritual community. A particular sect or community may recommend these activities,[8] but if the penance is practiced to the point of sadomasochism, it results in neurotic self-absorption, instead of the containment of the ego. The consequences of such actions can change the chemistry of the body, as well as the brain. They can even create narcissistic regression that becomes idealized self-destruction. These practices may enable people to carry on morbid self-harming activities, which are physically dangerous and create a discharge of intense emotions that is difficult for an individual to manage. Those who are numb inside may feel some connection to the pain, but the release in this particular kind of sacrifice creates only a momentary catharsis, instead of an inner awakening.

Anorexia or the use of physical devices like ropes, hair shirts, clamps, or knives on the body is part of a warped continuum of religious self-abuse. These "austerities" can become addictive ways to release tension and to gain a sense of control. The pain of the practices themselves produces feelings of euphoria mistaken for spiritual experiences, but the body's endorphins are actually inhibiting its responses and kicking in to create the release, a bitter paradox as the self tries to protect itself from pain.[9] For many, these kinds of austerities can be unconscious reenactments of previous trauma that have nothing to do with spirituality at all. Ironically, they can provide a way to physically express what is happening either in the present and in secret or something long ago.

For Shimon, self-mutilating was an unconscious opportunity to show on the outside what he had been suffering all along.

> I remember the first time I really started self-harming, something that I had been silent about my whole life was visible on the outside. There was something so compelling about having made concrete something that had been silent my whole life. It was very much that I was also saying, "I am not okay." It was the first time I had ever dared to make concrete the fact that something is not right, and so there *was* something. And it was an ability to bring that out. . . . I had been killing parts of myself all these years. So I was making that self-aggression external, where I could examine it in a different way. (Shimon)

I ATE ALL THE BREAD, ALL THE MEAT, ALL THE SWEET

Probably one of the most insidious outcomes of chosen religious sacrifice (and its darker addictions) is piety, a trap for those who give most ostentatiously or indiscriminately without an interior compass. While piety may come from an earnest endeavor to manifest the divine by thought, word, or deed, it can be a tricky manifestation of shame's most stubborn shadow. Frederick Douglass, in his *Slave Narrative*, describes how Christian piety was misused to defend slavery, sacrificing one race for the comfort of another: "I can see no reason but the most deceitful one, for calling the religion of this land, *Christianity*. I look upon it as the climax of all misnomers, the boldest of all frauds, and the grossest of all libels. Never was there a clearer case of 'stealing the livery of the court of heaven to serve the devil in.' I am filled with unutterable loathing when I contemplate the religious pomp and show, together with the horrible inconsistencies, which everywhere surround me."[10]

Under the mask of piety, the devout may blame the victims, demand further sacrifice, and even punish them instead of those who have perpetrated the abuse. This does not eradicate the abuse or erase the pain—for anyone. It only exacerbates the moral collapse the abuse has already incurred.

When the leader of a Hindu community had been accused of sexually violating one young nun, the community's response was to turn the tables and demand that *she* either make amends for what had been done to her or leave the community. There was no question of responsibility or accountability on the part of the spiritual leader. And, in the end, she had no recourse but to leave.

> And some of the nuns were saying beg his forgiveness for whatever you did, it'll be okay. The ones who encouraged me to seek forgiveness assumed I had done something horrible to bring on his really vicious attacks and accusations. The situation was growing intolerable—being expected to appear contrite while carrying that knowledge. (Diana)

No one should be called to sacrifice honor or integrity for the sake of community homeostasis or to keep the peace. No one should ever have to be punished for telling the truth, no matter how unbecoming it is for the community's public persona. In the words of Abishiktananda, a Benedictine priest who became a wandering Hindu swami, "piety is the ego's last stand."[11] Its spiritual pretentiousness masks injustice, and, in an unconscious turnabout of supercilious pride, it can provide justification for physical, psychological, or even sexual abuse. Piety plays good with its silence or heavenward glance, but it is often a cheap masquerade for authentic spirituality and cannot ever hide the moral betrayals, coverups, or lies of the "devout."

THERE WAS MORE, THERE WAS ALL, "GIVE ME MORE, GIVE ME ALL . . ."

In the history of religion, there have always been religious movements. There are some that celebrate a definitive sacrifice that is given in exchange for the ultimate gain of salvation or honor; there have always been people who have willingly sacrificed their own lives for the good of the cause or by being associated with it.

Martyrdom, either by choice or by affiliation, is the sacrifice of life for one's religious beliefs. In light of the current religious climate, it is of note that those who choose to die by killing themselves or others in the name of *God* are usually idealistic young men and women who appear to be unattached to the preciousness of their own lives. The ones who direct that course of that sacrifice are often the elders. Perhaps their twin fears of death and replacement make it easier to dictate the value of such ultimate sacrifice for the young, especially if they are unable or unwilling to sacrifice themselves.

The sacrifice of martyrdom may come in response to something that has failed—reactivity to modernity and marginalization, a call for revolution, or a desire for a dramatic change. Yet, dying for a cause by suicide or while committing violent acts against others or those in one's own faith is also indicative of the deep despair and hopelessness of those who see no future in the lives they lead.

There is yet another kind of sacrifice that is never requested, never negotiated. It is the sacrifice that is made under the terrible conditions of ritual abuse. In such a sacrifice, through an aberration of religious ritual, victims are forced to atone bodily or to give back to a deity or a demonic force something of themselves in order to create a "right" relationship between themselves and the "sacred order." The rites of ritual abuse can involve human blood, burning, being buried alive for some time, and witnessing violence or sadistic acts committed on other people or animals. This is a profound aberration of human rights and an unconscionable violation of any man, woman, or child. We will return to the subject and the "sacrifice" of ritual abuse in chapter 6.

Every holocaust, every pogrom, every genocide that has occurred under the banner of faith is evil at its most unimaginable. Extermination in the name of God through the sacrifice of a race or a religious body to restore religious, racial, or spiritual "purity" is a trauma often endured by an entire community. Though it can take centuries for a people to reclaim their spiritual place, the safety to practice their religion, or even the freedom to speak, it is often under such persecution and with enormous unspeakable loss that profound spirituality grows. This is the opposite response from hopelessness, which is the secondary loss generated from despair.[12]

Victor Frankl, as a young Austrian doctor, survived his way through the depravity of the Nazi concentration camps by finding meaning beyond bitterness and something beyond the physical or mental abuse that he suffered. He found that this *something* could sustain him in the face of losing everything. In his profoundly personal response, *Man's Search for Meaning,* he writes, "Each man is questioned by life; and he can only answer to life by answering for his own life; to life he can only respond by being responsible."[13]

Like Dr. Frankl, even amid such powerful losses, people find ways to restore themselves and those they care about. They may become activists; they may empower others to think for themselves, or practice fierce compassion. Recovery can be rooted in an action or a stance, as it is for Victor, a psychotherapist and a survivor whose restoration is not simply an intellectual exercise. He has dedicated his professional life to service and to others' recovery. But he challenges those in religious authority to answer for what they themselves do, with the same authenticity and rigor they demand of others.

If it's true that we all have to reckon things at the end of our lives, then why don't you let the reckoning happen and get on with your life? You know, take care of poverty, end war, um, you know, *be kind!* Help people who are in trouble. (Victor)

Be kind . . . What would it mean if *this* were the ultimate criterion for sacrifice? It would be no small matter—kindness is a decision, more than an emotion. It would entail sacrifice at its most *un*dramatic: it would not exclude. It would mean consistent action beyond sentiment and the development of character without performance. It would be a quiet activism in the open, in the house, in the church, and in each of us. Kindness is not a show of niceties or the piety of acceptance ("Well, it's *God's* will. . . ."). Real kindness must come from a place of courage and human caring, where real trust can be generated.

At its best, sacrifice is surely the gift of a life, a way of living. It is uncompromising compassion. Yet, in the end, the most powerful antibiotic for the corruption of sacrifice and restitution for the abuse of it will is compassionate but rigorous transparency in religious life. It is this unflinching transparency that will be most urgently required as we bear witness to those who have suffered sexual and ritual abuse in the ecosystem of religion.

RECOMMENDED READINGS

Corwin, Marla A. "Meaning in Suffering," guest sermon delivered at the Columbine Unitarian Universalist Church, January 31, 2005, http://www.columbineuu church.org/sermons/corwin_sermon1.html.

Flinders, Carol Lee. *At the Root of this Longing, Reconciling a Spiritual Hunger and a Feminist Thirst* (San Francisco: HarperCollins, 1998).

Goodwin, Jan. *The Price of Honor: Muslim Women Lift the Veil of Silence on the Islamic World* (New York: Plume Books, 1995).

Hassan, Steven. *Combating Cult Mind Control: Guide to Protection, Rescue, and Recovery from Destructive Cult* (South Paris, ME: Park Street Press, 1988).

Lerner, Gerda. *The Creation of Patriarch* (New York: Oxford University Press, 1986).

Thandeka, *Learning to Be White: Money, Race, and God in America* (New York: Continuum, 2001).

RECOMMENDED FILMS

For the Bible Tells Me So. Daniel G. Karslake, First Run Features (2007).

God and Gays, Bridging the Gap. Kim Clarke (2008).

A Jihad for Love. Sandi Simcha DuBowski (2008).

Latter Day. FunnyBoy Films, Davis Entertainment Filmworks (2003).

My Father, My Lord (*Another Abraham's Story with a Different Ending*). Kino International (2008).

Priest. Antonia Bird, Miramax Films (1994).

Trembling Before G-d. Sandi Simcha DuBowski (2001).

CHAPTER 6

———— ✠ ————

This Is My Body: When Religious Violate in the Name of *God*—Sexual and Ritual Abuse

Listen, or thy tongue will keep thee deaf . . .

—Native American saying

What had happened? It was a man of *God* that did this and told me it was special love to bring me closer to *You*. Where were *You?* I prayed longer and harder than ever before. Was this priest right? *You* didn't love me? *You* couldn't love me? Why? How? Help! I prayed less and less. Started to fake sick not to go to church. Lied during confession—told less, other times exaggerated—still no response from *God*. The sky was never as blue, the clouds never as white. It was over between me and God. (William)

Living through a sexual trauma is hard to describe. The memory of those events may not be linear. Past and present interchange; often there is no future tense. Many individuals interviewed for this book still struggle with their syntax, because the past can be so unbearably present.

Some days—it's past, some present, some future, some unknown—that is why it is so very hard to answer questions about how and where I am, how I feel. (William)

Survivors risk further pain and estrangement in speaking about what has happened to them; sometimes there is little secondary gain by unveiling their experiences, especially if it has been a kind of spiritual death for them. But people *do* tell their stories and find their way in surprising and profound ways, nevertheless.

When air hits an abrasion after the bandage is removed, there is a burning on the skin. But the air is a necessary element for repair. These stories and their storytellers burn, but they need the air to heal; they need to be heard and seen.

There is a *truth* that was supposed to be the ultimate Word, but another truth made a travesty of it. The *truth* would have set the world free, but this one weighs heavy. *Truth* is one, but sometimes it has been broken into pieces and splattered across the pavement in the name of ideology. The *truth* is a balm; often a salve feels hot to the touch before it soothes.

Truth burns. Truth heals.

So we listen, even if what we hear is difficult to bear.

THE WOLF IN GOD'S CLOTHING

Sexual abuse in a religious context is a double breach of sacred trust and space. It occurs when sexual activity is forced or coerced by a person in some position of power on another. It is not necessarily direct physical contact. Sexual abuse in a religious context can include voyeurism, exposure to sexual material, inappropriate and erotic sexual conversations, or sexual exposure in the context of a religious activity. But it is an act of aggression nonetheless, whether one is forced or seduced, whether it is painful or pleasurable.

Sexual abuse by a member of the clergy in any religion is tantamount to incest. No violation other than with a blood relative combines such profound intimacy with intense betrayal. The breach is all the more serious because the abuse is under the auspices and in the company of the *sacred*. Circumstances and context can differ whether the victim is a child or an adult. But, for anyone violated in this manner, regardless of age, the malevolent exploitation of trust, dependency, and affection leads to a mind-numbing decline into alienation, secrecy, and spiritual chaos.

> He made it seem like I was going through some kind of special sacrament, and always wore his full black priestly garb . . . He told me everything's going to be all right, and we were going to start our training . . . He made me feel very special. He pulled my pants down and my underpants and told me to be quiet, and he bent me over my bed. I remember I didn't know what was going on, and the next thing I knew, I felt something up my rectum. And he told me to be quiet. I remember how it hurt, and I remember seeing my tears drop onto the bedspread, and he was holding on. I remember telling him it hurt, he told me not to anger God. And I didn't know what to do. I just kind of froze. I could see his reflection in the mirror, and he was just happy. He kept repeating the "Our Father." I would have to say it with him—as I said, "Thy will be done," that this [was] God's will—"Thy will be done, this is God's will." Then it was over. (William)

THE MEMBRANE OF MEMORY

When the dynamics of power are out of balance, a forced or seductive sexual contact by a representative of the divine can distort reality and the naming of it. Most profoundly, a sexual exchange like this can alter one's sense of self. Sexual abuse is so morally and emotionally confusing that one often splits from present experience and even memory, shutting down the body's responses just to survive. Sexual abuse is always invasive, even if it does not appear to be violent. It can flood a person with sorrow, rage, and, sometimes pleasure, which is all the more confusing. It almost always creates inconsolable isolation. Often, there is no technology to talk about it to any-body else. One may try over and over to let someone else know that some-thing is wrong, even by performing abusive acts on others or doing something self-destructive; yet, it might be difficult for anybody else to understand what is really being communicated with all this acting out. This can create further isolation or worse—it places the victim in the role of aggressor, often creating a scenario that obscures his own experience of trauma.

Sexual abuse can make its victims feel numb or hypervigilant. Victims sometimes lose track of time or become out of touch with natural body re-sponses. They may become either oversexed or completely asexual as a result of what has happened. They may cling to obsessive thoughts and behaviors, suffer flashbacks, or become dissociative. Sometimes the abuse stays below the radar of consciousness, locked in cellular memories for decades and show-ing up only later in locked joints, immune suppressed illnesses, and neural muscular pain.

Will Michaels's sexual abuse did not surface into consciousness until he was an adult. The sexual abuse by his parish priest always took place in si-lence. These silent memories were stored like holograms in his body until he was on the massage table as an adult.

> We started to do some massage around it, and that's when that stuff just came. The masseuse was tender and said, "Your body doesn't lie. Muscle memories are powerful." And then the memories—it was like the floodgates just opened up: this man who raped me when I was 10—that all came back, the priest came back. And I remember my masseuse saying to me, "It's almost like . . . little Will—(he's still inside)—realizes that Will the adult is now ready to get this information." (Will Michaels)

Sometimes the shame or horror of abuse can hold someone captive for decades. Francis kept his sexual abuse by another member of his religious community a secret until he was past 50 years old.

> It was in the seminary. He was also a scoutmaster, and there was grooming beforehand. One night he had me sleep in his tent and then molested me; and I knew it was abuse as it was happening. I froze. You know, the next day, I felt awful. I put the face on like everything was normal and pretty much wore that for 30 years until—I needed to address it. (Francis)

Francis consequently expected nothing more for himself until the sexual abuse of children he served took its toll on him.

[The abuse had] occurred for two and a half years. I entered religious life to spite that and continued to live with people who were accused of being abusers. Eventually I went to a place where they had an abuser as a youth minister; the guy had been convicted and done jail time—and all the stuff I buried came to a head. (Francis)

The truth has a way of seeping through the pores of silence. It can take years for it to bubble up, either because of the fear of repercussions or because of post-traumatic lapse of memory. That is why the statutes of limitations in common-law legal systems, which usually set three to seven years as the limit when offenders can be persecuted, are deficient and actually harmful for victims of childhood sexual abuse.

THE MEMBRANE OF CONTROL

For those who have lived through religious sexual abuse, the circumstances of addiction, work, or even sacrifice in other parts of their lives sometimes create powerful reenactments of the conditions of the abuse. It may be easier to do what is most familiar, recreating the abusive situation in one form or another rather than imagining how living could be otherwise. Some people simply withdraw from any human touch or contact altogether because they can no longer trust their natural instincts about love or safety. Religious sexual abuse breaches a sense of trust and can obliterate the belief in human goodness.

This is the psychological fallout.

But there is another consequence, as well. Sexual violation can contaminate the deepest sense of one's spirit.

If the abuse has been an intrinsic part of the culture in one's particular community, the buffer around physical and emotional integrity may be decimated without much resistance from the one being harmed. This creates confusion about both sacred and personal space.

In communities where there is plural marriage or polygamy, for example, women may be both stepmothers and sister-wives to one another, and children grow up with multiple mothers and siblings. Polyandry,[1] the practice in which a woman may be married to more than one man, happens more infrequently. Polygamy is practiced in Muslim communities throughout Africa and the Middle East, in fundamentalist Mormon sects, and, occasionally, in isolated circumstances among African American Muslims.[2] In some of these communities, there are situations when polygamous marriage is not only permissible but actually advisable.[3] Sex ratios, thrown off because of war and the wish to aid widows with children, are often cited as reasons for plural marriage, but the practice of polygamy is not without restrictions. Sometimes the outside community steps in to oversee what is deemed a questionable situation.

In 2008, for example, 400 children were seized from a polygamous fundamental sect of the Latter Day Saints in Texas after allegations of forced marriage and sexual abuse of minors. The children were removed from their homes and their mothers. The sect, which believes polygamy is ordained by God, found itself in conflict with the law and with the standards of the outside community about the protection of children and of women. This has raised a major ethical and moral debate between religion and the greater community about values, family, marriage, children, sexual practices—and sexual abuse.

Some children who live in polygamous families may learn a protocol of incest that is passed from generation to generation. Those too young or too isolated from the outside world may not understand how their lives could be any other way. Under these conditions, girls can be groomed to be victims and boys to be predators. The sexuality may be introduced too early and often, with the loss of safety being imperceptible to some in the community. The one who abuses is often a caregiver; he may be sexually exploitive or overwhelming, yet remain a primary source of love and comfort and, ironically, even overprotective. Authentic love, loyalty, and prayer may blur the sexual boundaries, especially if the incestuous contact is so familiar in the household that it seems that nothing out of the ordinary is going on.

To deconstruct or to reveal what happens behind the closed doors of such an insulated community may be extremely difficult, even unthinkable. Exposing a sexual violation, a childhood rape, or a forced childhood marriage seems an insurmountable task unless individuals are willing to risk alienation from the only family and community they have ever known. But despite great difficulty, there are resources and support for those members who wish to speak out, find places of safe haven or have their stories be heard. Finding even one person in the community who can name what is happening, or see behind the veil of silence, can be the first step toward taking the risk of disclosure.

THE MEMBRANE OF DESIRE

Sometimes sexual aberration in community living arrangements occurs on the opposite end of the spectrum. Religious congregations that espouse a life of sexual abstinence present a similar problem when it comes to sexual abuse.

Celibacy involves an honest and sustained attempt to live *without* direct sexual gratification in order to serve others productively for a spiritual motive. In the religious communities that are supposed to be continent,[4] this vow of chastity is often imposed rather than freely chosen and frequently creates considerable challenges for those who are not sufficiently prepared or willing to live it, especially if sexual abstinence is practiced without education, psychological balance, or community support.

When celibate men or women have an inappropriately erotic or sadomasochistic relationship in the name of *God*, they corrupt their vows and the persons with whom they engage.

Both the arousal and the exhaustion of such relationships are often fed by an adolescent push-pull of sexual teasing and magical thinking. While these may be earnest, albeit sick, attempts at intimacy, they are based on dominance and submission, perverted gratification, or humiliation. If both parties are not equal players, the outcome is especially disastrous for the one who has the least power. Submission is confused with surrender, even if the abuser mistakes him for the one who has sacrificed. But the real casualty here is the soul. Such abuse deadens the spirit and corrodes authenticity because it has so degraded the deep longing to know and be known.

Mary Gail Frawley O'Dea calls this form of sexual gratification a false-self masquerade. "Arousal, nerve jangling excitement and ultimate exhaustion play perverted understudy roles to transformational erotic excitement, sensuality, and reimagined life."[5]

Occasionally, a strictly friendly same-sex relationship or spiritual kinship devolves into a situation where the older religious or spiritual mentor grooms a younger, less sophisticated student or community member. Physical and sexual lines become blurred and double messages abound, especially when the contact is in a "spiritual" context.

In her book *Sexual Abuse and the Culture of Catholicism*, Myra Hidalgo writes about her long-term sexual relationship with her eighth-grade teacher.

> When Sister Ann and I discussed the nature of our relationship, it was always in a spiritual context. She believed that our connections was very personal gift from God and should be cherished and celebrated. This explanation seemed somehow to justify the secrecy of the relationship, since others would not be capable of understanding its "sacredness." (Myra Hidalgo)[6]

The relationship with her teacher progressed over time, though the imbalance of power was clear from the beginning. At various points, Myra became uncomfortable and tried to pull away, but the Sister would cry. Then the girl would try to comfort her teacher—and the sexual contact would resume. Besides, "My body would respond in ways that were foreign to me, but I was too scared to ask questions."

Often, after a sexual violation, there is no further mention of what has happened. If the matter is discussed at all, it is often put in a spiritual context. Myra Hidalgo said that her perpetrator maintained that their connection was a very personal gift from God to be cherished and celebrated.

Of course a "celebration" like this had to be kept secret. When Myra Hidalgo realized she had been in a homosexual relationship with a person under vows, she "felt sinful, like a pervert and an adulteress."[7]

For a member of a religious community to honestly practice sexual continence and remain psychologically and spiritually integrated, she must have a system of vigorous self-assessment in place as a way to transform sexual energies without repressing the life force. She needs to resolve the reality of living without physical intimacy and possess an ability to see *God* in others and in herself—or, at least, have that intention.

Within the covenant of celibacy is the resolution to actually abstain from all sexual contact with others. It is supposed to be a gift of religious life. This *gift* should release the body and spirit into a love affair with *God*. Celibate life provides a way to love others safely, unfettered by a sexual agenda, but it requires an understanding of the spiritual ideal and the capacity for emotional balance and maturity.

Persons who wish to practice their commitment to celibacy need living conditions and colleagues who also keep their obligation with compassion, integrity, and transparency. They need leaders who not only model and observe their own vows but also can give direction and balance to the celibate community. When the leadership is missing the ability to really nurture healthy and stable sexuality, religious formation itself creates and feeds the *persona* or mask of sanctity. When the leadership does not embody a standard of self-vigilance and honesty, there is only a caricature of sexual purity. Religious systems may even use the particular vocation of celibacy as a callous parody of itself for power and sexual subjugation.[8]

Celibacy requires an active inner life and a demanding honest sense of self. It must be nourished by spiritual longing, which can translate in any spiritual practice as hunger for the ideal. The choice of celibacy brings detachment, which does *not* mean being disconnected or disinterested in relationships. Detachment here means letting go of the desire that creates an exclusive sexual relationship in order to be utterly, deeply connected with all. It incorporates a level of freedom that engages all of one's creative energy and expression in order to find joy in the many other experiences that life provides.

Unfortunately, there are those Christian, Hindu, and Buddhist celibates who have little education and even fewer outlets to talk about sexual matters.[9] Therefore, when abuses occur, silence caps the lid of scandal—or, as we will later see, members demonize the person who reveals an impropriety or any concern about sexual matters because of their own ignorance or fear.

In those religious communities of women where sexual mistreatment of children and other women is kept under the radar, the reason is not always cultural or sexist bias. Sometimes the mechanics of the abuse and the particular manner of touch are bewildering, not only because these women have more malleable boundaries for physical contact but because their lack of awareness around sexual matters makes the violation difficult to name. This ignorance extends outside the convent or monastery walls and into other relationships, especially those with children and adolescents. A sexual boundary can be crossed under the pretext of spiritual friendship, special circumstance, or the erroneous notion that if the sex is not with the opposite sex, it isn't sex.

For any child or adult sexually violated by a religious figure who professes celibacy, often the insidious progression into sex begins with a confusing initial grooming and seduction. The abuse may be called *love, vocation training, spiritual education,* or *prayer*—but in reality, it is an undeclared and unacknowledged invasion of the body and the soul.

> And that all grew over time, the young, very handsome, very charismatic priest arrived, and I don't think as children we really understand why there is this kind of special energy that happens with the young. So I think everybody got affected by his presence. I wonder now because I don't really know. I spent a lot of time trying to connect the dots and at some point said, "I don't have to." I don't need to know how I went from spending some time there to spending most of my time there and how it would be to show up to help out with things at the parish—to—he and I having dinner together alone in the rectory and so on and so forth. And, just in my mind's eye, there was just this kind of almost seamless progression from not being a part of that world to being more a part of that world, which was being explained to me as my "vocation." Now at seven or eight, who the hell has a vocation? (Victor)

THE MEMBRANE OF TRUST

Sometimes sexual abuse occurs in the context of a nurturing relationship specifically because the perpetrator is supposed to be sexually off limits. This connection may be full of confusing tradeoffs, as it was for Victor, with gifts or kindness, escape from terrible neglect or violence, or exposure to beauty or other pleasures that would be otherwise impossible to experience. The perpetrator may be charming and compelling. He might even give off a spiritual elegance that is all the more confounding to his victim. But an abuser may not be developmentally mature enough to be self-aware or capable of having genuine respect for others. For an individual like this, there are no borders. The needs of others are filtered only through his own stunted instincts, where the limits and demands of dignity or humanity do not apply. But it is never simple. What he often gives in terms of friendship, beauty, wisdom, or even spirituality makes the bargain of sex an impossible dilemma. This holds true for adults, as well as children.

In every religion, people are put into these impossible moral and ethical dilemmas. One woman described how, as a nun, she tried to keep her integrity and her vow of celibacy, despite her spiritual director's pressure to have sexual relations with him.

> Somewhere in there in that first year, he asked me if I would get contraceptives. I told him that my doctor knew that I was a nun and would think it odd if I asked for a prescription. I also told him, "You know, you have a heart con-

dition and if you get involved with sex, you could have a heart attack." By doing this, I was trying to protect myself against what was going on in his head. (Eleanor)

The priest who raped William as a boy was supposed to be training him for the celibate priesthood. He confused the boy by calling the abuse "counseling." He had even covered his tracks by asking for compensation from William's mother after each session. His comings and goings left no room for questions. The perpetrator knew what he was doing; he had had plenty of practice with others.

> So the first "counseling" session, as he called it, was that afternoon. He had told my mother to make sure nobody came upstairs (my bedroom was upstairs at the far end of the house) while I was being counseled. He also laid the groundwork. He said, "It's a very tough thing to become a priest," that I would be upset when it was done, but that "it's God's way and God's will," and in the end I'd be the priest he wanted. So if I came downstairs from counseling and was upset or whatever, it was just because I was starting to prepare myself for the priesthood. "It's a tough journey." So it happened that way. Then we went upstairs. And, looking back at it, I can see how this wasn't some random act of violence; this was premeditated rape. (William)

There are times when a child (or an adult) is put into a situation of powerlessness because other victims are involved. The witness wants only to help with what seems an unsolvable situation.

> There were a couple other boys, a couple times. I got to sit in the front right next to him, but I didn't know their names. They looked at each other. As soon as their eyes would meet, they would turn and divert them away. I remember one of them. We would all go to the [priest's] brother's house; there'd be a whole plate of cookies and three glasses of milk. We'd drink our milk and eat our cookies, and then he'd take us back and do what he did. One of the other boys was really upset ahead of time. I tried to ask him. He said he forgot his tissues and his toilet paper. He didn't know what he was going to do then. So I gave him as much as I thought I could spare. Then I always packed extra from then on in case somebody else was short. We were never to use his [the priest's] brother's tissues or toilet paper. We were supposed to bring our own. (William)

For William, this was an impossible dilemma in a profoundly disturbed environment. Like a small prisoner of war, he was trying his best, in the only way he knew, to give some care to the other boys in a situation he was told was for their own good.

The consequences of a rape, an affair or liaisons with a member of the clergy can alter or destroy any semblance of an inner life. However, once the "contract" of such a relationship has been made, the moral and spiritual fallout almost overpowers the psychological damage. The person who is the representative of *God*, who sometimes *is God* to his community, has made a claim on another's body and violated the sacred trust.

Few people really talk about this kind of ultimate betrayal—the betrayal of the soul.

THE MEMBRANE OF LOVE

Because the sexual contact has often happened in a "spiritual" environment, it also may have provided what is invaluable to anyone who feels invisible, especially a child: attention and care. Victor, assessing his relationship with the priest who abused him, acknowledges the complexities the connection held for him. He had been a quiet, intensely intelligent child who lived in the chaos of a large family.

> For me, you know, [with] a large, chaotic problematic family, being able to escape to the sanctuary of the church, with either small group of peers or no peers sometimes, was a gift in a way. It took away a lot of the chaos and the noise that made up the rest of my life and gave me a place that was pretty quiet much of the time, because, as you know, I would be there before anyone else would be there, sometimes before the priest would actually be there, and often after. (Victor)

The sexual abuse by the young priest was unfortunately just one part of an experience that was also profound and meaningful. The abuse only intensified his bewilderment and pain. He can look at what happened now with more complexity.

> It's weird being a child with an adult; even though he was very young, I was considerably younger. I would say, more than anything, it was confusing. There was this specialness, but there were also secrets. There were benefits that came with that liaison, and this is something that I think shows up later. And, even in my work today, it helps me be more thoughtful and more sober about how complicated these experiences are, and how complicated it is working our way through them. When the person who is amusing you is changing your world, is giving something that leaves you feeling real separate and not like other of your peers—is also the person who's introducing you to some wonderful things: the grand music of the Church, our dinners at the rectory where I was waited on—there was somebody who served *me* dinner! Of course I started drinking too young, as most altar boys do. (Victor)

Victor was a soulful child. The most devastating part of the "bargain" was that the exchange also polluted his emerging spirituality. Eventually, he had to find a way out.

We prayed together. He taught religious classes after school. If we were preparing for mass, then he would be talking about his sermon or the form of mass. And then at that time the Mass was also changing, going from Latin to English, the very traditional back to facing the congregation. I mean there were lots and lots of transitions happening in that time. I think in some ways that made it even more confusing to figure out what was going on. Then the sixties happened. So you've got all of these internal and external—turmoil is too strong a word—but transition, trying to figure out what is it that's really going on here. "Who am I really?" Clearly, at some point, I wanted to be with my peers, not separate from them. On a subtle level, I think the hypocrisy of the Church was beginning to come through pretty clear to me. Again, I don't think I had a lot of language about that; I had a lot of feelings. So I was starting to do my own rebellion which really fast-forwarded when I got my license, because then I could say I'm going to church and not go. (Victor)

The spirit can be strong despite compromising events. Victor was becoming an adolescent, trying to do what normal teenagers must do: questioning, rebelling, refusing to comply. He had little technology to understand the elements or the ramifications of what had been happening to him. He knew only that he had to break away.

THE MEMBRANE OF POWER

Sexual abuse is often a series of double binds, where the abuser gives the abused conflicting messages, one message denying the other. The abuser creates a situation in which the abused will be put in the wrong no matter what he does. The abused cannot comment on the conflict, resolve it, or opt out of the situation.

Chris's abuse already set him up with a system of beliefs that promised punishment and disgrace for explorations of his own body.

I was a boy scout. I remember getting the medal for Catholic scouting called *Ad Altare Dei* in the eighth grade. I remember one day in the eighth grade before serving mass asking the priest [the scouting chaplain] to hear my confession. I told him that I had touched myself impurely many times. He then asked the question that I'll never forget. He said in French, "Ton corps t'a coulé?" In other words, "Had I ejaculated?" I remember feeling embarrassed by the question. No priest had ever asked me that before. It took me by surprise, and I said, "No!" I lied. That was wrong, and I was taught that it would make every subsequent confession unbinding and sacrilege. However, that didn't stop him from inviting me to go with him to another scouting award ceremony. (Chris)

Later, what happened to him with that same priest corroborated what Chris had been taught: that *he* was the sinner and responsible for what had happened.

I remember nothing of that evening until he had me call home and get permission to stay overnight with him, coming home the following morning. We traveled to a deserted wooded area at the end of a long dirt road. There was a cabin visible in the headlights of the car. There were no other lights anywhere. The cabin door led into a small common living room/kitchen area with a table and chairs in the far left corner and a couch by the front door and directly in front of a window. He said we could go swimming in a cool stream not far away to cool off but first we could have something to drink. He took out a bottle of wine and poured some for both of us. When he saw that I was under the influence of the alcohol, he told me to go into the little room next to the kitchen and change into the bathing suit that was there. (Why did the bathing suit fit me so well?) When I came back out into the open area, he was sitting on the couch next to the door. He told me to come and sit next to him. He was to my left. He began to giggle a bit and said how nice I looked. Then, in what seemed like a flash, he had his hand inside my bathing suit and pulled the suit off of me. The second he touched my penis, I remember saying to myself that *God* had sent his priest to punish me for being sexual, and I can remember making a vow to never do this terrible thing to anyone. I remember crying because of my shame. I had been caught by *God*, and I was going to be punished. (Chris)

Chris's perpetrator had turned the tables, using the sacrament of atonement against him. It only added to the confusion in his already troubled mind.

I remember sitting at the table again with him telling me how we could *both* confess what had happened, how he went to confession, too, and that everything would be okay. I remember nothing of the ride home, how I felt or what I thought about. I only know that I never told my parents what had happened until 30 years later. They weren't safe for me then. And, besides, why would I want to tell them about *my sin*? (Chris)

Chris was left not only with misbegotten shame but with the lie that comes with sexual abuse: that *he* was simply guilty and responsible *because* of his sexuality. He never initiated anything sexual, yet he was stuck with the shame of the priest's calculated sexual intrusion.

The next morning, after the abuse was done and I was no longer drunk and we were sitting at the little table in that little kitchen area and he said we could both go to confession and confess what had happened . . . I don't remember exactly what I told [the priest], I'm sure I told him that I had done something wrong, because the priest had *nothing to do with it.* That is what comes screaming through my head isn't "What's this person doing to me?" What's screaming through my head is that *God* has sent his priest to punish me for being sexual. (Chris)

Nobody set the record straight for Chris. He worried that what had happened had stained him for life. He condemned himself, renouncing intimacy with others in ways those on the outside simply could not begin to comprehend.

> [I knew] it would be nice to have some other people around, but like a mystic, I was going to be pretty much alone, that I wasn't going to let—I *couldn't*—let anybody else in. I mean, what if I wanted them? What if I flirted with them? What if I touched them? What if? You know, I can't do that. That's wrong, and not only if it wrong, but it is a thing I swore I'd never do when I was molested. When he put his hand on me, what screamed through my head was that I would never do anything like this to a human being. So, my sense has always been that if I pursues someone I'd be a perpetrator, that I'd be violating the very oath that I took when I was being molested. (Chris)

Sexuality, sexual desire, and intimate sexual contact are natural human experiences. The cruelty of such abuse is that what was supposed to be an innocent exchange had been corrupted by a celibate priest. But sexual abuse by non-celibate clergy also happens in every religion, and the results are just as disastrous for survivors molested by married clergy as for those abused by celibates. Abuse is damaging, confusing, and insidious no matter who commits it or how.

Jacob speaks about how surprised he was about sexual abuse in the orthodox Jewish community.

> I was really shocked, enough to motivate me to make a film. I knew that if I made a film like this and it got out, it would be super controversial. (Jacob)

The Awareness Center[10] is an organization that reaches out to Jewish survivors of sexual violence, parents of sexually abused children, family members of alleged and convicted sex offenders, rabbis, cantors, and other community leaders. They report incidents of rabbinical sexual abuse in *all* denominations of Judaism.

Jacob wanted the Jewish community to recognize that sexual abuse by clergy happens to Jews, as well as adherents of other faiths.

> We were pretty much like everyone else . . . Sexual abuse is our problem, too, and it's not something people should be ashamed to talk about. People should seek help for it and that there are resources and there's hope for them, and this is to kind of break that silence has been going on forever. (Jacob)

Sexual abuse of children is reported in Orthodox communities, but also by elders and bishops, clerics and cantors, swamis and roshis—and it is always controversial because it is never supposed to happen in any of these places. The Right Reverend William Persell, Bishop of the Episcopal Diocese of Chicago, comments: "We would be naïve and dishonest were we to say this is a Roman Catholic problem and has nothing to do with us because we e married and female priests in our Church. Sin and abusive behavior ow no ecclesial or other boundaries."[11]

There are some who argue that pedophilia is a natural sexual preference for certain people. Cultural relativists argue that the appropriateness of sexual relations with a child depends on location and custom and that various cultures have differing criteria for when a boy or girl is ready for sexual relations. (One elderly French Canadian priest joked about the practice of sexual relationships between priests and young boys referring to them as "little sins.") But children are never in a position of power when it comes to sexual contact, even if they want or initiate it. While such relations are part of certain cultural initiation rites and arranged marriages, it is a complicated situation because children usually cannot advocate for themselves or make complicated decisions about their well-being.

Sexual contact in a pedophilic relationship like this can even feel good or right to the child. It may be the only "caring" relationship in an otherwise violent or chaotic life. But children need to be loved without condition or exploitation no matter how their relationships are framed, where they live, or what religion they practice. In the Bible, there are strong words from Jesus about protecting children: "Obstacles are sure to come, but alas for the one who provides them! It would be better for him to be thrown into the sea with a millstone put around his neck than that he should lead astray a single one of these little ones. Watch yourselves!" (Luke 17).[12]

Those who feel they need to use children for their own sexual pleasure are usually in a pathetic but spiritually bankrupt position themselves.

Christopher Hitchens is an antitheist[13] who takes the position that religion is a morally collapsed institution, responsible for most of the evils of the world. Hitchens may be a controversial figure when it comes to the polemics and politics of religion, but his cynical indictment of pedophilia by clergy makes its point. "To need love or sex only from the innocent, or to be able to express your needs only in that way, is obviously a terrible punishment in itself and can, in some circumstances, even call upon our pity (and our dearly bought secular and scientific knowledge about the possibility of care and help). But to become a hardened exploiter of children as part of your vocation, and to be defended by a coalition of stone-faced, ignorant patriarchs and hysterical virgins, is a privilege known only to the most devout."[14]

There are no excuses, no defense, no rationalization for pedophilia. And, there should *never* be legal protection for religious pedophiles, no matter who they are. They deserve the same treatment under the criminal justice system as any other perpetrator.

In the eleventh century, a monastic order in Spain published a momentous document titled the *Rule of Compludo*. It was devised to specifically address the issue of pedophilia in a religious community.

A cleric or monk who seduces youths or young boys or is found kissing or in any other impure situation is to be publicly flogged and lose his tonsure. When his hair has been shorn, his face is to be foully besmeared with spit, and he is to be bound in iron chains. For six months, he will languish in prison-like confinement, and on three days of each week, shall fast on barley bread in the evening. After this, he will spend another six months under the custodial care of a spiritual elder, remaining in a segregated cell, giving himself to manual work and prayer, subject to vigils and prayers. He may go for walks but always under the custodial care of two spiritual brethren, and he shall never again associate with youths neither in private conversation nor in counseling them.[15]

Imagine if current religious institutions took this template for treatment of the sexual predator seriously. Imagine if bishops actually took responsibility for known repeat offenders by permanently removing them from the ministry and by expediting prompt and ethical legal action, instead of failing to report criminal acts to police or moving offenders from parish to parish but allowing them to continue to have personal contact with children.

Imagine if religious bodies did not participate in the obstruction of justice in connection with grand juries or criminal proceedings when there has been an allegation. Imagine if full participation in the criminal justice system resulted in open, transparent, and full cooperation instead of perjury, false affidavits, or destruction of documents.

Imagine if the Catholic Church, for instance, actually addressed the practice of *crimen sollicitationis*, which translates as the crime of solicitation, which occurs when priests abuse the sacrament of penance by sexually propositioning penitents.

Imagine if the Church (or any other offending religious institution) paid off those who have been violated by priest perpetrators *not* to silence them but to make honest amends by commitments to compensation for therapy and medical treatment for post-traumatic stress.

Imagine if pedophiles were administered custodial accountable psychiatric and psychological care in prison that included zero-tolerance cognitive-behavioral therapy and treatment for their own sexually abusive histories.

Imagine if seminaries, convents, and monasteries actually offered balanced and rigorous preparation to those who are preparing to live a lifetime of celibate sexuality.

Imagine . . .

THE MEMBRANE OF THE MEMBERSHIP

Religious communities often operate as if sexuality does not or should not exist among their membership, much less sexual abuse. In this environment, it may seem useless for those victimized to report sexual abuse of adults, especially if it is prevalent from the top down or made shamefully unspeakable.

When Myra Hidalgo told a priest what had happened to her, he gave *her* absolution for *her* sexual sins. "He never once qualified my experience as sexual abuse, and he never made a report on my behalf to help me or my family cope with this trauma."[16]

Myra later joined the same community of sisters where her perpetrator was still working. Once she was there, the community's response to her report of the sexual violation was lackluster at best. Members never clarified that what had happened between the nun and Myra was *not* Myra's fault. They did not acknowledge the exchange with the nun as sexual abuse at all, much less share in any responsibility for failing to protect Myra. Instead, they recommended that she seek spiritual direction—from a man.

Deficits and further abuses like this often take place for both women and for men because either nobody in the community sees what is happening; or those who do see lack the courage to blow the cover of the perpetrator and create a scandal in the community. They protect the perpetrators at the expense of those who really need their protection.

When Francis finally revealed that the reason he was struggling in his missionary work involved the abuse that was still happening in the seminary, the community's response was to declare *him* unfit for ministry because he had been abused and to send him to a home for elderly priests.

> They made me the identified problem, because it was easier to have me as a problem, than to address the issue themselves. I was clear to go back to ministry. [But] I was told, "Nope, you can't go back to ministry because some can go back and some cannot." That was just wrong! That's people who abuse, not people who have been abused! Basically, they don't know how to handle it. So the support I should've gotten, I just kind of got dumped. (Francis)

The alienation that Beth experienced in her community is an example of one of the worst consequences of sexual abuse by religious figures. It is a cruel testament to the power of denial and fear. When the community is more attached to rituals and protocols or simply too busy to protect its own people, harm is inevitable.

Beth had tried again and again to find people who could help her sort out her dilemma with her young teacher. In an isolated location far from home, she could find no support or feedback about her situation, except from her perpetrator, who was intent on achieving his own agenda. There was nobody to give Beth a reality check or to help her process her way out of an exceptional and difficult problem. She was caught in her own spiritual hell.

> I tried to talk to an older American woman who was also living in the center about my feelings that this man's actions weren't right, but it quickly became clear to me that this woman had a lot of psychological problems. She didn't make sense a lot of the time. Meanwhile, the teacher said about this woman,

"Oh, she's crazy, I just have her here because it's the compassionate thing to do." Then I tried to go to the guy who was doing his 100,000 prostrations [a spiritual practice in Tibetan Buddhism undertaken to counteract pride]. He just didn't want to talk to me. He was involved in this really intense religious practice, visualizing this tulku who we were living with as the Buddha. Then, I went down to find one of my teachers. I walked down the mountain, got onto a bus, rode over to the other side of the valley, and went to his house to find him. The trip took two or three hours one way, but when I finally got there, he wasn't home. So I wrote a letter to him, saying, "I just came down here because some stuff is going on and it's making me uncomfortable. But I don't know if I'm just misinterpreting things. So I really would appreciate some guidance, and to talk to you. If you could come up or call or something, that would be really great." So I left this letter. Then I went back to the center—and I heard nothing. (Beth)

Beth wanted to make sense of her situation and to get some support, yet the community around her was either too self-involved or complicit with the abuser himself to be of any help to her. This is truly the secondary trauma of sexual abuse, the denial and protection of the abuse and the abuser.

One part of me is shocked and another part is outraged that I reached out for help with no success, even just some little token of validation to so many people that I wasn't crazy. It was just nothing—just nothing, nobody. It was bizarre, when I think back on it—that I reached out so steadily to so many different people and just got nothing. (Beth)

Diana's devastating experience with her religious teacher made her feel increasingly more estranged from her religious community. What was happening seemed to be invisible to them, and therefore she could no longer participate in the culture of adulation that surrounded the teacher.

But then I wondered, "Is that absolutely true?" Did somebody not really know? But either way, it worked to break that bond I was developing with these people. I could no longer make an outward life of devotion to him. (Diana)

Diana's decision to reveal her story of sexual abuse to a member of her own religious community only exacerbated her pain and alienation. Later, she was thrown out of the community because of this revelation.

You know how terrible it made me feel, and when I told a nun in the community what had happened, she didn't react with shock, she didn't make any attempt to try and get me to reinterpret the experience. She really acted like she had heard it before or had experienced it before. And that that made the place so rotten. When it all came right down to it, of course she was going to protect him. And she denied that this could've possibly happened. She's never

ever acknowledged that there was anything to it. Those were the really hard parts. (Diana)

THE MEMBRANE OF SPIRIT

When an adult is pandered to, seduced or raped by a clergyperson, whether by a person from her early religious tradition or in a new chosen path, the result can be no less devastating than if she had been molested as a child. Even the most spiritually evolved person can be tempted to seek out those without power for comfort or to satisfy sexual or emotional needs. It can leave the designated caregivers believing that they are collaborating in ministry, providing support, or even receiving a blessing.

> I had put this very innocent interpretation on it. In fact I didn't really think of it much, except I knew I had the old explanation—this kind of brief, intimate physical contact was some kind of blessing. (Diana)

In the relationship between spiritual director and aspirant, or between teacher and disciple specifically, the transaction is supposed to be unlike any other kind of connection, even with lovers or family. That first blush of the spiritual relationship can often feel like falling in love. But the objective is to fall in love with the divine, or the path—not with the teacher's personality or with him. As the Qu'ran says, there is an intimacy in *God* so personal that it is "closer to you than your jugular vein." The love affair is not about the teacher. He must facilitate and represent a much larger relationship.[17] He is supposed to be there as witness to the sacred journey and as a sacred friend. His exchange with the student should be based on mutuality and respect.

At its best, the tender link between the spiritual mentor and his student replicates that between mother and child. In fact, Buddhism uses the Tibetan word *lama* (defined in English as the male priest, the teacher, or guru), which actually translates as "soul mother." Sometimes what happens in the connection between the guide and the student can bring both to a kind of spiritual ecstasy in which there is a physiological, almost orgasmic component. But, unless the director is fully grounded, self-vigilant, and aware of the dangerous force of emotion and sexual energy that this exchange can elicit, the experience they share may be more hysterical than mystical, more corporeal than consecrated. Even if the original intentions are initially pure, the result has the potential be disastrous.

This is carefully described by Shirley du Bouley. The spiritual relationship between Abhishtananda, a Benedictine monk who eventually took vows as a wandering Hindu monk, and his disciple, Marc, was a profoundly deep and ecstatic connection. Both master and student were vigilant about their experiences in high states of meditation. Yet, in a state of "holy inebriation," a complicated and ecstatic experience between master and disciple, Marc's diary reveals that what had happened had included some sexual expression, which du Bouley says should not seem surprising in that such ecstatic union would "need to take physical form." It is difficult to say whether the experience was spiritual or simply overwhelmingly sexual, because, shortly after the incident, the disciple left a message with a senior monk and then literally disappeared into the Himalayas, not to be seen again.[18] These are incidents that are difficult to deconstruct, especially between two consenting adults. But the imbalance of power combined with an intensely loaded rapturous exchange could have easily deteriorated to something that might not have been spiritual at all.

Even if what happened is interpreted, as an enlightened experience shared by master and disciple, there can never be an ethical rationale for the sexual exploitation of another. Whether or not permission is given, even if the aspirant is seductive or there is mutual consent, the teacher always possesses the power and the responsibility to hold the sacred container. He is obligated to keep the boundary—or leave the relationship.

Sometimes a teacher can recognize an almost translucent quality about a student in an early stage of spiritual practice. Such a state is not unlike the luminous innocence of a child. Perhaps it is in such a sacred and vulnerable place that someone is most attractive to the spiritual guide, who may be unaware or in denial about his own potential dark side. The temptation to pluck the beauty of the student's spiritual progress off the flower of her soul can be unconscious and powerful.

> I would sit on the ottoman, facing him, I mean that's what he asked me to do, and I did—and he was looking at me very intently. You know, I thought this is leading to some grand, spiritual thing . . . I didn't exactly think it objectively, but it was a very intense moment for me. And suddenly he reached out and put his hands on either side of my face and drew my face toward him and kissed me right on the mouth. Not only did he do that, he stuck his tongue in my mouth and I just froze, you know, I just froze. (Diana)

The bitter irony is that, for some, the only person it would seem safe enough to talk to about situations this confusing is the same pastor or spiritual director who is doing the abusing. He may have been one's only confidant in truly personal matters and perhaps the only resource for not only support but also spiritual guidance. The abuser is often a spiritual partner with profound access to the most intimate parts of the student. He can be a fount of spiritual knowledge and a source of love. But such love is *not* conditional.

> [It was] confusion, total confusion. It was very strange because one of my friends who was also a victim, said, "You were so devoted to him." And it is very strange, because when I look at photographs of myself . . . I'm horrified to see myself standing there saluting and adoringly looking at him, the man who

I knew . . . on the other side was sexually molesting me, and no one knew it.
I basically lived a double life. (Eleanor)

If the teacher is kind or gentle in his demeanor, one might feel the relationship means something more than it really does, especially if there is a
prior history of molestation or sexual violence. Many housekeepers, parishioners, disciples, and nuns feel at first that closing the door to the office or
the sacristy creates a confidential and "sacramental" space that is sanctioned,
safe—and intimate. They may have to disconnect from the reality of what is
happening altogether by spiritualizing it.

> And I'm actually having an out-of-body experience, so to speak. . . . I'm sub-
> tracting myself from my body. I thought that I was going out there like it was
> supposed to be a spiritual experience. (Eleanor)

Sometimes the moment of transgression is hard to decipher, especially if
the sexual contact is at first invisible, with a gradual progression of touch.
It may seem incomprehensible that the abuser would not question his own
motives at this point. In the beginning, he has some control of the victim's
perception of reality, which ultimately can leave that person feeling complicit. This compliance may affect the person's thinking, action, identity,
and prayer. It can be inconceivable or simply too scary for the person to
question what is happening, especially if one is committed to a sacred path
and devoted to the teacher, whom one believes has transmitted spiritual
gems.

If there is any physical pleasure or even a small piece of caregiving involved, the relationship may become even more needy. Because of Beth's
connection with her young teacher, for example, her mind had to morph
itself into an opposite way of thinking just to make sense of a confounding
situation. She was in an isolated situation in another culture with no emotional safety net or feedback from the outside.

> I just reversed my position and went from saying to myself, "This is not right"
> to saying to myself, "Fuck it, I'm just going to stay here. I'll just sleep with
> the guy. Whatever, I'm just going to do it, whatever, it's fine!" So I ended up
> sleeping with him. But the part of me that had objected just disappeared. It
> wasn't like I was consciously doing something that I knew that I didn't want
> to do; it wasn't that I was doing something but feeling resentful about it. My
> feelings just completely reversed. I started to act as if I adored this man, like
> he was some sort of enlightened person and that I was lucky to be able to be in
> this relationship with him. And this is where again, I hear myself recounting
> this story, and I just can't believe that I ever thought these things, you know?
> I don't understand where the part of me that found the situation so objection-
> able went. I still don't. (Beth)

Perfectly reasonable people being compelled to do unreasonable acts in psychologically and spiritually compromising environments—how can one make sense of all of this? What would make someone who possesses the capacity to inspire or to transmit something so sacred do so much harm and create such suffering?

THE MEMBRANE BETWEEN

Many survivors don't care *why* the abuser does what he does. Those who are survivors have already given enough energy to the abuser's needs and *his* concerns. The reasons—"it was God's will, it was your *karma*," "it is a mystery"—do not suffice. Survivors just want to find meaning for themselves and others and a way out of their pain.

But it may be important to understand how it is that a perpetrator can become what she is, especially because often there is a lingering notion that survivors and perpetrators are one and the same—which they are *not*.

Occasionally, there are celibate individuals who find themselves unable to keep their vows or control their impulses. Their backgrounds do not appear to be dysfunctional; in fact perhaps they have been made into models of perfection by families and communities that would have fed the narcissistic idea that they were above human frailty. They themselves may be so horrified or ashamed of their acts of violation that they deny that their actions either took place at all, or worse, had any negative impact on others, especially if their abuses were with adults.

Victims rarely become perpetrators; however many incorporate the humiliation and harm that they have experienced and inflict it on themselves. Mary Gail Frawley O'Dea notes not only how sexual abuse survivors and their perpetrators differ but how important it is to recognize "that the clay of the survivor's abuser self is molded quite literally by the hands of a master— the sexual and relational victimizer." Therefore, the survivor may mimic the same lack of respect for herself (and others) that was initially shown by her perpetrator, who had no boundaries when it came to his own desires.

Dr. O'Dea painted another picture of the sexual perpetrator's impact on the survivor in her address to the U.S. Conference of Catholic Bishops meeting in Dallas in 2002:

> Coexisting with the violated, terrorized, grief stricken victim self, the adult survivor of sexual abuse has within [him] her a state of being that is identified with the perpetrator. Through this unconscious ongoing bond to the predator, the survivor preserves her attachment to the abuser by becoming like him in some ways. When threatened by experiences of helplessness, vulnerability or anticipated betrayal, the survivor unconsciously accesses this self-state to gain a sense of empowerment. Subjectively experiencing herself as righteously indignant, the survivor may enact at times breathtaking boundary smashing, cold contempt, and red-hot rage.[19]

Often a victim may sabotage himself or treat others poorly, but when a victim himself does turn into a sexual perpetrator, the transition usually involves a number of specific factors.

Psychoanalysts point to the stage of development when the formation of the ego gets stuck at a highly conforming orderly (anal-retentive) or cruel and sadistic (anal-aggressive) place. It is here that a child may absorb both passivity and aggression as a personality style, making it easier for him to re-enact his own abuse as an adult at another's expense in a smooth downward spiral from an "innocent" touch to a sexual breach.

The perpetrator as victim was often introduced to sexual activity in a seductive, covert, conditioning process within his own family. A perpetrator of abuse against children, especially, is usually developmentally stunted himself in perpetual pubescence, probably because he was deprived at an early age of relational intimacy and nurturance. He may identify more emotionally with children or adolescents than with his peers and sometimes can seem quite childlike himself because he is fixated at a point in development where he had to be highly conforming and orderly. Alternatively, he may become cruel and sadistic toward others as a response to his own situation. When the innocent and age-appropriate curiosity of a child is contaminated by overstimulation and eroticization, the child cannot metabolize what he has experienced. He may do what every other child does to process his experience: practice the offending behavior or foist it on somebody else.

The perpetrator may have learned to molest by observing some kind of sexual abuse inflicted on someone else. This is especially complicated when certain cultures validate this kind of behavior with others by calling the abuse "initiation," "getting lucky," or interpreting it as preferential treatment. Sometimes, if a child or adolescent witnesses the abuse of another child, he aligns himself with the abuser, not the abused. He may have harbored the wish to be singled out as special, or to incorporate the power he never experienced by reenacting the violations on others.

In some cultures, a religious perpetrator might have experienced sporadic or routine sexual abuse, which could have involved extreme ritualistic acts, especially in a context of religious rites. The perpetrator's own abuse may have included gross sadistic or forced masochistic behaviors, or he may have been subjected to threats of harm or outright violence if he did not comply with the abuser's wishes. Perhaps he was exposed to a religious community's Petri dish of hyperaroused sexual energy and contact, secrets, misinformation, or inappropriate touching.

Elder members of a religious brotherhood or sisterhood may have overwhelmed the perpetrator with confounding sexual experiences at an early age. If the family or religious community minimized, denied, or renamed the abuse, the perpetrator-in-training was conditioned to believe that it was not wrong or did not see it as abuse at all. One factor that seems to distinguish the profile of a perpetrator is the utter lack of any loving *balanced* role model or caregiver in early life. Because of this lack, the perpetrator can generate little empathy for the ones he violates or perhaps feels entitled to soothe himself without considering how his behavior impacts victims and their families.

Many offenders have also been trained to believe that they have been called to a special vocation and are entitled to deference.[20] The religious institution may encourage those stuck in a perpetually stunted adolescence into its membership by mixing their pastor's grandiosity and entitlement with community secrecy and shame. This provides an ingrained sense of invulnerability, which is even encouraged by the congregation. Such behavior is considered above the norm because the leader has been called to a special, more meaningful vocation in life than have "ordinary" people. When critical thinking is alien to a religious culture, the community's ability to make mature assessments or difficult decisions is severely weakened, and the possibility of harm increases.

Whether the offender violates a child or an adult, the exploitation may be intentional, calculated, or just unconsciously selfish. The abuser may delude others and even himself that what he did came out of a special need, or for love. Victims may be double-crossed by being led to believe they are special or holier than others, but then are left to sort it out for themselves because there is no one they can tell.

The perpetrator is often compartmentalized; he may do the deed in full secrecy, fearful of being exposed for what he really is even to himself while maintaining an effective and even positive spiritual face. He may dissociate from the abuse and even go to great lengths to "protect" his relationship from others. He may keep up his façade, while punishing or flooding his dependent and vulnerable victims with affection, eliciting pity, or telling lies. He may threaten blackmail or violence—even death, if the victim should reveal what is going on.

But the perpetrator may not have to work very hard to get what he wants, or to hide what he does. The very communities whose members are supposed to protect and support one another are often programmed by religious fervor or ignorance to compensate for the perpetrator, instead.

> I waited for him to leave before I came downstairs. My eyes had to be flushed out. My mother had to see that, to tell me how well father said this session went. He'd be back; he said we'd be working on *it* for a regular basis for an undetermined amount of time. When I disclosed this to my mom back in 2002, [she said] he would put his hands out for some money, my mother would slip him in his hand some money as he left. That kind of makes my mom an inadvertent pimp, I don't know. (William)

Chris's unfulfilled dreams and the unspoken betrayals of his childhood predetermined that he would suffer more sexual violation as an adult, occurring during the ritual of a private liturgy with a newly ordained priest "friend." The priest invited him to celebrate mass as a co-celebrant. The setup was in place, and the cycle of abuse resumed.

> I remember going to his ordination and crying my eyes out because it was the kid in me who knew that that was his dream—and the four-year-old would never get to have it—and so when I got that close to be able to do it and go that close to hold the cup and say the words with him—you know, he used the very ceremony to set up being able to kiss me and shove his tongue down my throat afterward. That was the payoff for him. And I had just froze and tried to keep him out of my mouth, but I was *not* 30 years old in that moment. That went on for months, probably a year. (Chris)

A perpetrator's shamelessness can override any boundary. In his mind, the unthinkable abuse is justified as he projects his shame onto the victim.

Perpetration in a religious community and the denial and shunning that often occur in its aftermath lead us to another discussion that is distressing precisely because there is such denial about the topic. We now explore *ritual abuse* both as a real phenomenon and in response to how the larger community relates to it. Avoiding this subject would be a devastating hole in our treatment of religious abuse.

RITUAL ABUSE: THE BROKEN MEMBRANE

Ritual abuse[21] by a religious person is the darkest jewel in the vile crown of religious violation. Ritual abuse is the deliberate, systematic infliction of severe physical or mental suffering or an inhuman procedure of cruelty using ritual or indoctrination. It has been a system of dehumanizing violence inflicted on children, minorities, homosexuals, and women for centuries. Ritual does not necessarily mean *satanic*[22] abuse, although both include intimidation and often brutal violence. While it would be impossible to give an adequate or even remedial exploration of ritual or satanic abuse here, it is important to note that diverse anthropological evidence points to its existence in many cultures; elements of ritualized abuse have been reported in American churches, temples, and schools.[23]

The psychological and physical aspects of abuse can include ritualized sacrifice of animals or people, torture, or the witnessing of such things. Forcing victims to participate in or to witness heinous acts can be accompanied by threats of punishment or violence to one's loved ones or pets if the victim objects. The sexual abuse is usually sadistic and humiliating, intended by the perpetrator to gain dominance over the victim and to instill terror. Disclosing the abuse can seem futile to the victim because "no one will believe you" or because "*God* no longer loves you." The combination of the excruciating circumstances of physical, mental, and sexual torture can produce severe dissociative disorder and multiple personality.

When ritual abuse is carried out in religious settings, sacred words, liturgical practices, and props are often used as instruments to torment victims. The supposed need for exorcisms or for "punishment" of sins provides the rationalization for torture and sexual degradation. In William's situation, for instance, the combination of ritual and sexual violence was sadistic, disorienting, and utterly shameful.

> He [the priest] said, "It's God's will." God wanted this. The rapes continued, for all that time. And he would point to the crucifix over my bed and say, "God suffered and died on the cross for me; that's true suffering. What I'm going through is nothing, don't anger God anymore than he already is at you." I wanted God to love me; I would do his will: "It will be done." I was thinking, "Good, my pants are up, maybe we're going to pray." He put his hand on my head, once again said stuff in Latin—I didn't know what the hell he was saying, with one hand on my head, unzipped his pants with the other. (William)

Ritual abuse is specific, organized to obliterate the personality of the victims and to diminish their physical and mental capacities; it is nearly impossible for persons to find a way out for themselves, if they think they will survive at all. Often, a child like William is made to feel responsible for his actions as though he had freely chosen them. Psychologically, there is a kind of disbelief and paralysis—and hopelessness. When one is forced to participate in a ritual or procedure that hurts or kills others, there appears to be no escape. Victims are often too small or too threatened to resist. They may have to perform these activities just in order to survive.

For some, concern for their own survival has had little to do with it. Many children or adults who have had to inflict harm on others would have gladly given their own lives rather than be forced to do what they did. They seemed to be in an unthinkable dilemma of having to choose between two equal evils of participating in harming or killing—or facing incomprehensible torture or death. Having to make such choices or to participate in horrible acts so compromises one's psychological and emotional integrity that it is difficult to put the shards of memory back into coherent recognition of facts or to understand what or how such events could have occurred at all.

In the torture chamber of sexual or ritual abuse, one can become more and more dependent on the perpetrator because of a bizarre and confusing combination of affection and neglect. This is known as the *trauma bond*, something based on a double bind of reverence, fear, and, ironically, attachment. A connection like this creates severe obstacles to entering into a trusting or meaningful relationship with another person ever again. But that is not all.

For William, breaking off with the abuser also left him full of confusion, fearing being a *failure* and that the abuse might pass to someone else, possibly a loved one.

He [the perpetrator] confused me all along. He'd been telling me that I would be on my way to priesthood and . . . that God would start loving me once I developed hair. In the spring . . . I started getting body hair, started getting pubic hair. I was all excited. In my "warped" little mind I thought I was becoming a priest, and [Father] was telling me how I would have to do this to other little boys when I was a priest, because that's what a priest does. And I said, "How am I going to know?" He said, "God will inspire you; you will know who to choose to bring." Then the day he came over when I had the first signs of pubic hair, he was disgusted and told me I was worthless. And he left. I could hear him tell my mother what a disappointment I was down in the kitchen. He was visibly upset, his voice was louder than usual. [I had] probably wasted all his time. I did this and I did that, and now it's worthless. I heard him drive away that last day. I went downstairs. My mother's in the kitchen, cooking or baking something, and she's crying. I told her, "I'm sorry," and . . . she said how disappointed she was in me. She said, "There's always your brother Liam, I guess—if you can't do it." (William)

William was trapped. In his young mind, it was dangerous to tell his mother what had really happened or to warn her about the possible harm to his brother. The community, of course, unwittingly protected the perpetrator, and William was at the mercy of the priest, the system, and his own programming.

It is natural that anyone who listens to this story or others like it, might react by calling the abuses something other than ritual abuse—an indication of a survivor's psychosis, manipulation, or paranoia. Sometimes, the survivor *has* manifested psychosis, manipulation, or paranoia, but they are a result of severe post-traumatic stress. The memories of a ritual abuse survivor are sometimes so incomprehensible that witnesses may reject the possibility of the existence or "creativity" of such evil. Some therapists, doctors, clergy and members of the community may diminish the content or completely discount the credibility of a survivor who has actually experienced it.

I'm so sick of being told it was inappropriate touching and inappropriate contact and inappropriate—or a mistake. That's what really hurts. I'm not a mistake, for Christ's sake! A mistake is getting off at Exit 10 when you should've gotten off at Exit 9! (William)

The *mistake* of this response illuminates yet another demoralizing violation of rapacious and sadistic abuse. A community's callous denial or ignorant diminishment of what has happened becomes the devastation, or "second rape," which is as bad as or worse than the first.

REPAIRING THE MEMBRANE

Those who have suffered any permutation of sexual or ritualized abuse are often profoundly terrorized and even incredulous about their own memories, which can be almost surrealistic in quality and content. Survivors may have been programmed to think that there is no way out regardless of their actions and to therefore keep silent about it. They may sincerely believe themselves to be evil, with no hope of redemption, even when they are later told otherwise. They may not believe there is any way to protect themselves and feel irreparably stained, despite what anybody says or does to make them feel otherwise.

Keith was brutally raped as an adult by a priest. When he attempted to talk to another priest about what he had experienced, however, the exchange may have been as traumatic as the rape. He tried twice to speak of what had happened to him in the "safety" of a Catholic confessional.

> The priest asked a number of questions, which got more and more graphic. I started answering them as I thought he needed to know in order to forgive the sin. Then he asked how big the priest's penis was (his breathing was very heavy, and he appeared to be getting very aroused). I then ran out of the confessional. I next told a priest about it several years later when I went to him for counseling. I asked if I was going to hell. He told me "he didn't know what God did with these things." He never asked who, what, when, where—nor did he encourage me to report it. (Keith)

Survivors often appear to be tough on the outside, but it is often difficult—if not impossible—for them to trust anyone by being vulnerable again. A man who has chosen to be known as Coach sought out a minister to sort out the terrible abuses he had suffered as a child from a member of his own family who was a convicted pedophile. The minister failed him on two counts: by not understanding or acknowledging his struggles or his pain and by using the religious position to condemn and blame, especially in a space that had been designated to be sacred and safe

> [The minister] questioned me regarding the sexual abuse that had happened. When he inquired regarding the specifics, he did not understand the complex nature of it. However, he wasn't fearful or intimidated like the majority of others that I had sought help from over the years. . . . When I asked him about how he was going to help me, his response was "I'll do the heart work and you do the hard work." When I asked him to be more specific, that is when he condemned me for using my mind. . . He asserted that I was responsible for the sexual abuse and I had lured the abuser. (Coach)

Later Coach was "baptized," which in his mind was the best thing to come out of his experience. He was willing to deal with whatever had caused him so much confusion. Yet, the minister's response and, later, his refusal to deal with Coach at all only solidified the experience of isolation and betrayal.

Maybe it was more palatable for the minister to blame the victim than to face the unthinkable reality of what had happened to Coach. It is as if the transfer of blame neatly removed the minister's own culpability or that of the community, for failing to see, failing to respond, failing to rectify the abuse.

Caregivers, therapists, or other religious persons may be well meaning when listening to survivors, but they can also create more pain if they are not trained or ready to deal with the material. Occasionally, pastoral counselors or therapists are captivated with the drama of the material, becoming enthralled with the sordid and fantastic details. If they overreact, report irresponsibly, or operate without supervision or grounded clinical and spiritual direction, it can be further damaging to the survivor.

If ritual abuse is part of the story, it is important for professionals to seek expert counsel before advising spiritual action of any kind. Although it may seem indispensable for spiritual healing, asking an untreated survivor to do a practice of prayer or meditation can compromise her cognitive and emotional capacities unless there is some gradated and specific structure in that spiritual practice. Blessings or even exorcisms can actually have a negative effect because the rituals themselves trigger the abusive memories.

Listening to the stories of sexual and ritual abuse is often unbearably painful for anyone. While an authentic response from a caregiver, therapist, or practitioner can bring some resolution to the utter dishonor a survivor has experienced, it can also make matters worse if delivered with platitudes, ignorance, or incompetence. However difficult it is for anyone to sit with such sorrow, mere empty words from a caregiver do not comfort.

> Tears were coming from this man's eyes; I saw tears coming from his eyes. He sat there; he didn't really know what to say to me. He said, "You don't have to think about this anymore," which is absurd. It doesn't go away, it never goes away! (Eleanor)

If survivors speak about what has happened to them, the very least they need is safety and respect from the listener. In fact, sometimes silence is the best response one can give to any survivor. Quiet listening itself can generate a kind of sacred space. This sort of silence is not the same thing as the silence of secrets or shame. In fact, it is appropriate that those who listen be perhaps dumbfounded and humbled by what they hear. It is a tribute to the survivor.

But those who are survivors deserve even more than this. What they merit from the community, as well as from the counselor, should be the birthright of any human being: compassion, and perhaps even outrage on their behalf.

> The issue is not a private issue; it's really a huge human social justice, human rights issue. When people say what happens to someone's faith, what happens to someone's soul, his or her soul gets buried. [The] soul gives humans dignity, and when you are violated on that level, you begin to perceive yourself as less than human. (Delicia)

There are stages of survival *after* abuse, similar to the stages of grief. They may sequence in a variety of ways: disbelief, realization, bargaining, with-

drawal, possible self-sabotage, depression, anger, and either acceptance
the abuse or a resolution to find a way to stop it from happening to othe
Whether or not the events that follow entail a confrontation with the perpetrator, a confession from him, or prosecution, there is often another series of
conflicting emotions and inner states that follow in the aftermath.

For Diana, the violation of sexual abuse has profoundly damaged her ability to trust another person about her spiritual life. In a tradition that placed
an emphasis on the sacred nature of the guru-disciple relationship, she felt an
irreparable loss.

> I mean to me, for me he really killed the guru-disciple relationship so that
> I don't think I can really properly have that with anyone, not that I even want
> it anyway. (Diana)

It is easy for some survivors to be frozen in a childlike relationship with
the abusing father or mother figure of *God* because of what has happened.
And, in the "child" mind, either *God* has abandoned them or there is no
God.

> I tried to think of how they say He exists and I keep going back to the Bible,
> but maybe those are just stories or fairy tales. I think of myself praying, doing
> something back when I was ten, just bawling my eyes out, thinking what
> I should do; and I picked up the Bible. They ran out of booze at a wedding, and
> Mary says to her son, "They have run out of booze, and would you change the
> water into those casks to wine for us?" "Okay." He snaps his fingers, and the
> vases are filled with the finest wine they've ever had. What kind of God is that,
> that won't come to the aid of a 10-year-old, but yet he'll make a vase of booze
> if people run out? Is this the kind of God I want to pray to and worship? This is
> just a family story we've invented because we need something bigger than us.
> Maybe none of it exists. We just want to know that there is a creator, there is a
> heaven and hell. (William)

Although the dreams and ideals of childhood may have almost been
crushed by what has happened, the human spirit is fierce. Even as adults,
people may still search for new forms of spiritual nourishment.

In the aftermath of sexual and ritual abuse, or even in response to what
others have suffered, individuals may be at a loss as to how to find meaning
or purpose or to get back to what they once felt. They may worry how about
how to protect themselves—and others. They may wonder what to make of
the sum of their experiences with an abuser and about his impact on the community. They might question their own inner lives or whether any of what
they once experienced was valid.

> If he could do this to me, then all the good things he was doing to other people
> or for other people, how real were those things? I mean, during those first early

years, of course, I had this burden that I felt I had to protect everyone, you know, or most people. And I called into question the very reality of *the* spiritual experience, you know, or *a* spiritual experience. (Diana)

Survivors may need to create some meaning out of their experiences; to keep their ideals, their vocation, their faith, and their soul.

But the next few days were some of the most panicked days I've ever had in my life. You know, playing through all the possibilities of what I should do, what could I do, how could I remain a nun because this is what I wanted to do. So, I convinced myself that I would stay. I said, "Okay, he's got this problem. I can take that if ultimately what he seems to want is to really want *God*." I was rushed. You see, I can't even describe what I was trying to do mentally. I was trying to find some reason not [to go] running out and screaming into the night, you know? (Diana)

Survivors also need to know that they do not have to live like this for the rest of their lives. The abuse does not have to be the only part of themselves that they identify with. They need to see that they are more than their abuse or even their survival.

I mean for a long time it defined me, and I would live for the day—I was tired of this dark cloud—being a survivor—having sexual abuse just hanging over my head. I just wanted it to be integrated into who I am as a human being. And, I'm getting there. You know, it's not done yet. There's some new things that have come to light in my life which have made it more difficult, but it's coming there, so, I have no doubt I'll get there. (Will Michaels)

Those who have had a life-changing experience with a spiritual teacher or guru may have wished to hold their initial encounter intact, without risking disillusionment. They may not wish to consider how someone of this stature ever could have ever broken sacred boundaries with them or with anyone else. But, if individuals are honest and if what they have learned was important in their spiritual life, then they must hold the teacher to the same standards and accountability that all must meet.

What has happened cannot remove the transmission, the spiritual gems, the life-changing power of words, or the value of the practice, though it can stain these gifts so that they are no longer recognizable. In the end, if a spiritual leader has truly possessed greatness, he will want transparency and resolution. He will want those who have followed him to remember that the real teacher is the one within us. Though others may still insist on silence about a scandal—silence outside, or silence within—silence protects no one. The community that fears the truth loses its own soul.

Natalie Goldberg is a writer and a Buddhist teacher. For years, she manipulated the story of her master's sexual improprieties with her and with others.

It was painful and terrifying to have to admit that the man she had followed and who had been so profoundly important to her was capable of the very behaviors his teachings despised. But, she had to be faithful to her teacher and to the legacy that he had given her: to write honestly. She speaks of the enigma of her experience, as she put the truth about him into print:

> Nothing will ever change how this man opened my life. And not only mine—all the people who practiced with him were forever helped. We forsook him by freezing him in some image of our own selfish need, even when we had learned otherwise. To not be real about our teacher is not to be real about ourselves. It is to twist the dharma.[24]

So it is for all of us: we would not want any other outcome but to respect ourselves and to fiercely honor the truth.

"What is truth?" said Meister Eckhart, the thirteenth-century Catholic theologian and mystic. "Truth is something so noble that if *God* would turn aside from it, I would keep to the truth, and let *God* go."

So be it.

The truth can break our hearts. But it breaks us open.

It heals.

The truth—it sets us free.

RECOMMENDED READINGS

Bailey, Charles L. *In the Shadow of the Cross: The True Account of My Childhood and Ritual Abuse at the Hands of a Roman Catholic Priest.* New York: iUniverse, 2000.

Frawley O'Dea, Mary Gail. *The Long-term Impact of Early Sexual Trauma,* paper presented to the National Conference of Catholic Bishops, Dallas, Texas, June 13, 2002.

Gerber, Paul. "Victims Becoming Offenders: A Study of Ambiguities," Hunter, Mic, ed. *The Sexually Abused Male.* In Mic Hunter (ed.) *The Sexually Abused Male, Vol. 1: Prevalence, Impact, and Treatment.* Lexington Books (1990, pp. 153–76).

Mansfield, Victor "The Guru-Disciple Relationship: Making Connections and Withdrawing Projections" (lecture at Hamilton College, New York, 1996), www.lightlink.com.

RECOMMENDED FILMS

Celibacy, Anthony Thomas, HBO (2008).

Deliver Us from Evil, Amy Berg (2006).

Hand of God, Joe Cultera, PBS, *Frontline* (2007).

In the Spirit of Honest Inquiry (a dialogue between the Dalai Lama and the Western Buddhist teachers, Dharmasala) 1996.

The Narrow Bridge, Israel Moskovitz (2006).

The Scarlet Bond, Jbird Productions (2008).

The Secret Swami (BBC documentary) (2004).

Vedanta Catalogue, http://www.vedanta.org/reading/bookstores/catalog.html.

CHAPTER 7

———— ✸ ————

The Water You Want: Recovery in Four Directions

Someone may be clairvoyant able to see
the future, and yet have very little wisdom
Like the man who saw water in his dream,
and began leading everyone toward the mirage.
"I am the one with heart-vision.
I've torn open the veil."
So they set out with him inside the dream,
while he is actually sleeping beside a river
of pure water. Any search moves away from
the spot where the object of the quest is.
Sleep deeply wherever you are on the way.
Maybe some traveler will wake you.
Give up subtle thinking,
the twofold, threefold
multiplication of mistakes.
Listen to the sound of waves
within you.
There you are,
dreaming your thirst,
when the water you want
is inside the big vein on your neck

—Jelaluddin Rumi
translated by Coleman Barks

The oldest recorded myth about recovery was written on clay tablets in the third millennium B.C. It is a Sumerian story about Inanna, the beautiful Queen of Heaven and Earth and Goddess of Light. As the story goes, Inanna feels obliged to visit the underworld to attend the funeral of the husband of her sister Ereshkigal, who rules the dark realm. Inanna is not in the habit of going below and has had no contact with her sister or this realm since Eresh-kigal was raped as a child and then exiled—an unjust consequence of her trauma. Ereshkigal is not only grieving for her husband. She suffers in labor, unable to give birth. And, she is raging. She lies on her bed, furious because of her circumstances, fearful of more loss, and desperately lonely.

Inanna believes she can easily make the trek to the underworld, pay her respects, and come home. But Enki, the God of Wisdom, knows it might be more difficult than Inanna believes and gives her the holy *me*, a gift of knowledge to help her make the journey. Inanna also brings her crown, her lapis lazuli beads, some sparkly stones and a fashionable robe, which she considers both necessary and alluring. She leaves instructions for her servant: if Inanna does not return in three days, the servant must beat the drum for her, and go find help.

Inanna arrives at the gates of hell after a long journey. Meanwhile, the dark Queen of Death, groaning in misery, is enraged that her sister has blithely entered her realm without an invitation. Her presence is hardly welcome. In fact it seems a bit self-serving. Her sister's visit is but a reminder of all that Ereshkigal has lost.

"What does the Queen of Light want from me? I am the Goddess of Death. I weep for infants taken before their time. Does she want a piece of that? Or does she just want the Water?" For there in the underworld, it is Ereshkigal who also holds the Water of Life.

Ereshkigal declares that even the Queen of Heaven must abide by the same regulations as everybody else. She instructs the gatekeeper to systemati-cally remove Inanna's garments as she descends. He takes Inanna's crown, the lapis, the jewelry, and the royal robe at each of the narrow consecutive gates down to the realm of death, until Inanna arrives in the underworld utterly naked. But it makes no difference that she has been stripped and shamed. Inanna is still quite lovely, which only infuriates the miserable Queen of Hell even further. Ereshkigal, embittered as she is, pronounces Inanna guilty—guilty of the ignorance of death. And, with a cry, she fixes her eye of death on Inanna. She turns Inanna into a rotting corpse, left to hang on a meat hook.

Now Ereshkigal is truly miserable. Her husband is dead, she has killed her only sister, and she is still in the pangs of labor, unable to give birth.

Meanwhile, Inanna's servant waits outside the gates. After three days, she appeals for help from the two men who should care the most, Inanna's hus-band and father. Inanna's husband has quickly moved on to other distrac-tions, found another love interest, and forgotten about his wife. And Inanna's father, like a company man fearful of rocking the cosmic boat, says he can do nothing to alter fate.

So the servant again approaches Enki, who gave Inanna the blessing of knowledge for her journey. Enki is quite troubled to hear what has become of Inanna and agrees to do what he can to rescue her. He takes some dirt from under his fingernails and creates two little unobtrusive genderless demons, called Mourners, that can sneak through the cracks of the underworld. When they arrive, they do not even bother with Inanna's body but instead go to Ereshkigal, who is moaning on her labor bed.

"Oh, my inside. . . ."

"Oh, oh, your inside!" the creatures moan back.

"Oh, my outside. . . ." She weeps.

"Oh, oh, your outside. . . ." They weep with her and do not leave her side.

The Queen of Death falls silent. This is a new experience for her. No one has ever seen or acknowledged her pain. Relieved and flooded with gratitude, she finally gives birth.

In appreciation, Ereshkigal offers the little Mourners a boon of their choosing. They simply ask for Inanna's corpse. Ereshkigal agrees—and then mercifully sprinkles some of the Water of Life over the body of her sister.

Inanna, now revived and alive, returns to the earth and its heavens. But she is no longer simply the Queen of Light and Joy. She has been touched by the eye of death and experienced the decay and darkness that are her opposite. She has been stripped down and left for dead, and yet she has learned something down there in the cave. She has also found the Water of Life and so returns to her kingdom a wiser, humbler Queen.

Yet, Ereshkigal's story is perhaps even more significant to us than Inanna's. Ereshkigal does not leave the dark realm; she continues to be the ruler of the underworld, the one who must accept and hold death. Yet, something has transformed her. The little Mourners cannot erase what she has endured. But they witness her pain and resonate with it—and, because of this, she is finally able to give life.

It changes everything.

This is one description of grace. It does not make the pain go away. There are no magical solutions. But something has happened in the exchange: presence—or Presence—stillness, a joining, a knowing, a listening.

Grace—a ladder from Somewhere to gather us up.

THE GIFT

In my life I have found that the disillusionment I have experienced through spiritual hardship has often brought an odd sense of relief. For a short time—a minute or a decade—there is a delicious absence. The noise in my head may momentarily roar to a halt before the next wave arrives. I investigate my inner world differently, because what once determined it has been swept away. It is true that I still do not always know where I want to be, nor am I clear about what I wish to leave behind.

I may still grapple with the big questions.

Why does God allow evil?

Why did God allow this to happen to me?

Is there a God at all?

Does it matter?

There is a restlessness that is never satisfied by money or success, old habits, or new rituals. A dark blank of longing lingers for something I can barely voice. But I have yet to be spent with this wretched thing called hope. Hope is at times an aberration and at others a kind of knowledge in the face of no viable or reasonable fact. Hope is a bubble, a geyser, a spurt of optimism, or a trickle of faith. Hope sees prospects in impossibility but it is not always easy to find. The details are as much in dreams as in waking life.

Perhaps it is a human thing to hope. Plants respond to sun and water. Animals are creatures of conditioning and know how to wait. I am a human being. I do all of these and more with hope, even if there seems none to be had.

Thomas Merton writes in his "Letter on a Contemplative Life":

> I have been summoned to explore a desert area of man's heart in which explanations no longer suffice, and in which one learns that only experience counts. An arid rocky dark land of the soul, sometimes illuminated by strange fires which men fear and people by specters which men studiously avoid except in their nightmares. And in this area, I have learned that one cannot truly know hope unless he has found how like despair hope is.[1]

LOSING THE CROWN

Spiritual loss and betrayal often causes confusion and emptiness. For many, it is extremely uncomfortable to be left with fewer rules, little feedback, and nothing to push against. People may carry a divine or not so divine rage; it is hard to be without a faith community or without faith itself. There is often grief, not only for what has been lost but for what was assumed to be a constant in life.

Many look for relief from their abuse by seeking some kind of justice. Some confront their abusers directly or look for restitution from the institutions that hurt them. Sometimes this helps. But, perhaps, like Ereshkigal's attempt at striking back, it does not always do as much as they hope.

> It was agreed that I would have my friend with me, and the priest would be accompanied by another priest who was second in charge from the bishop. We met in a small study. I sat across from my perpetrator who was then in his early seventies. He was noticeably nervous. I remember saying that I wanted to read a prepared statement from my memories of the night of the abuse. And I had two sworn statements from my best high school friend and my ex-wife, who were the first two people I told about the abuse. I read the statement and waited for a response. He said that he was an alcoholic and didn't remember

anything that I was saying had happened. However, he did take issue with my memory that it wasn't a Boy Scout function that he had taken me to; it was a wedding. Interesting that he remembered that and not what followed in the woods. I then read the sworn statements to prove that I wasn't making up these charges so many years after the fact. He simply repeated the same denial of the abuse and said he was an alcoholic and was subject to blackouts, with no real admission of guilt. I asked for a few moments alone with the priest. My request was granted, and the others left the room. Alone with him, I told him about the harm that this had done to my life, and he began to repeat the same mantra. I cut him off. We sat there for a few moments, and then he made two statements. He said, "I was always very fond of you," and, "Your mother asked me to look out for you." I felt nauseous and felt it best to stop before I assaulted him. (Chris)

The hope of resolution is not always met, even if the litigation is successful and a check is signed. Restitution is often more difficult because the money does not replace a lack of moral accountability from the institutions guilty of housing, ignoring, or enabling the abuse.

> Just ask yourself why not a single bishop, cardinal, or pope has ever been indicted for any crime, even though district attorneys all over the country have sufficient evidence to arraign them on criminal charges of conspiracy in actively covering up crimes of sexual abuse of children. (Chris)

Survivors can be bitterly let down, and still do not feel safe, even long after the abuse has ended. Like Ereshkigal, they may rarely get an apology or acknowledgement of what has happened to them, which is probably one of the most essential parts of the resolution. For people like Chris, the power of the Church that abused him lies in its ability to convince people that it speaks for *God*. This "authority" is in part what keeps so many survivors of religious abuse silent for so long.

> It isn't about holiness that we need or want more of. It is to remove these people from their cathedrals with their holy books, bring them to courts like any other men, and have them tried, judged and punished just like any other criminal. When someone from the Church steps up and does this, then I'll feel safe knowing that if there is a *God*, then *God* will once again be *God* and not the men who act as if they were gods. (Chris)

History has shown again and again how difficult it is to purify religious institutions. It can take centuries for a system that invests in power and fear to produce a lineage that is committed to rigorous spiritual practice and accountability. These are often the tasks of reformations and revolutions. However the leadership behaves, transforming the institution ultimately rests with the community. It is the people themselves who must challenge the inertia or the hubris of their leaders and if need be prosecute them for their crimes.

> If you are a janitor in a school, you're held in a jail, but if you're a priest, a bishop, a physician, a lawyer, a judge, you're allowed to get away. And as long a society and the community are collaborating, in the coverup, you know, there's not going to be anything to bear on the Church to change its behavior. Grant you, the Church should be leading society in how it deals with this, but, you know, there's so much collusion between the two, it just boggles my mind that that could be done. (Delicia)

There is often a paralysis in those communities already engulfed in rage, despair, or disappointment about the ones who were trusted with their souls. It can take decades, even centuries, for the pot to simmer enough to boil into change. Fear may be masked by an imitation of stability or by the inertia that keeps communities from doing anything about the betrayals. Eventually, when enough people are dissatisfied or demoralized, there may be a revolution. Sometimes a mystic or a visionary will spark a light with a radical life or perhaps an untimely death, which sets off the blaze. These individuals may initially be regarded as unlikely candidates for the job of spiritual revolutionary and even be considered blasphemous, irrelevant, or insane. While one is often mistaken for the other, madness and mysticism are essentially different because of the source from which they spring.

Jalaluddin Rumi was a whirling dervish who made a meditation of active devotion to God through his mystical poetry. Once he whirled for three straight days, but, as his poetry and his life indicate, this twirling was not born out of psychosis. Rather, Rumi was moving on an inside track toward his experience of God, which had little to do with outside physical limitations.

Rumi wrote, "Move within, but don't move the way fear makes you move." His life was the essential witness. He also said, "We are the mirror as well as the face in it. We are tasting the taste this minute of eternity." His devotion was as mundane as it was holy. "We are pain and what cures pain . . . the sweet cold water and the jar that pours."[2] There is no distinction. He communicated the palpable immediacy of experience and how to deeply connect to either side of pain and pleasure. This perception cuts open the screen that fear and hubris erect and keeps it from shielding people with their security of wealth, academics, or familiarity.

Francis of Assisi, another apparent madman in his time, was thrown out on the street by his own religious community after they instituted a congregational Rule, finding his unconditional surrender to the divine too radical to endorse. His uncompromising poverty and unmitigated love initiated a particular kind of revolution in a twelfth-century Church that confused material wealth and scholarship with spiritual accomplishment.

It can sometimes take a century or two for the power and vision of the mystic like St. Francis to filter into a religious organization, especially if the formal institution is already in place. Habits are hard to break and traditions difficult to dismantle in any Church or religious body. The challenge of a religious community to live the truth without compromise is not a popular or natural task. Religious arrogance easily overwhelms holy institutions and specific individuals long before the cyst of corruption can be lanced and the infection cleared away. Human beings are creatures of convenience, and change can be excruciating. But, once in a while, a Rumi or a Francis—a rural village woman or a street merchant—create an inner revolution in the community that takes hold and the system gets a power wash, even though the community may have difficulty catching up to the ideal.

> But I also believe that the Holy Spirit, or however you want to define it—every once in a while—cleanses the church, you know, whether it's Buddhism or whatever. There's a great wind that comes in, and it's often extraordinarily painful. But often the benefit is that the purging of the evil leaves another open door. And it's going to take another 40 years because society still isn't coming to terms with it. (Delicia)

Raising awareness about what happens in one's religious community is both dangerous and necessary. It provides a model for those who feel they have no voice and offers them the possibility of taking back their power. As the mystic or the prophet would verify, this can be a lonely and dangerous position. Survivors, or those who have witnessed abuse, bear an enormous burden in disclosure and advocacy. To expose even the most glaring and visible offenses has resulted in expulsion or annihilation for many.

For Eleanor, trying to seek spiritual guidance and resolution about her sexual abuse resulted in being told by another minister "I never want to see you again."

> He wouldn't allow me to speak. Within the first five minutes, he started shouting at me, "There's no proof that this happened," and, "It's your fault. How come you didn't bring it up when it happened?" We don't use the word "excommunicated." But, after decades, I literally walked away. I suppose I would say I was shunned. When I walked away from that appointment, I realized that I would never put foot on that land again. Every once in a while, it just shocks me to think that a place that was so much a part of me for so many decades was literally sliced away that day. (Eleanor)

Those who have the courage to reveal what has happened or is still happening now deserve the assurance that their report will be respectfully heard and investigated. They need to be safe enough to trust there will be no revictimization because of their disclosure. While they know that speaking out may horrify and shake the faith of the community; being silent protects no one but the abusers. If an organization turns on the survivors of its own religious abuses or those who speak out about them, it abandons the very people it is supposed to serve and forfeits its integrity. And the community loses any real spiritual home.

THE BEADS UNSTRUNG

Losing a religious community can be like losing a family. For many, it *is* losing one's family.

For Diana, alienation from her religious community meant a profound disconnection from a spiritual home. Because there are few centers in the country where her tradition and spiritual lineage is practiced, she felt completely isolated.

> My goodness, at least you can go to another Catholic church in another city. I mean, we were cut off from any kind of connection to this force of spirituality. (Diana)

It is not so easy to replace those spiritual ties. Rasan and Irit also know well how difficult it is to live without the sustenance of deep connections with their own people. Their tenuous association with their Muslim and Jewish communities has factored into their concern for their two adult children. Each of their children, in his or her own way, struggles to bridge the two different worlds of their parents.

> I told my daughter, "You have to find people like you, to create your own community that will give you a sense of social support which most of us need." As long as they find that social support system, whether that support group is made of Hindus or Americans or Chinese or whatever, I really don't mind. But I think it's essential for their health, psychological health and mental health, and stability in life. (Rasan)

As survivors look for other meaningful connections, the new relationships they do find may be very different, perhaps having nothing at all to do with religion but found through political action, scholarship, art, or community service. As we look for community we want to be welcomed, nourished, and, hopefully, inspired to be connected to a purpose. We need to know that we are not alone in our struggles and in our inner quest. Even those who choose to be hermits or live in solitude count on the support of the larger family of humankind in some way to live.

While some may believe it best to compartmentalize the investigations of an inner life and try to recreate those original connections and practice in other associations, experimenting with new communities or possibly new religions means also engaging with the human beings in those places. We all bring our emotional luggage to a community along with our gems. It is interesting to note whether and how we replicate family scripts or previous religious pathologies with the new cast of characters.

New processes can be strangely reminiscent of old familiar patterns of abuse, often with similar results. It is always important to consider how much to bring to each and every relationship and whether they seem to recreate the same problems over and over again.

If new communities remind survivors of their old organizations and end up with the same unsatisfying or even triggering results, they may not only cease to seek communities they can belong to but discard the notion of community altogether.

> I have not found and no longer look for a community, because none can meet all my criteria, which are, grounded in spirituality but utterly free of dogma and utterly free of materialism and one-upmanship—not a quasi-religious interpretation of the leaders, or how you're supposed to dress, or what language you're supposed to use, or how you're supposed to arrange the chairs in the room. (Joseph)

There are times when some people have to unhinge themselves from *any* relationship with the institution, even in the association of adversary. Otherwise, they can get stuck in the struggle, unable to move out of their identities as victims. Whether or not they discard the system entirely, it may be important to keep what has been valuable and remember what brought them to their spiritual path in the first place.

> I think the basic teachings of Buddhism are true for me and help me understand who I am, how I am, and how the world is around me. That is a good thing: to return to those basic principles, rather than getting caught up in all the different personalities of teachers and schools and the drama that goes along with that. (Beth)

Sometimes it seems that there is no choice but to throw out the baby with the bathwater even though the prospect of real change and uncertainty is hard to imagine. Yet while survivors of religious abuse want to be free of their pain, they often continue to use old habits in an attempt to lock it away in a drawer without ever fully addressing it. Many of us can spend years trying to dissolve our frustration and dissatisfaction without really altering anything in our own inner lives.

Jack Kornfield, a psychologist and Buddhist teacher, gives one perspective on how people try to separate themselves from personal pain simply to survive.

> The walls of our compartments are made of fear and habits, ideas we have about what should or shouldn't be, [or] what spiritual life is and what it is not.

Because certain aspects of life have been overwhelming to us, we have walled them off. Most frequently we don't wall off the great and universal sufferings of the world around us, the injustice, the war and bigotry, but rather our own and immediate pain. We fear the personal because it has touched us and wounded us most deeply.[3]

But the personal is perhaps the only part we can ever really change.

UNROBING THE SELF

For many, the powerful journey of psychotherapy is invaluable as they recover from the abuses of religion. In that process, there can be deep support, a shared intention to transform one's encoded fear into new possibilities, and new ways to find meaning again. But it is a humbling experience for a professional to stand over the blind crevasse of the soul with another person. Unmasking the deep fissures of spirit takes a long time. The exploration of emotion goes only so far unless some attention is given to the inner life. One cannot avoid the pain, though it is natural to want to resist it. Survivors want to believe that, although suffering is inevitable, misery is optional. They want to count on the therapeutic process to give them a safe space to look at the past and present with the added intricacy of religion. This is why the choice of a clinician is such a personal and important decision.

When survivors enter into new emotional or spiritual terrain, it can be terrifying. There is a distinction between comfort and safety and the way each of these interacts with fear. Some survivors may be comfortable in an extremely unsafe circumstance because the situation is so similar to an old pattern of injury. Other times, when they are actually safe enough to push toward growth, they may instead hesitate or resist change because the process of psychotherapy can be so uncomfortable. The challenge is to experience freedom or choices, even when one is afraid, and to recognize what is truly safe for oneself, whether or not it is comfortable.

This is one of the most essential therapeutic goals for the survivor: to be safe *enough* to be uncomfortable with new input and to trust the process as she pushes through fear toward change and recovery. If the client cannot first set the parameters for her emotional and physical safety, she will never know her limits or understand how this relationship is any different from earlier abuses. There may have been clergy or counselors in the past who promised and nevertheless violated her safety. The therapist needs to ask what the client needs to be safe enough to begin to do the work, rather than dictate the conditions. That the therapist might ask *first* can be a revolutionary concept to the survivor.

Hypervigilance and the old emotional entrenchments often paralyze survivors' capacity to absorb new or positive experiences. They face a minefield of emotional triggers, and the enterprise of psychotherapy can feel dangerous or overwhelming even when the space is secure. It seems as if the entire process could backfire with a single interchange. Many do not know what words, gestures, or stances of others will set them off. Some imagine that the therapist can magically extrapolate everything about them just by sitting there, so they do not easily risk their vulnerability. They find themselves alone in a room with someone who appears to be in a position of power, awkwardly trying to talk about what is almost unspeakable. It is a familiar setup.

> Imagine if you had no skin and everyone could see inside of you, exposing all your private thoughts and experiences. The priest, through the confessional, knew exactly how to get to me, and I didn't realize that because it was supposedly God I was talking to in there. Now fast-forward 30 years later, to me seeking a therapist. As soon as I entered the room, I would completely dissociate and have no access to any of my feelings. I would go completely numb. There I was, back in a confessional experience, and the boy in me would come forward and completely freeze. (Chris)

Even the logistics of therapy can seem threatening. Survivors initially have to assess what might make it work; then they actually have to somehow ask for it. The request is not always verbal. The client may need to sit on the floor, stand in the corner, or face the wall, to shout or curl up in a ball. The survivor might not even know what he needs from anybody else, especially if his boundaries have been badly defined and violated. He may need the space to have his emotions, to be furious or sacrilegious. He may even need to be combative but then must learn that this is different from being abusive. He still has to be able to say whatever he needs to say about *God* or the organization or whomever the culprit was without being judged. While a survivor may need to have the space to be combative, a therapist also requires respect and safety so both she and the client can be in a position to do the recovery work together; *neither* survivor nor the therapist ever need to tolerate verbal or physical abuse. Some exchanges in therapy are never legitimate: a sexual relationship, a dual relationship that involves money lending or other business transactions, or an opportunity for the therapist to proselytize. At times, there is a place for therapeutic nonsexual touch or for the pushing of limits towards healthy growth. But the responsibility for maintaining physical and emotional safety in the room and hence the potential for betrayal is *always* with the therapist. It is essential for her to create a clear distinction between bodywork, Authentic Movement, dance, psychotherapeutic use of touch—and sexual contact. Religious abusers often confused their victims with their touch, saying that what was happening to them was either not happening or that it was a holy act. Each survivor needs to know that he will not be pushed or touched without specific permission. In fact, even if *he* asks for these things, the therapist must tenaciously protect and hold the boundaries using touch and space, words and silence, with immense respect and skill.

Sometimes a clinical situation brings a person back to her own shameful feelings and have little to do with *who* is currently in front of her. Eventually, the survivor client may project some kind of old association onto the therapist. This can be a very productive experience if the transaction has a reparative outcome that is ultimately different from what happened in the past. If a survivor feels discomfort because of a transaction with her clinician or if, for instance, an action feels far too familiar or intimate, it is best for her to speak out. But if she has no words (which often happens when a memory of an early experience is triggered) or if what has transpired in the treatment room affects her only later in the hour, the next day, or the next week, she needs to talk about it before she puts herself in another similar situation where she will feel equally vulnerable.

Occasionally, the experience with the therapist makes the survivor feel he must leave treatment. It can take time to sort out. Sometimes a therapist has stepped in a therapeutic minefield and unconsciously reenacted a familiar abusive scenario; sometimes she has missed the point, or fails to connect. It would be invaluable and productive if the survivor could work through his feelings with the therapist, but he may not feel safe to enter the space again. Ideally, the survivor would let the therapist know what felt wrong and why he left the therapy and find another resource as soon as possible so that the experience does not become embedded as another impassible trauma.

However, if the same dynamic happens again and again,— it may be necessary for the survivor to take a closer look at the exchange and what in order to investigate what was recreated in the therapy that is reminiscent of the past. Sometimes a transaction has less to do with the specific content of the abuse than with the larger landscape of past history that has been recreated in the room.

Unlike in psychotherapy, dual relationships often occur in religious communities with pastoral counselors. It is commonplace for clergy to be friends with members of the church, mosque, or temple. Food, celebrations, favors, and gifts are shared and treasured. Members of religious communities, especially the clergy, are often as much a part of our daily rituals and personal connections as our families. These relationships may have been loaded with sacred and intimate meaning, which further complicates why the roots of betrayal are so deep and the conditions for abuse so entrenched and confusing throughout one's life.

The relationship in psychotherapy or pastoral counseling is both profoundly intimate and *not* social. The therapist, in particular, is not a part of the friend or family network, whether or not he shares the survivor's deepest values, spiritual foundation, or even religious community. A pastoral counselor may actually be a part of one's spiritual community, but unless a clear boundary is established as an indispensable part of safety in the initial interview, the survivor will have a lurking concern about possible violation, whether it is consciously acknowledged or not.

For a survivor of religious abuse, it can be enormously comforting to share the perspective and principles of a particular tradition and community with one's therapist, because there is so much religious data that does not have to be explained. But it is important that there be a clear and unmistakable contract regarding the relationship, money, and confidentiality, especially if there is ever any interaction between the two outside the therapy room.

However it goes, the process of finding a good therapist involves time, possible missteps, negotiation, and chemistry. Even so, it is not ever possible to find *the* perfect person. In fact, seeking perfection may stall the search. The point is to find someone with whom the survivor can be herself to do the work, with whom she can build trust, and who will challenge her to grow.

Therapy may emerge as the only place where the survivor can safely speak of spiritual matters. The work that is done in the sacred space of therapy rides on the delicate teeter-totter of trust and vulnerability. Other techniques and wisdom from other spiritual traditions such as yoga, mindfulness practice, and meditation can also be quite beneficial for treatment and for rethinking the spiritual journey. Survivors need a special kind of container that will enable them to negotiate the ambiguities and ambivalence of not only the past but also what is ahead.

> After a very long time, I found a dance therapist four hours from my home who became my therapist. It was with her that I came closest to what I guess others experience when they feel they can finally trust someone enough to let the "self" be seen. And still even with her not everything was shared, and the ability to shut it all down could happen with lightning speed. I have always needed someone who could let me know that they are prepared to sit with me in the horror of my world and hold the light up ahead of me so I can see where I'm going and that I'm not walking the journey alone. (Chris)

The link with a therapist can be a profound connection or a disastrous reenactment of an old destructive paradigm. The work has to proceed within a new power structure of deep respect, safety, and mutuality. The therapist cannot manipulate the process to suit his agenda, especially if it is a religious one.

Adam, a psychologist and a survivor of religious bigotry, recognizes how his old belief system can affect his clinical work with others.

> There's the missionary part of me that believes that the right way is you doing it my way; my way *is* your way, and happiness only comes when you conform, when you're like me. "I have the truth. I've figured it out, and if you don't accept it, there's something wrong with you." So that's where it backfires on me: I shut down clients' process of exploration or avoid or ignore avenues that they

wanted to talk about, but they never felt safe enough, because I'm telling them what to feel, how they should feel, what they should think. So my eagerness or my sureness that I have all the answers and truth—which is definitely a Mormon belief—gets in my way of connecting to them and allowing them to be who they are. (Adam)

Adam's self-awareness as a psychotherapist has helped him respect whatever his clients need to do or be in the process of the therapy, to do the powerful work of recovery with them.

I really try to focus in on them and allow whatever is coming from them to be, and honoring their "craziness," honoring their truth, honoring their wisdom, honoring whatever is in the room, and understanding it. (Adam)

Like those in the religious ministry, therapists who have an undigested sense of mission may find that their enthusiasm, love, or kindness can sometimes contaminate therapy. Shadows of histrionics, overidentification with the material, or cynicism can be the result of the therapist's own history and have little to do with the client. The process also falters if the clinician minimizes the spiritual damage that the trauma has caused or fails to remember to go only as fast as the slowest part of the survivor.

The challenge for any clinician is to encourage curiosity, not judgment. This distinction is absolutely essential for recovery, especially because survivors of religious abuse have been degraded at such a core level.

Survivors' memories, life decisions, and relationships with their abusers have often been complicated by love, as well as shame. It is difficult (and should be) for therapists or anyone else to jump to slick interpretations about their relationships and history with their abuser.

Victor understands such complexities both as a therapist and as a survivor.

I think one of the more difficult things for me and for the survivor, is to be able to hold the piece of this that has to do with love, and how confusing that is, and how much they want it back still, even now. If I dismiss it too easily, too quickly, I've lost that person or made our work that much more complicated. And if I overemphasize it too soon, it infuriates [or] terrifies the client; that might be a loss. Someone will take a hike right there. There's no opportunity to repair that. (Victor)

Delicia also touches on the complications for those in the community who both witness the evil that has been done to their members while still recognizing any benefit the abuser may have given to them or others. It is often difficult but important to come to grips with both realities: one does not necessarily cancel out the other. Delicia reminisces about what it meant for one particular woman to get the larger perspective in the wake of a clergy abuse scandal in her church.

We went into the corner and held a conversation so that we could have privacy, so that no one can pick it up on TV, and just talked about what did this mean for her own faith journey and how important this person had been. I fully believe no matter how wretched a person's behavior is, there are times when they do enormous good. And to help her process out that the church and her faith were much larger than her relationship with this one priest. (Delicia)

It takes a large lens to see the big picture. The challenge is to have the patience to take the time and to allow the space to include the full measure of good and bad. Survivors do not have to do this in one session, or one year, or ever. It can, however, be an important piece of the healing process, when and if they are ready to take in the large view.

LEAVING THE DARK REALM

One of the most important psychological and spiritual end goals of psychotherapy is to accept the self in all its convolutions, in its loves and its hatreds, in the best and the worst. There are other considerations in the recovery process, as well: the issues of forgiveness, the problem of *God* or whatever we call It, and how we make meaning. These are tasks that can go far beyond the limits of a therapy office.

Perhaps the most complicated issue in recovery from religious abuse for any survivor is the matter of forgiveness. Indeed, it is a complex and individual question. Forgiveness of a perpetrator cannot be mandated by a religious or psychological agenda. There is no checkoff point that a therapist, counselor, or community has a right to determine when it comes to forgiveness. Forgiveness cannot be made a requirement in order to "move on." In fact, sometimes pushing survivors to forgive only increases their anxiety and rage, which further perpetuates the trauma of the abuse.

Forgiveness is usually a process, rather than a clear-cut decision. It can happen in stages or not at all. Sometimes, the offense has been so profound that absolution is not even the survivor's alone to give. How does one tackle personal forgiveness within the story of the Holocaust or within any intentional annihilation of a race or religious community? How does anyone easily come to terms with the calculated abuse or torture of a child?

There are occasions when one is stuck with the burden of pity: pity for the conditions of the abuse, pity even for the perpetrator. Surely, it seems pathetic and almost inconceivable that any person could be so morally or spiritually ravaged as to commit intentional harm or profoundly neglect another, less powerful person. One may take the expansive, empathic view to see that the perpetrator has his own particular history of betrayal, and his own particular sorrow. But none of these excuse the violation.

While the perpetrators were probably a complicated mix of light and shadow, we shouldn't expect them to thank us for exposing their abuses, much less acknowledge what they have done. But one's truth is more important than the myths, even myths of God.

Of course, there are always two sides to every story. There are times when the victim has been too psychologically compromised to provide a full or accurate explanation of his abuse. Pieces of memory do not fall into a linear order. As we have seen, recollection and recall can play like a broken movie reel, especially when it comes to trauma. Sometimes, the one who has been deeply compromised even accuses other innocent people of terrible deeds for various, even curious reasons. Leonard Shengold, in his classic *Soul Murder Revisited*, asks, "Does it matter if it really happened? The answer is yes—and no."[4] No matter what or how it occurred, it is important to responsibly establish that *something* happened between the accused and the survivor and take exquisite care to acknowledge it, as well as any contradictions in the relationship. The task is not simply to determine culpability. All involved must grapple with the delicate process of the soul's recovery, how or whether forgiveness should ever be encouraged (if even in that order), and what will help a survivor recover his inner life.

There may be much at stake when a survivor decides to speak out. It is never easy to bear the brunt of his or her own indictments, especially if those accused are beloved by their communities, not held accountable, or have no compunction to be so.

Even if the offender makes amends, it cannot be assumed that the survivor automatically should or could absolve the offense. Deciding to forgive a perpetrator, a community, or an organization requires an examination of the heart. One can do this only with the intention and with enough time to gauge one's authentic "response-ability" to the individual situation.

One can learn something from the principles of *aikido*, a Japanese martial art form that emphasizes harmony and control of the self. In such a discipline, the point is not to attack but to redirect the force of the attack. In that way, one circumvents the energy of aggression, fear, and constriction, responding instead from relaxed awareness. Maintaining control over oneself, the situation, even the source of suffering, takes practice.

Of course, *aikido* is a practice. It develops over time and requires both intention and action. Forgiveness, like the discipline of *aikido*, has an edge. It is a balancing act involving justice and, ultimately, compassion. While forgiveness cannot exonerate the abuse or negate the harm done, one needs to tease out the sense of revenge from inappropriate rage so that he can eventually be free of both.

It is up to the survivor to decide whether *or not* he chooses to forgive face to face, by himself, in his own mind, or only after the perpetrator is dead. The point is to release the power of the perpetrator on every level and to let go of the notion that the survivor did anything to deserve what happened to him. He didn't. He has been bound to the abuse and the abuser long enough.

The process of forgiveness is best accomplished with balanced and compassionate support from the community, the therapist, or a safe spiritual mentor. In certain practices, the act can even include gratitude to the abuser for what one has learned. For others, this is impossible. They may acknowledge what was good or even holy in that person and what was valuable to their lives and spirits, but they never need to view the evil done to them as a holy or righteous act.

In Eastern traditions, there is often an undigested notion of *karma* and how it plays out during abuse. *Karma* involves the notion of cause and effect—not fate—and one's own responsibility for what happens through actions past, present, and future. It is sometimes grossly and callously misconstrued as a kind of "blame the victim" rationalization for events where one's traumatic experiences are seen as manifestations of past behavior. It would be inappropriate to try to deconstruct the theory of *karma* as it relates to abuse in this book. But, as we factor this into the discussion of forgiveness, let us strongly caution against indicting anyone who has suffered at the hands of religion as somehow deserving his or her violation.

It is a challenge to look at forgiveness in all its incongruities. Those in the process of recovery must be honest, take their time, and recognize that they will probably feel all over the place about it. And, in the end, it is *their* decision when and how they free themselves.

Most imagine what it would be like to be relieved of the burdens of their past but may be confused as to how to leave behind what has colored so much of their identity. They may want a witness to see them in these complexities but are often ashamed when anyone actually does. They may desire compensation for their suffering only to recognize how truly complicated it is to let go of the pain.

Tears and words may be the best attempt to circle an experience, but, in the end, there are still ragged paper cuts of unfinished business that afflict any person struggling to recover.

> I started therapy in 19__, and that was something. I really feel like I took care of myself in those two years. They were intensive, and I cried a lot and talked a lot. So, I took care of myself. But the thing is, the stuff never goes away. I mean like I just told you that I haven't thought about this—but isn't it interesting—how it's right there. (Eleanor)

No matter what the process entails, survivors may only begin to confront what Stephen Levine calls their "untouchable sorrow."[5] Such sorrow is marbled in the tissue along with resistance: resistance to life, resistance to risk. One may resist having to bear another collapsed promise or the habits of tension that religion and its disillusionment evoke. How can anyone make meaning after that and begin to risk other possibilities beyond the fullness of pain?

There is a fearful silence that comes at the end of hope or, even during the closing stages of a fruitful inner journey. One may be struck with the terrifying possibility of *not* being numb but utterly broken open instead. Yet, light can still pass through the cracks in the heart. Something can still draw outward from the reverie—and inward—far deeper than tears and words ever go.

> It's really difficult to let go of that fear, which is what I look at a lot. I recognize that falling apart is what happens first. If something happens with the falling apart thing even here, I'll be okay because coming together will come after it. (Shimon)

How do people know this? They begin to listen more deeply. They may notice that they are more flexible and less rigid about how things ought to be. They may begin to recognize a profound resonance with kindness or an outrage when they hear religious platitudes; this particular sensitivity may drive a mischievous or even sacrilegious sense of humor that rails against injustice and discrimination in the name of *God,* even when that particular *God* has had nothing to do with any justification for intolerance.

For one who has shared a profound spiritual connection with the person who abused her, it may be difficult to come to any resolution or spiritual connection without the excruciating opposite experience of abuse and the spiritual experience.

> When I still try and to meditate, I think there is a great welling up of some kind of pain and sorrow, so I feel in a way that meditation in the mode of that particular tradition has been taken away from me. (Diana)

What survivors have experienced through their struggles, even through their deep spiritual losses, can also be the soil for recovery and for immense understanding. Though we can never trivialize or rationalize what happened to us, we can begin to recognize that, on some level, even the suffering was essential to our particular spiritual story. *We are pain and what cures pain . . .*

Coach says that his spiritual life is best described in a Puritan prayer entitled, "The Valley of Vision." With the vision, "in the daytime stars can be seen from deepest wells, and the deeper the wells, the brighter Thy stars shine," Coach holds the darkness along with the light and struggles to find an exquisite balance in opposite realities.

But, of course, it is always up to each person to choose how to do this.

> I can choose a path of suffering, or a path of healing. I choose both. I waver back and forth. I move and break and carry the broken pieces within me to reintegrate into a new whole. I cannot face it but cannot avoid it. It is the very essence of existence. All the forces of healing and destruction in the universe wrestle in my soul. I stand like Jacob on the banks of a new and old life and wrestle with an angel. I will not let it go until it has blessed me. (Shimon)

Shimon mentions a quote from Jung that is on his desk: "One does not become whole by imaging figures of light; it's by making the darkness conscious." His challenge to see beyond the pain and embrace that even the darkest part of himself seems to bring a far wider lens to the full picture of his recovery.

> My deepest wounds then become the very ground on which I must work. I must learn to see G-d in my suffering; I must learn to see G-d even in the very institution that crushed the Divine within me, for, if I cannot see G-d in my abuser, I cannot bring G-d forth from within myself. This is incredibly difficult. It requires that I love my enemy even when I am still being hurt. It requires that I love myself (which is often just as hard or even harder). In the end, it requires that I realize that *I* am the Mormon Church and that they are me: that we are all part of the same G-d, each of us a face of the universe, each of us whole and complete. (Shimon)

Of course, not everyone can see a *God* in the struggle at all. Sometimes the notion of *God* has been so polluted that we relinquish the idea altogether. It may be difficult to let go of the child-size disappointment in a kind of *God* that seems as though he is no longer interested.

> What's different? What's changed that makes it more important to listen to me now then back then. To me, it's nothing. If you didn't listen back then, why listen now? (William)

Some of us may find another way to connect with God in traditional religion or other spiritual paths. For others, the anthropomorphic idea of *God* may shape-shift out of the concrete and develop into another kind of experience altogether. Will, minister and survivor, has found the experience of connection as a way of also reclaiming his spiritual self.

> That idea of the Peeping Tom God in the clouds—I abandoned that completely, that just wasn't what it was for me. And now, as a minister, I can use that prayer as God, but it doesn't necessarily mean this divine, all-powerful being. It means a connection. (Will Michaels)

Will's ministry becomes the homeopathic remedy, the "pain and what cures it."

> And I think in many ways, I remember when it first started to come up and I was dealing with it in seminary and some of these things. You know, this was like a circle of healing—like I healed myself as it were. It was a sign of healing that here I was. abused by a priest, and I found myself as a clergyperson. What a circle! (Will Michaels)

That inner life may have no name, but it still moves the outer one. It drives wonder and curiosity; it lets us watch things, listen to things, experience things, and wonder about something that is larger.

It's within me, I mean, it's the love that flows from within me and the pain that flows from within me and the things that connects me to all those things; my pain, my joys, my sorrow, that's what I call *God*. (Will Michaels)

But whether *God* means a connection, a question (Kate insists "It's the question in my life; it's just a nonstop question.") or no question at all, something else may be moving through the aisles of our mind that satisfies the inner wakings.

While some may struggle with demons like hopelessness or despair, contending with "nothing" may be most unsettling experience of all. *Nothing* is what we imagine it to be, but *nothing* also presses in. This is not just word play. Despite all the pain, the lack of self-esteem, the attention deficits, the addictions, the endless self-sabotage, the shadows and potholes, this *nothing*—is always there, like a brook under the ground. So we may have to come up with a different picture of *It*.

Deep inside me, I sense that *God* probably exists. I hope that, when I die, the wall that separates us will disappear—but I'm not certain. (Eleanor)

Some of us decide the only *it* is us. Still we trudge along with ourselves and find something special along the way, whether it is a listening within or a prayer, even if we no longer believe in *God* or, at least, the one we thought was *God*.

I think my inner life drives my wonder and curiosity about my outer life. It's probably what gets me up and going in the morning and keeps me moving through the day and often what interferes with my sleep that night, which still happens. And, for somebody that doesn't believe in *God*, I have a spiritual practice, and in a way I think living is a spiritual practice for me now. Sometimes, I remember that I have my books around to pick up and read, my daily readings; sometimes, I don't. Sometimes, I build in time for meditation; sometimes, I don't. I mean, a lot of people would find it quite humorous that, for somebody who doesn't believe in *God*, I probably say "*God* help me" more often than people who actually do believe in *God*. (Victor)

Some of us may find another way to connect with God in traditional religion or other spiritual paths. Perhaps we may still be listening but not necessarily to sermons or lectures. We may have an active inner life—but it might not have a thing to do with anything we *know*.

To me, to look at a nautilius shell or a sunset, a newborn baby, the way a flock of birds will coordinate their motions, or a school of fish, and to deny that there's something going on that we don't know about—that just denies the evidence of the senses. But I think that human weakness and fear and the need to scare away those dark things skittering around outside our tent at night—the more detailed cosmology, the fantasy—the more comforting it is for some people. I do believe deeply in some spiritual component to existence. I just utterly reject the notion that any group has exclusive marketing right to it. "You can't get it wholesale—we're *God*'s sole authorized retail agent!" That's what Meister Eckhart[6] was trying to say: that you could have a direct experience without intermediaries, without an alms-collecting priest. (Joseph)

A direct experience. . . . It is hard to describe. One can usually define it only in roundabout ways. There is term in art theory called the *fleeting effect*,[7] which describes the qualities of movement and time as they apply to a painting or a two-dimensional object. These ethereal qualities appear to be inferred, like metaphors. They are not directly visible on the canvas but are communicated nevertheless. The qualities of an inner life give off this *fleeting effect*, because what is experienced is not always definable in concrete terms—yet is palpable, even so.

Diana calls it "advisory presence."

> There is a kind of almost energy or something that happens, where that inner presence feels like it's permeating you. (Diana)

This energy or presence can breed restlessness but not the restlessness that comes out of monotony. It is a kind of agitation that births creativity and invites sensitivity to beauty. It can drive activism but also the search for quiet. That search may move deeper still—to listen to another voice that is different than the noisy mental dialogue filling the top of the brain. It is not always easy to tolerate this particular form of silence, because with it often comes a self-awareness that is starkly different from self-absorption. There may still be this grappling question of evil, confusion about *God*, a persistent inner dialogue, or simple longing.

Survivors might use other varieties of distraction, aggression, or even condescension, whatever it takes to avoid their pain. But eventually they might instead slowly begin to breathe in and out without as much resistance to the question. They might begin to soften that inner stance toward themselves with receptivity and kindness.

Besides generosity, compassion, and fearlessness, there may be other surprising repositories within to discover and resources to cultivate community as one pulls his outer lives together.

It is a strange freedom to be adrift without a place to call one's own.

Howard Thurman, a twentieth-century mystic, writer, and minister, speaks eloquently of this.

> There is a spirit in man and in the world working always against the thing that destroys and lays waste. Always, he must know that the contradictions of life are not final or ultimate; he must distinguish between failure and a many-sided

awareness so that he will not mistake conformity for harmony, uniformity for synthesis. He will know for all men to be alike is the death of life in man, and yet perceive the harmony that transcends all diversities and in which diversity finds richness and significance.[8]

Even doubt and ambiguity carry their own treasures.

So, having the ability to stick with it and ask questions and look for alternatives and consider options has really been the thing that has brought me to a place of being able to hold these things that are seemingly contradictory: good things and bad things, transcendent self and shadow self, doing the right thing and doing the wrong thing sometimes. (Victor)

Joseph runs a writer's group for men in prison. One summer evening, he is thinking about the riches of uncertainty aloud and shares something he dedicated to the guys "in the joint":

I kept track of certain things, toy soldiers on the shelf
cracks in the sidewalk
in front of the school
a number of streets between the bridge
and my family's house. But now the list of things
I've lost or forgotten or thrown away
sometimes seems longer than the list of what remains.
This thought visits often late at night
when each breath is a footstep measuring a mile of dawn.
But this morning, when I walked across the yard
the sun suddenly set through a cloud to warm my face,
and later I was surprised by a small kindness from an unexpected source,
This is not the life I would have chosen, but I would try to keep an open hand each day
for the gift.
It spreads across my path like Easter eggs hidden
in the grass. (Joseph)

What stirs the heart can seem quite mundane from the outside. Sometimes we don't even know what to make of these ordinary but actually quite extraordinary inner awakenings. Yet, they may come as close to the spiritual as other, more traditional or "lofty" experiences.

It surprises me how certain forms of music nobody would necessarily consider elevated forms—American minstrel music or the older folk music—it is totally surprising to me, but it connects. In unpredictable ways, certain melodies, rhythm, and qualities of voice can bring about intense feelings and awareness that I would have formerly associated with spiritual experience. (Diana)

Chris did not tap some of his own inner riches until later in life, when he began to dance. It came through the practice of "Authentic Movement" and improvisation. Authentic Movement is a simple form in which a person moves with eyes closed in the presence of a witness and symbolic meaning is manifested in the mover's action. The movement may begin as an impulse, a sensation, as in gesture, image, or memory. The witness is present to simply "see" the mover without judgment, attending fully to both the mover and her own inner experience.[9] Chris discovered a talent for dance, as well, something he would have never imagined in his life.

> It is where the dancer came from; it is where my creativity comes from. I guess my inner life, when I allow it to happen, is pretty rich. But it is in stark contrast with my outer life, which really is only beginning to show itself. (Chris)

Still some of us might be restless or bored as hell. We may not know what to do with our time or may be afraid we will run out of time. But something can happen—some situation or a dream—for us to pay attention and check in. We might notice it in odd ways: while we listen to a corny piece of music, when we are laughing hard about something sacrilegious, silly, or dark—or as we encounter utter and noble silence. It is not always the content, but the context that seems significant. This particular awareness may show up in qualities of joy, gratitude, or simple well-being that is quite distinct from pleasure. Like grace, theses qualities present themselves in big moments and in little things. They may drench our hearts with sweetness, even when things are not so good. Experiences like this also work like a muscle. They need to be accessed again and again, like wonder or humor. It may take practice for them to grow and ripen into a daily part of our lives.

Some folks swear that going to a Red Sox game is as close to a spiritual experience as they could imagine. Runners, dancers, artists, and musicians passionately lose themselves in what they are doing. When action and awareness come together, the sense of *I* is overtaken by the immersion in the experience and a loss of self-consciousness. It is a way of being innocent; to be as freely *unself*-conscious as freedom itself. The sense of time and even space seems to shift and there is often a flow within that is akin to the experience of a deep and active inner life.

Is everything holy, then? What is the difference between entertainment and joy? Is there a distinction between indulgence and nourishment?

In American culture, for instance, food, television, or the Internet have often been used as numbing drugs or comforting addictions when there has been overstimulation from violence, neglect, or a lack of affection. We may use them to mitigate the fear of being alone or of having to think thoughts or feel feelings. We may eat in the car, in front of the sink, or in secret; we may sit and munch in front of the computer or television, without connection to the food, the information, or the company. Or we might use the Internet or the cell phone, compulsively jumping from subject to subject or person to person just to fill time. One can use television, the computer, even books as "deities," insisting on certain commitments to shows or Internet chats in lieu of real connection in real time. Once again, context trumps content. We all have to eat and can experience pleasure and relaxation in the process of cooking, sharing, and eating meals. Computers, cell phones, and televisions are invaluable in the world we live in, often bringing communities together instead apart, but their value may depend on why, how, and how much they are used.

There may be another way to use our time alone. Instead of eating a solitary meal in front of television, a book, or a steering wheel, for instance, we might take the time to sit, smell, chew, and taste. It can be a new olfactory journey to simply and thoughtfully eat.

We might experiment with turning off the computer or flat screen or shutting off the cell phone just to stare into space. At first, just making the opening for such an endeavor can be rather uncomfortable; confronting the space inside may feel like tumbling into a chasm. But there is a value to falling into the abyss of our own mind, even if the "chattering monkeys" inside get noisier at first and continue to shout out their bad advice. Eventually, we might be able to let the babble be, like background noise or the roar of the ocean. Silence may begin to fill more and more of the space even as thoughts race about, releasing us from the compulsion to do anything about them. Eventually, the "monkeys" might even settle down into a kind of richness in the quiet.

To sit with another in the midst of an impossible dilemma, unbearable sorrow, or profound wonder, without doing anything but being present, can also be a sacred act. Many of us know how to do this already; listening with empathy has been a natural process for us because it is all some of us knew how to do and perhaps would have wished for ourselves. Finding or being a friend who listens is a precious experience and perhaps one of the best ways to recover one's soul.

Intimate lovemaking with full heart and surrender can be a playful, joyous, or spiritual experience. If there has been some sexual abuse in one's background, however, these encounters can also be a bit like taking poison as a remedy. Shame often shows up as an almost physiological state for many survivors. Survivors, independently or with help, may have to reconfigure the skin, muscle, and olfactory memories with help so that they can reclaim their sexual selves with their partners and inside themselves. It may take patience, trust, and tenacity to create a safe connection with one's partner and to reclaim one's body and the soul of sexuality again. This is when good therapy, bodywork, and loving presence are most needed.

For survivors of religious abuse, especially sexual violation, to deliberately practice vibrant and responsible celibacy in monastic or intentional living depends on support not only from those who practice it but also from the larger, interdependent connection with the community. But members of celibate communities can and *must* support each other's emotional lives to be balanced and deeply loving—and accountable. Celibacy is like a monogamous sexual partnership. It has to be lived as a conscientious practice, even if it is sometimes a messy "gift." Releasing oneself of sexual contact can free the celibate to become capable of interrelatedness with all humans. As Richard Sipe says, "the aloneness of celibacy is to be embraced. It is based on a resolution, a deep relationship with the transcendent, and an ability to see the transcendent in other people."[10] It is a gift that is dependent on a strong spiritual practice and an immensely balanced community.

If those in recovery look for spiritual nourishment in themselves or in others, from new mentors or new communities, they will have to take some risks again. And those who react to old traditions might even have to contend with the G-word or reinvent it—perhaps a little poison as the remedy. Will Michaels takes this to heart. As a survivor, he knows how religion polluted the force field of his inner world—and, as a minister, he wants to do what it takes to dilute the poison and reclaim the word *God*.

> In order to heal a wound, you have to be able to open it up. I remember my congregation would count every time the word *God* was said in a sermon. I thought, "Oh my *God*, how sad. All you're doing while I'm preaching is counting the number of times I used the word *God* because it's such a loaded word." So I said, "I hear how much pain that causes you, so if you're comfortable, let's sit together and go into that wound as to why it's so powerful. It's just—a word!" I think I need to create a safe enough place for the people to do that, and safety is utmost in my ministry. (Will Michaels)

Individuals may need the safety to be able to go straight to the source, whether they use the G-word or not. If one is experimenting with a new community or another tradition, he or she always has to ask the hard questions again and see what happens. Survivors of religious abuse most often have a strong intuition based on years of hypervigilance, knowing what they need and able to smell trouble if patronized or stuffed with platitudes.

Those of us who have survived a violation may also not want to admit that any good came from connections with our abusers. But there yet may be some gold in the mud as we try to come to terms with what has happened to us.

> It's the complexity of people who did both good things and bad things. I can think of a lot of people, like my crazy grandmother, who could be awful in so many ways, who also did some truly wonderful magical things for all of us. You know, I can't take her out of the equation. I can't take the handsome young priest out of the equation. I can't take the murky old priest out of the equation. I can't take the bitchy nun out of the equation. (Victor)

In Tibetan Buddhism, there is a practice called *tonglen* that increases compassion and deep understanding. It is a way of confronting pain and opening the heart. In this practice, one breathes in the suffering of others—even of those who have harmed—owning it, instead of avoiding it. Then the practitioner breathes out fear and resistance, sending calm and nourishment to the source of suffering. At first, such a practice seems almost impossible, because the mind is often hard-wired to feel tightness, anger, or revulsion in response to painful circumstances or difficult people. The practice of tonglen appears to be the opposite of how anybody would ever imagine he could ever deal with pain or hold himself together. But *tonglen* is a practice of gradual steps: acknowledging the pain in oneself and/or others and holding some kindness around the injury.

When Inanna leaves the dark realm, she does not forget what happened in the cave once she surfaces into the light of day. What has happened in the dark has changed her perspective and made her wiser and more complete.

> The other side is, I know the darker side of *God*. The absence, the *God* who doesn't reward and punish here, the *God* where there's *not* going to be justice. Not every story lives happily; they don't always live happily ever after. I've been abused. I've gone to the *MaleSurvivor* Web site,[11] and I'm really grateful. Some guys have gone through a lot more hell than I have, so not every story is happily ever after. We've got to put that into our image of *God* and in our spirituality. (Francis)

Whether some of us are accompanied by demons or friends or only ourselves, whether there are new names or forms of *God* or no names and no forms whatsoever, we may discover or rediscover the exchange best called *prayer*.

We keep dreaming about thirst even when the water is right there. We keep praying, when the prayer is praying itself.

CHAPTER 8

The Water of Life

We are the sweet cold water and the jar that pours.

—Jalaluddin Rumi

My soul is a mosque for Muslims
A temple for Hindus
An altar for Zoroastrians,
A church for Christians,
A synagogue for Jews,
And a pasture for gazelles

—Ibn Arabi

I met Howard Thurman in 1974. The Reverend Thurman had been a mentor to Martin Luther King and other leaders of the civil rights movement and had co-founded one of the nation's first interracial, interfaith, intercultural congregations. To him, the inward and the outward journeys of a human being were inseparable.

Dr. Thurman had grown up with his mother, sisters, and grandmother, a former slave. He told a story about himself as a little boy in the then-segregated Daytona Beach, near the edge of one of its many swamps. As a boy, he loved to go out and explore by himself. He loved his solitude. I like to imagine that these times were the beginning of his rich contemplative life. One day, the young Thurman ventured off into the swamp singing to himself, fingering the goop and the slip of leaves and moss, immersed in the sounds of the birds and crickets, and losing track of time or markers—losing track altogether—until it was dark.

He looked around in the gloaming mist to discover he was lost. A cloud cover had thickened over the stars, and it started to rain. What began as a trickle soon became a downpour. This being the south, the monsoon of a summer storm can be quite relentless. So there he was in the stormy night, a small boy groping in the dark to make his way back home. The lightning opened the sky—then a pause before the thunder. Although it was quite frightful, Howard realized something: if he paid attention to the split-second flash of light, he could take a step or two in the dark, tracing from memory what he had just seen until the next lightning burst gave him his clue to where he was. It went on like this all through the night—Howard waiting for the lightning, finding his way by that little flash of memory. He trekked between the trees and the swamp, barely missing the bolts of lightning. Eventually, he found his way back to his grandma's house. Seventy-odd years later, he recollected how he had remembered the flash in that dark night and followed it home.

"We travel in the dark," he said. "Now and again, there are flashes of light. They pass. We cannot cling to them. We still have to go on in the dark, in the light. But we remember what it is that we have seen, all the way home."

I have discovered I am not alone. Even in solitude, which is a precious ingredient of any intentional inward life, I experience a presence within myself. There is no way around it. No spiritual connection includes all the unique ambiguities and uncertainties of my existence, but sometimes the attachment to how different I am only keeps me separate from connecting even within my self.

I imagine how it could be safe enough to be unafraid, or at least, honest enough about what we fear. I imagine how it might be if I did not have such distance between myself and everything else. I could live without the worry about what I said or how I looked even to myself. I might live without the worry of separation and feel safe enough to risk connection and not have to carry paralyzing shame.

I would like to witness simple kindness as a political stance. I wonder how it would be if people lived with a sense of humor, but not at the cost of anybody else. I would like for us not to be afraid to be kind, not to flinch from the suffering of others, and, like Enki's little demons, not feed off their pain either.

I imagine how it could be if leaders could admit their mistakes and attempt to make amends. I imagine how it would be if every single one of us enjoyed the same civil rights and religious freedoms as anyone else. I imagine how church leaders and the rest of us could encourage one another not to be self-involved and fearful and instead would model open heartedness, self-vigilance and authenticity. We might encourage one another to be brave enough to stand for our convictions. We might support each other in an intentional spiritual practice.

I imagine how it would be if religious, racial, and sexual safety was a priority in each and every church and community, not simply in name but conscious and transparent practice.

Although I sometimes still contract into the habits of security or cynicism, I imagine that we all can expand into an endless sky of possibility for our souls. The options before us have more to do with our questions than with the pat answers that have always been offered by others.

None of this could happen at once, in one place or one person. But I imagine that the possibility is out there and that the possibility is also inside me.

I have discovered that the search for *God* (or whatever I call it) and for meaning, or community, or for myself—and the process of recovery—is often long and difficult, when at times there seems to be so little to cling to and so much to risk. But I also know that the burden of it can lift.

From a place of darkness, what is there to lose? So many of us have looked into the face of evil itself, have been hurt, and yet here we are—fighting, screaming, singing, eating, praying, being, searching. If we waited for fear to pass, we would probably never move.

In therapy, people are sometimes given affirmations or small self-care tasks to help meet the needs that were lost in trauma. But these self-care projects often fill only the small tank of the ego, which has a hole at its core. In the cultural irony of indulgence and neglect so prevalent in the West, many are dogged by an obsession with visibility, especially because they have had to struggle so much to matter to someone or something. Sometimes we project an enlargement or caricature of who we are, even to ourselves, simply to diffuse our shame. I imagine what it would be like to empty myself of these considerations.

I imagine releasing the need to be *something*, other than simply to *be*, I imagine how it would be to be free from some of these burdens of self-absorption. Emptiness, in this case, would not be nothing. It would, instead, be a kind of fullness that seals the cracks of the poor, dilapidated ego. Like darkness, which is not simply the absence of light, emptiness would be full of space. That space would invite a kind of inner journey that would have no end in sight and bring awareness to interconnectedness, rather than alienation.

I imagine that it is right here: a wide infinite spectrum of space for all magnificent and endless souls, even mine.

"One does not discover new lands," says André Gide, "without consenting to lose sight of the shore for a very long time." Though I may seem to be traveling with no end in view, I want to remember what light looks like. I imagine that it is not so different from the dark.

Every so often we get some small blink of radiance like Thurman's lightning: a word or a look, a bar of music or some surprising perfume, maybe a silent presence that goes deeper than memory or time.

We step out into this odd dark heaven. Noelle Oxenhandler says, "It's as though, having once belted out *Amazing Grace*, we have to sing it backwards, 'For I was found, but now I'm lost, could see, but now I'm blind.'"[1]

But, amazing . . . this grace.

It is fierce, and as simple as breath.

We may still be in Erishkigal's dark cave, but we are not alone.

RECOMMENDED READINGS

Chodren, Pema, *The Places That Scare You: A Guide to Fearlessness in Difficult Times* (Boston: Shambhala, 2001).

Khan, Hazrat Inayat, *The Inner Life* (Boston: Shambhala, 1997).

Smith, Huston, *Why Religion Matters, The Fate of the Human Spirit in an Age of Disbelief* (San Francisco: HarperCollins, 2001).

Wiesenthal, Simon, *The Sunflower* (New York: Schocken Books, 1998).

Resources

The following Internet resources are recommended for survivors from all faiths and are only a fraction of what is available to help those recovering from religious abuse. These resources can be adjuncts to the dimensions of spiritual recovery, but they are not final destinations. Some resources here may be considered therapeutic but not necessarily spiritual; others are spiritual venues without psychological material. None of them are nor should be considered recommendations for "treatment."

Web sites are often obsolete almost as soon as they are created, so use the following as a reference and research guide only. Many of the Web sites are targeted to survivors who belong to specific religious organizations, but none advocates a specific religious agenda. I have been careful to leave out Web sites that proselytize and for that reason did not include some excellent organizations and Web sites that, although valuable for individual recovery, have a specific philosophical or evangelical agenda.

The listings include educational and outreach services. The content provided is informational and does not imply a personal endorsement. Much of the wording was adapted or quoted from the original sources.

Though some of the material included in the Web sites can trigger difficult memories or feel overwhelming, especially the survivor pages and the chat rooms, these venues are invaluable for those who have been silenced or expelled from their particular religious communities. Please take care of yourself as you peruse the information and engage in conversations. Investigate carefully, ask questions, and look for ethical transparency and safe boundaries within the community. You can explore further—or you can simply close the Web site. How you utilize this list or this book is up to you. It is your journey of recovery, and you can do it any way you wish.

ORGANIZATIONS, SERVICES, AND WEB SITES

Abuse by Nuns

Abusebynuns.com provides a network of support for people who have experienced sexual or other forms of abuse by women religious. On the Web site, there is a section entitled "Answers," which is dedicated to exposing the issue of abuse by nuns, supporting those personally affected by it, and advocating for responsible and healing approaches in addressing it: "We recognize that any form of exploitation, be it sexual, emotional, physical, mental or spiritual is wrong and can profoundly affect one's life in many ways. We represent those who were abused as children, youth, or vulnerable adults while in the care of nuns or within the charge of a religious community of women. We call upon the leaders of all communities of women religious, the organizations and dioceses that support them, and the Church hierarchy to take responsible action to deal with this issue and its tragic consequences."

www.abusebynuns.com

Abuse Tracker

Abuse Tracker is a digest of links to media coverage of clergy abuse in all religions.

www.bishop-accountability.org/AbuseTracker

Adult Survivors of Child Abuse

ASCA is an international self-help support group program designed specifically for all adult survivors of neglect, physical, sexual, and/or emotional abuse.

The Morris Center
P.O. Box 14477
San Francisco, CA 94114
www.ascasupport.org

Advocate Web Helping Overcome Professional Exploitation

Advocate Web is nonprofit organization that provides information and resources to promote awareness and understanding of the issues involved in the exploitation of persons by trusted helping professionals. "We publish information about advocacy work, new legislation, links to news stories, updates on what professional organizations are doing (or not doing) to address these problems, and in the future: publish newsletters, provide resources for the news media, foster the formation of local survivor support groups, provide referrals for victims seeking professional (counseling or legal) help, host retreats for victims, and organize regional and world conferences for professionals and victims."

Advocate Web
P.O. Box 202961
Austin, TX 78720
www.advocateweb.org

Affirmation

Affirmation serves the needs of gay Mormon women and men, as well as bisexual and transgender LDS and their supportive family and friends, through social and educational activities.

AFFIRMATION: Gay & Lesbian Mormons
P.O. Box 46022
Los Angeles, CA 90046-0022
661-367-2421
www.affirmation.org

The Awareness Center for Sexual Violence and Spiritual Abuse in the Jewish Community

The Awareness Center is an extensive Web site dedicated to providing education, information, and resources to Jewish survivors of sexual violence, family members of survivors, religious leaders, rabbis, and all Jewish communities globally. It also has a comprehensive list of resources for survivors of other religious denominations.

Vicki Polin
P.O. Box 65273
Baltimore, MD 21209
info@theawarenesscenter.org

Bikers against Child Abuse

BACA exists to create a safer environment for abused children. "We are a body of Bikers to empower children to not feel afraid of the world in which they live. We stand ready to lend support to our wounded friends by involving them with an established, united organization. We work in conjunction with local and state officials who are already in place to protect children. We desire to send a clear message to all involved with the abused child that this child is part of our organization, and that we are prepared to lend our physical and emotional support to them by affiliation, and our physical presence. We stand at the ready to shield these children from further abuse. We do not condone the use of violence or physical force in any manner, however, if circumstances arise such that we are the only obstacle preventing a child from further abuse, we stand ready to be that obstacle."

www.bacausa.com

BishopAccountability

BishopAccountability aims to facilitate the accountability of U.S. Catholic bishops under civil, criminal, and canon law. "We document the debates about root causes and remedies, because important information has surfaced during those debates. We take no position on the root causes, and we do not advocate particular remedies. If the facts are fully known, the causes and remedies will become clear."

www.bishop-accountability.org/
staff@bishopaccountability.org

Call to Action USA

CTA is an independent national organization of more than 20,000 people and forty local organizations that believe the Spirit of God is at work in the whole Church, not just in its appointed leaders. They believe the entire Catholic Church has an obligation to respond to the needs of the world and to take the initiative in programs of peace and justice.

Call to Action
2135 W. Roscoe
Chicago, IL 60618
773-404-0004
cta@cta-usa.org

CEASE

CEASE has been created by victims and survivors of sexual, physical, and spiritual abuse committed by employees and volunteers of the worldwide Seventh-Day Adventist Church. "Devoted to educating church leadership about the prevalence of these abuses within the denomination, we want to bring about changes to church policy in order to protect others from the devastation we experienced."

CEASE
P.O. Box 251
320 Seventh Avenue
Brooklyn, NY 11215
wawknboots@yahoo.com

The Center for Action and Contemplation

The Center for Action and Contemplation serves as a place of discernment and growth for activists and those interested in social service ministries—a place to be still and to learn how to integrate a contemplative lifestyle with compassionate service. The Center's purpose is to serve not only as a forum for peaceful, nonviolent social change but also as a radical voice for renewal and encouragement.

Center for Action and Contemplation
P.O. Box 12464
Albuquerque, NM 87195
www.cacradicalgrace.org

Confronting Collusion with Abuse in the Faith Community, Takecourage.org

Takecourage.org is dedicated to illuminating the power of collusion in sexual abuse, especially when the perpetrators are members of the clergy: "*Takecourage* stands as a source of enlightenment, dispelling the darkness so often cruelly created when victims or advocates dare to speak truth about sexual and domestic violence to people of faith. It is unique because it primarily offers insights into collusion, rather than the primary abuses of perpetrators."

www.takecourage.org

Cult Awareness Network

Cult Awareness Network is a mediatory organization. "We gather useful knowledge and the best sources for help and information to freely distribute to the general public and the media—in other words, we are the go-between for quality professionals, their research and the public; we are a neutral source of support, compassion and insight standing between conflicting parties—in this respect, we are similar to professional mediators in the legal & social spheres (except our services are free)."

Cult Awareness Network
1680 N. Vine Street
Suite 415
Los Angeles, CA 90028
800-556-3055
www.cultawarenessnetwork.org/

Dignity USA

Dignity USA is "organized to unite gay, lesbian, bisexual, and transgender Catholics, as well as our families, friends, and loved ones, in order to develop leadership and be an instrument through which they may be heard and to promote reform in the Church."

Dignity USA
P.O. Box 376
Medford, MA 02155
800-877-8797
202-861-0017
info@dignityusa.org

Exmormon.org

Exmormon.org is a resource for those who are or were Mormons to let them know they are not alone in their feelings and experiences as they seek to regain their lives after years in this religion. "We have e-mail groups to join, bulletin boards, gatherings and individuals to help with a transition to a post-Mormon life. We advocate no specific religious preference or religious activities after Mormonism. Our active participants are diverse and from differing cultural backgrounds throughout the world."

www.exmormon.org

Factnet.org

Factnet helps survivors heal abuse caused by religions or cults. It deals with all areas of financial, sexual, physical, psychological, theological, and indoctrinational abuse by any religion or cult. "We provide survivor recovery resources and survivor peer to peer healing. We hold that fully making both the abuse and the abuser transparent the abuse recovery process can be faster and far more effective. This is because others can also learn, heal or be inoculated by this transparent openness. We proactively research and provide information on the many healthy non-pathological aspects of religion and religious practices."

Factnet, Inc.
P.O. Box 1314
Ignacio, CO 81137-1314
www.factnet.org

FaithTrustInstitute.org

Faith Trust Institute is a multifaith training and education organization that works to address the religious and spiritual issues of sexual and domestic violence. "We provide communities and advocates with the tools and knowledge they need to address the religious and cultural issues related to abuse. Faith-Trust Institute works with many communities, including Asian and Pacific

Islander, Buddhist, Jewish, Latino/a, Muslim, Black, Anglo, Indigenous, Protestant and Roman Catholic."

Faith Trust Institute
2400 N. 45th Street #101
Seattle, WA 98103
www.faithtrustinstitute.org

Fortunate Families

Fortunate Families ministers primarily to Catholic parents of lesbian, gay, bisexual, and transgender (LGBT) persons. "When parents explore and value their stories, they are empowered to share that story with their family circle, their faith community and the larger society."

Fortunate Families
PO Box 18082
Rochester, NY 14618-0082
585-698-6100
www.fortunatefamilies.com/

Freedom of Mind Resource Center

The Freedom of Mind Resource Center is dedicated to respect for human rights, spirituality, and consumer awareness. "We endeavor to be a safe and responsible place where you can turn to for resources, news and information about destructive cults, and mind control techniques, as well as learn how to help yourself and others." Freedom of Mind Resource Center has excellent resource pages and a comprehensive bibliography for cult abuse survivors.

www.freedomofmind.com/resourcecenter/

FreeMinds, Inc.

FreeMinds, Inc. is a nonprofit organization that keeps a critical eye on the Watchtower (Jehovah's Witnesses). It is not affiliated with any religious organization.

FreeMinds, Inc.
P.O. Box 3818
Manhattan Beach, CA 90266
www.freeminds.org

Gamofites

"Gamofites are men united in the joys and challenges of being fathers, gay, and Mormon. They are dedicated to fostering and supporting the needs and individual growth of members in an environment of confidentiality, trust, and unconditional love."

www.gamofites.org
gamofitetex@gmail.com

Gay and Lesbian Arabic Society (GLAS)

The *Gay and Lesbian Arabic Society* (GLAS), an international organization, serves as a networking organization for gays and lesbians of Arab descent or living in Arab countries. "We aim to promote positive images of Gays and Lesbians in Arab communities worldwide, in addition to combating negative portrayals of Arabs within the Gay and Lesbian community. We also provide a support network for our members while fighting for our human rights wherever they are oppressed. We are part of the global Gay and Lesbian movement seeking an end to injustice and discrimination based on sexual orientation."

www.glas.org

Interfaith Sexual Trauma Institute

The *Interfaith Sexual Trauma Institute*'s mission is to facilitate the building of safe, healthy, and trustworthy communities of faith. It promotes the prevention of sexual abuse, exploitation, and harassment through research, education, and publication. "In areas of sexuality, it offers leadership, gives voice, and facilitates healing to survivors, communities of faith, and offenders, as well as those who care for them."

Interfaith Sexual Trauma Institute
Saint John's Abbey and University
Collegeville, MN 56321
www.csbsju.edu/istirevival
isti@csbsju.edu

Karamah

Karamah is an educational charitable organization committed to developing a comprehensive, just, and thoughtful Islamic jurisprudence that takes into account the current concerns of Muslim women worldwide. "We have rooted this jurisprudence in the best of the classical Islamic jurisprudential traditions. Our various educational and grassroots programs are guided by our vision and directed at implementing our mission. Karamah is founded upon the ideal that education, dialogue, and action can counter the dangerous and destructive effects of ignorance, silence, and prejudice. We are committed to supporting human rights worldwide, especially the rights of Muslim women.

Our overarching goal is to promote the well-being of Muslim communities worldwide through legal education and leadership development, and to increase respect and understanding of Islamic law and civilization in other communities. In particular, we try to provide women with a better understanding of their rights under Islamic law, and respond to their needs through legal advocacy, education, and grassroots activism."

Karamah
202-234-7302
www.karamah.org
karamah@karamah.org

MaleSurvivor.org

MaleSurvivor is an organization committed to preventing, healing, and eliminating all forms of sexual victimization of boys and men through support, treatment, research, education, advocacy, and activism.

MaleSurvivor offers Weekends of Recovery for survivors of sexual and clergy abuse to discover a personal sense of community as they connect in safety to other men on personal healing journeys: https://www.malesurvivor.org/weekends-of-recovery.html.

"It was the safest retreat I've ever been to. I never felt, for even an instant, that anyone was at risk. The process was empowering and supportive. I connected with other guys powerfully. . . . Our boundaries were respected, defenses were respected, and the ability to take a time out to get grounded was respected and supported. I thoroughly recommend this retreat to anyone wanting a fuller, happier, healthier, more fulfilling life."

www.MaleSurvivor.org

Next Step Counseling and Small Wonder Books

The *Next Step Counseling and Training* is located in Brookline, Massachusetts. Co-directors Mike Lew and Thom Harrigan offer individual therapy, couples counseling, group therapy and clinical supervision as well as experiential workshops, professional trainings and public lectures not only in the states but throughout Europe, Australia and New Zealand. A primary focus of the work at *Next Step* is adult male recovery from the effects of sexual child abuse and other trauma.

Next Step
P.O. Box 301146
Jamaica Plain, MA 02130, USA
617-277-7172
nextstep.counseling@verizon.net

Postmormon.org

The mission of *PostMormon.org* is to provide and maintain systems that facilitate the growth and development of a safe and supportive community for those who leave or are considering leaving the Mormon Church.

Postmormon.org
P.O. Box 3782
Logan, UT 84323
www.Postmormon.org
email@postmormon.org

Queer Jihad

Queer Jihad is a resource for gay Muslims. "We are interested in the spiritual lives of gay and lesbian Muslims, and other queer Muslims. We are interested in encouraging queer people to remain true to their Creator, to grapple with the issues, to come to terms with who they are in whatever manner and fashion they are capable of doing so."

www.well.com/user/queerjhd

Red Circle Project

The *Red Circle Project* (RCP) at AIDS Project Los Angeles (APLA) is currently the only HIV prevention program in Los Angeles County that specifically targets Native American gay men (known by the culturally specific term "two-Spirit individuals").

Red Circle ProjectAIDS Project Los Angeles
The David Geffen Center
611 S. Kingsley Drive
Los Angeles, CA 90010
213-201-1311
www.apla.org/native_american/RCP/index.htm

Safe Space Coalition

The *Safe Space Coalition* is an initiative that works to ensure safety and respect for gay and lesbian Latter-Day Saints.

Safe Space Coalition
P.O. Box 522
College Park, MD 02740
202-213-9267
www.ldssafespace.org

Sharon's Rose

The purpose of *Sharon's Rose* is to give voice to clergy sexual abuse survivors by providing resources and information. Its mission is to provide awareness and understanding about clergy sexual abuse. "It is my belief there are thousands of cases of CSA that are not being addressed: cases involving the sexual abuse of adult women by members of the clergy, including pastors from all denominations, priests, and rabbis. This Web site is a means of support to these adult women survivors, whose lives have withered in the 'desert place.'"

sharon@sharonsrose.com

Sidran Institute Traumatic Stress Education and Advocacy

Sidran Traumatic Stress Institute is an educational organization that assists individuals in the treatment and recovery from traumatic stress (including PTSD), dissociative disorders, and co-occurring issues, such as addictions, self-injury, and suicidality. "Because we believe that *connection* is the active ingredient in healing, Sidran's philosophy reflects RICH relationships (Respect, Information, Connection, and Hope) in all our professional and interpersonal interactions. Recovery from the effects of trauma (especially human-caused trauma) requires growth-promoting relationships and the willingness of survivors to risk re-connecting over time with friends, family, treatment providers, and community. Simultaneously, those providing support must also risk connection, with colleagues, with the survivors in their care, and with their own, true inner selves. Sidran's programming emphasizes respectful, empathic connection and hope for the future."

Sidran Institute
200 E. Joppa Road, Ste. 207
Baltimore, MD 21286-3107
410-825-8888
www.sidran.org
help@sidran.org

S.M.A.R.T. Ritual Abuse Newsletter

"The purpose of *S.M.A.R.T.* is to help stop ritual abuse and to help those who have been ritually abused. We work toward this goal by disseminating information on the possible connections between secretive organizations, ritual abuse, and mind control, by encouraging healing from the extensive damage done by ritual abuse and mind control, and by encouraging survivors to network."

S.M.A.R.T. Ritual Abuse Newsletter
P.O. Box 1295
Easthampton, MA 01027
smartnews@aol.com

SoulForce

Soulforce is an organization that advocates freedom from religious and political oppression for lesbian, gay, bisexual, and transgender people through
the practice of relentless nonviolent resistance. "The mission of Soulforce
is to cut off homophobia at its source—religious bigotry. *Soulforce* uses a dynamic 'take it to the streets' style of activism to connect the dots between
anti-gay religious dogma and the resulting attacks on the lives and civil lib-
erties of LGBT Americans. We apply the creative direct action principles
taught by Gandhi and Martin Luther King, Jr., to peacefully resist injustice
and demand full equality for LGBT citizens and same-gender families."

Soulforce, Inc.
P.O. Box 3195
Lynchburg, VA 24503
www.soulforce.org
info@soulforce.org

Survivor Connections, Inc.

Survivor Connections—(True Memory Foundation) is a volunteer organization promoting activism by survivors of rape, incest, and sexual assault. "*Survivor Connections* is for all survivors, not just those abused by clergy."

Survivor Connections, Inc.
52 Lyndon Road
Cranston, RI 02905-1121
www.survivorconnections.net

Survivorship

Survivorship is for survivors of ritualistic abuse, mind control, and torture
and supports survivors of extreme child abuse, including sadistic sexual abuse,
ritualistic abuse, mind control, and torture. *Survivorship* provides resources,
healing, and community for survivors; training and education for professionals who may serve survivors; and support for survivors' partners and other
allies. "The organization functions as a lifeline for survivors who may be isolated emotionally or geographically. Through community outreach and training, *Survivorship* also raises awareness about these difficult issues."

Survivorship
PMB 139

3181 Mission Street
San Francisco, CA 94110
www.survivorship.org

Survivors Network of Those Abused by Priests (SNAP)

The *Survivors Network of Those Abused by Priests (SNAP)* is a volunteer self-help organization of survivors of Catholic clergy sexual abuse and their supporters that supports survivors and pursues justice and institutional change by holding individual perpetrators responsible and the Church accountable. "If you've been victimized by clergy, please know that you are not alone. You can get better. You can reach out to others who've been hurt just like you have. Together, we can heal one another. We are the nation's largest, oldest and most active support group for women and men wounded by religious authority figures (priests, ministers, bishops, deacons, nuns, brothers, monks, and others). We are an independent and confidential organization, with no connections with the church or church officials."

Survivors Network of Those Abused by Priests
P.O. Box 6416
Chicago, IL 60680-6416
312-455-1499
1-877-SNAPHEALS (1-877-762-7432)
www.snapnetwork.org

Tamar's Voice

Tamar's Voice is a nonprofit agency based in California that helps victims who have been sexually exploited by clergy to establish a support system. It also conducts seminars and conferences on preventing sexual abuse by clergy, dealing with a clergy abuse situation, and healing from the wounds of clergy abuse.

Tamar's Voice
P.O. Box 17442
Irvine, CA 92623
www.tamarsvoice.org/

TransFaith

TransFaith is "dedicated to supporting Transgender folks in their faith journeys, while providing useful resources to help Church folks become better educated trans-allies." This Web site includes resource links, exclusive content, RSS/XML news feeds, an e-mail update list, and special resource lists (e.g., book list, video list, study guide list).

TransFaith Online was founded by Chris Paige (formerly publisher of *The Other Side* magazine) in order to provide an index of Internet resources that provide insight into the transgender faith experience. Jewish and Muslim, as well as Christian, resources are included.

www.transfaithonline.org

Voice from the Desert

Voice from the Desert is a blog and newsletter for the often-divided Roman Catholic Church reform community: "We align ourselves with the legacy of the Old Testament prophets in our striving for social justice for all oppressed people. The oppressed include the survivors of those abused by priests and by others in authority in our Church; women and married men who are excluded from priestly ministry; women; the poor; priests who have left to marry; the powerless laity; gay, lesbian, bi-sexual, and transgender people; theologians who are not accorded appropriate freedom of inquiry and due process in Church proceedings; and whistleblowers who strive to tell us the truth about unchristian behavior of church officials.

Voice from the Desert
8064 W. Greensleeves Way
Tucson, AZ 85743
www.reform-network.net/

The Wolf in God's Clothing

The Wolf in God's Clothing is for survivors of religious abuse of all faiths. Religious abuse is the physical, sexual or mental damage suffered by members of a faith community when its leaders exploit them. Dale English and Mikele Rauch preview the journey of the soul on the road to restoration in the wake of religious abuse. "With respect, music, storytelling and humor, we will provide one another a container of safety that will allow enough vulnerability to risk sharing your truth, yet grounded enough to connect with your own inner life in the presence of others. The result will be new ways of reclaiming the spirit stolen from each of you. Boundaries and choices around participation will be shown the deepest respect."

Dale English M.S., C.A.S.
570-246-6600
www.youdeservesupport.com

Mikele Rauch, M.A., L.M.F.T.
617-244-4524
www.mikelerauch.com
www.healingthesoulfromreligiousabuse.com

YouDeserveSupport.com

Through experiential, expressive, and body-centered work, Dale English offers workshops and recovery weekends for survivors and professionals. In his workshop "Rhythmic Journeys," he utilizes authentic, contact, and improvisational movement that "acknowledges the unique way that every human being learns, processes, speaks and grows. "The entire process unfolds with the creation of a safe container in which one can work, connecting with your true self, hearing and understanding the self's language of feelings, sharing those feelings with others, and relating with others while remaining true to your self." Dale English and Mikele Rauch also offer a workshop for pastoral caregivers and professionals with vicarious trauma and compassion fatigue entitled "My Turn": "There is a price to be paid for being witness day after day to the pain of others. Accumulated exposure carries with it consequences for both client and caregiver. In this workshop, you will be encouraged to become aware of the physical, emotional and spiritual signs and symptoms that indicate your level of need for care."

Dale English, M.S., C.A.S.
RRI, Box 819
Dingmans Ferry, PA 18328
570-242-6600
www.youdeservesupport.com

PROGRAMS OF RECOVERY

Alcoholics Anonymous

Alcoholics Anonymous and other 12-step programs are about sobriety and recovery from addictions of all kinds. *Alcoholics Anonymous* is not a religious domination, but "a fellowship of men and women who share their experience, strength and hope with each other that they may solve their common problem and help others to recover from alcoholism." There are many conversations about the "higher power" in the program, but AA makes a point to use that term in a non-religious manner. The *Big Book* speaks about the concept of God, which is often troubling for some people in recovery who may be agnostic: "We discovered we did not need to consider another's conception of God. Our own conception, however inadequate, was sufficient to make the approach and to affect a contact with Him." (*Source:* Alcoholics Anonymous World Services, *Alcoholics Anonymous* (*The Big Book*) (3rd ed.) New York: 1976, p. 47).

A.A. World Services, Inc.
Box 459
Grand Central Station

New York, NY 10163
212-870-3400
www.aa.org

There are many variations of addiction, which can stem from the bankruptcy of religious abuse. The following are only a few of the resources based on the 12-step program that are important to list here.

Alanon

Al-Anon (which includes *Alateen* for younger members) offers help to families and friends of alcoholics. "It is estimated that each alcoholic affects the lives of at least four other people . . . alcoholism is truly a family disease. No matter what relationship you have with an alcoholic, whether they are still drinking or not, all who have been affected by someone else's drinking can find solutions that lead to serenity in the AlaAnon/Alateen fellowship."

Al-Anon Family Group Headquarters
1600 Corporate Landing Parkway
Virginia Beach, VA 23454-5617
757-563-1600

Al-Anon Headquarters (Canada)
Capital Corporate Centre
9 Antares Drive, Suite 245
Ottawa, ON K2E 7V5
613-723-8484
www.al-anon.alateen.org

Co-Dependents Anonymous

CoDA is a fellowship of men and women whose common purpose is to develop healthy relationships. The only requirement for membership is a desire for healthy and loving relationships. "We gather together to support and share with each other in a journey of self-discovery—learning to love the self. Living the program allows each of us to become increasingly honest with ourselves about our personal histories and our own codependent behaviors. We rely upon the Twelve Steps and Twelve Traditions for knowledge and wisdom. These are the principles of our program and guides to developing honest and fulfilling relationships with ourselves and others. In CoDA, we each learn to build a bridge to a Higher Power of our own understanding, and we allow others the same privilege."

CoDA
P.O. Box 33577
Phoenix, AZ 85067-3577
602-277-7991
www.codependents.org

Gamblers Anonymous

"*Gamblers Anonymous* is not allied with any sect, denomination, politics, organization, or institution; does not wish to engage in any controversy; neither endorses nor opposes any cause. Our primary purpose is to stop gambling and to help other compulsive gamblers do the same."

Gamblers Anonymous
P.O. Box 17173
Los Angeles, CA 90017
213-386-8789

Narcotics Anonymous

NAWS is an international, community-based association of recovering drug addicts: "Central to the Narcotics Anonymous program is its emphasis on practicing spiritual principles. Narcotics Anonymous itself is non-religious, and each member is encouraged to cultivate an individual understanding—religious or not—of this 'spiritual awakening.' NA has only one mission: to provide an environment in which addicts can help one another stop using drugs and find a new way to live."

Narcotics Anonymous
P.O. Box 9999
Van Nuys, CA 91409
818-773-9999
www.na.org

Sex and Love Addicts Anonymous

SLA is a 12-Step Fellowship of men and women who help each other to stay sober. "Sex and love addiction is a progressive illness which cannot be cured but which, like many illnesses, can be arrested. It may take several forms—including, but not limited to a compulsive need for sex, extreme dependency on one or many people, or a chronic preoccupation with romance, intrigue, or fantasy. An obsessive-compulsive pattern, either sexual or emotional, or both, exists in which relationships or sexual activities have become increasingly destructive to career, family and sense of self-respect. We offer the same help to anyone who has sex addiction or love addiction or both and wants to do something about it."

SLA
Fellowship-Wide Services
1550 NE Loop 410, Ste. 118
San Antonio, TX 78209
www.slaafws.org

The Society for the Advancement of Sexual Health

The Society for the Advancement of Sexual Health (SASH) offers resources to those seeking information about sexual addiction. SASH is especially helpful for people in recovery from the addiction to pornography. However. using the Internet can be difficult for persons who have a history with Internet pornography. SASH has this to say about sexual addiction as it pertains to censorship and Internet use: "The Internet does not create sexual addicts. However, it can and does provide a form of sexual acting out that can lead to the progression of sexually addictive behaviors . . . The Internet plays a role in educating individuals about healthy aspects of sexuality and there are many resources available for the recovering sexual addict. Email, online meetings, recovery discussion groups, and informative home pages are resources that recovering addicts use to benefit their own recovery. For some, the choice to utilize healthy Internet resources is not a problem, for others, it is a problem and abstinence must be applied to their Internet access. Those who are experiencing discomfort as a result of their Internet use should seek consultation with a professional knowledgeable about sexual addiction."

SASH
P.O. Box 725544
Atlanta, GA 31139
www.sash.net
sash@sash.net
770-541-9912

White Bison

White Bison, Inc. is an American Indian nonprofit organization of the Mohican Nation that offers sobriety, recovery, addictions prevention, and wellness/*Wellbriety* learning resources to the Native American community nationwide. "Many non-Native people also use White Bison's healing resource products, attend its learning circles, and volunteer their services."

White Bison, Inc.
6145 Lehman Drive, Ste. 200
Colorado Springs, CO 80918
719-548-1000
www.whitebison.org
info@whitebison.org

NONDENOMINATIONAL RETREAT CENTERS FOR SPIRITUAL RENEWAL

There are hundreds of retreat and conference centers in North America that offer spectacular programs for spiritual renewal. Many of them are operated by a particular religious denomination but are open to people from all faiths as spaces for spiritual recovery. (See www.RetreatFinder.com or www. FindtheDivine.com for an extensive list.)

Sometimes, however, survivors have problems with particular sites because of a spiritual ideology that informs the philosophy of the place—even the smells and iconography of these places can evoke memories of past injuries. Occasionally, a piece of artwork, a stick of incense, the use of music, water, or fire, or even an individual staff member can reawaken the old trauma. This can represent a difficulty *or* an opportunity to reclaim something sacred that has been lost; yet, the most important factor in reclaiming the sacred is having a enough safe space to do it with a supportive community around you.

The following retreat places are sacred spaces not affiliated with any religious organization. Some are large commercial enterprises; others are smaller, affordable venues. All of them offer spaces and programs for renewal without religious or philosophical agendas, although they may sponsor particular weekends for specific spiritual practices:

Center for New Beginnings

The *Center for New Beginnings* offers group retreats, experiential therapeutic process, spirituals explorations, or personal solitude in a natural setting. "We also welcome workshop leaders who want to reach out to others in healthy ways, promoting wholeness through balance of body, mind, emotions and spirit."

The Center for New Beginnings
129 Center Point Drive
Dahlonega, GA 30533
800-492-1046
www.centerfornewbeginnings.com

Golden Willow Retreat Center

Golden Willow Retreat in Arroyo Hondo, New Mexico, is a nonprofit organization dedicated to helping individuals, families, and communities effectively heal from grief. "Our mission is to heal, renew, and educate individuals in grief over personal losses including death, divorce, health issues, and many other life transitions. Golden Willow Retreat honors a path of spiritual growth by offering a sanctuary for those in need of respite."

Golden Willow Retreat
P.O. Box 569
Arroyo Hondo, NM 87513
505-776-2024
www.goldenwillowretreat.org

Hope Springs Retreat and Conference Center

Hope Springs Retreat and Conference Center in Peebles, Ohio, offers weekends and programs for women (and occasionally men) of all ethical, spiritual, and religious traditions. "Anchored by strong regional roots, supported by feminist values, and invigorated by a transnational perspective, Hope Springs appeals especially to individuals, groups and organizations."

Hope Springs Institute
4988 Mineral Springs Road
Peebles, OH 45660
937-587-2605
www.hopespringswomencenter.com

Omega Institute

Omega Institute in Rhinebeck, New York, offers spiritual retreats and continuing education in health, creativity, leadership training, and sustainable living. "Through innovative educational experiences that awaken the best in the human spirit, Omega provides hope and healing for individuals and society."

Omega Institute
150 Lake Drive
Rhinebeck, NY 12572
www.eomega.org

Peace Village Learning & Retreat Center

"*Peace Village* offers a variety of workshops and weekend retreats for people from all backgrounds to explore, reflect, and nurture the self. Our retreats offer relevant ways for people to explore and understand their own spirituality."

Peace Village
4 O'Hara Road (at Route 23A)
P.O. Box 99
Haines Falls (Hunter), NY 12436

Glossary

aikido: a Japanese martial art that uses the motion or the energy of the attacker and redirects the force of the attack rather than oppose it head-on, so that the opponent's strength and weight are used against him.

anthropomorphism: the attribution of uniquely human characteristics to non-human creatures and beings, material states, or abstract concepts.

antitheist: one who believes not only that there is no God but that religion itself is harmful.

Authentic Movement: a simple form in which a mover moves with eyes closed in the presence of a witness.

autism: a neurobiological developmental disability that impacts the brain in the areas of social interaction, communication skills, and cognitive function. Individuals with autism typically have difficulties in verbal and non-verbal communication, social interactions, and leisure or play activities.

bodywork: any therapeutic, healing, or personal development work that involves some form of contact, whether energetic work or the physical touch; a term usually involved in holistic healing practices.

celibacy: a state of being unmarried or abstaining from sexual relations.

chastity: in Western culture, an ethical code of practiced sexual abstinence.

codependency: enabling relationships that are one-sided, emotionally destructive, and/or abusive and that create or depend on neediness or addictive behaviors.

cosmology: a system in which relationships among people, nature, and the supernatural are presented as symbols.

countertransference: the projection of a therapist's or pastor's feelings about a client that stem from the therapist's own life experiences and issues.

culture: the complex system of tools, language, art, and beliefs of a given community.

dharma: Sanskrit term for one's righteous path or religious duty.

diaspora: the displacement of a population with a common ethnic identity from its settled territory so that the entire population resettles in areas often far removed from the former homeland.

disciple: a follower or student of a mentor or a teacher in a religious context.

divine: connected with the worship or service of a deity.

double bind: a dilemma in communication in which a person receives two or more conflicting messages and one message denies the other; a situation in which the person will be put in the wrong however he responds—he cannot comment on the conflict, resolve it, or opt out of the situation.

dual relationship: a term used in psychotherapy and/or pastoral care to describe a situation in which two or more roles are mixed in a manner that can harm the counseling relationship.

dzo: a male hybrid of a yak.

ego: the organized part of the personality structure that includes defensive, perceptual, intellectual-cognitive, and executive functions. It is accumulated by interaction with others. Conscious awareness resides in the ego, although not all of the operations of the ego are conscious.

elders: men who serve Mormon missions, so called during the time of their service. When they are no longer full-time missionaries they are no longer called by that title. LDS Church leaders who serve in the Quorum of Twelve Apostles, Seventies, and Area Presidencies are also addressed by the title of Elder.

enlightenment: in Buddhism, the discovery of the truth about life through meditation, deep thought, or concentration.

flashback: a psychological phenomenon in which an individual has a sudden, usually vivid, recollection of a past experience. The term is used particularly when the memory is recalled involuntarily, and/or when it is so intense that the person "relives" the experience, unable to fully recognize it as memory and not something that is happening in real time.

fleeting effect: a phenomenon described in art theory as the quality of movement and time as they apply to a painting or a two-dimensional object. This is demonstrated by the use of color utilizing light, symbol, and emotion.

flow: the mental (or spiritual) state of operation in which the person is fully immersed in what he is doing by a feeling of energized focus, full involvement, and success in the process of the activity.

fundamentalism: a deep and totalistic commitment to a belief system.

grace: the exercise or unconditional gift of love, kindness, or mercy.

grooming: the deliberate actions taken by an adult to form a trusting relationship with a child, with the intent of later having sexual contact with that child.

guru: a term often used in Hinduism for a spiritual guide or leader.

heresy: a dissenting opinion or deviation from the dominant truth in a religious system.

holocaust: a word of Greek origin meaning "sacrifice of fire." The Holocaust was the systematic, bureaucratic, state-sponsored persecution and murder of approximately 6 million Jews by the Nazi regime and its collaborators. Other groups were persecuted and killed by the regime, as well: Gypsies, homosexuals, the disabled, and political and religious dissidents.

ijtihad: a tradition in Islam of independent thinking and reasoning.

imam: a term used in Islam to denote a person with special qualities relevant to the religion, who leads the prayer during religious gatherings. The role and power of an imam depend on the sect in Islam (for Sunni Muslims, the imam is the man who leaders the prayer; for Shiites, the imam is a descendant of Muhammad chosen by God to lead the community in areas of belief and practice).

karma: literally means action or doing. In Hinduism and Buddhism, it refers to the law of causation. Any kind of intentional action, whether mental, verbal, or physical, is regarded as karma.

lama: Tibetan title for a teacher of the spiritual path or religious duty.

martyr: someone who dies, usually violently, for a sacred cause.

mitzvah: a concept in Judaism that describes any act of human kindness.

moksha: Indian term for liberation from the cycle of death and rebirth.

mythology: a legend or allegory that people create to understand the world; myths are often linked to the spiritual or religious life of a community.

nirvana: the ultimate goal of Buddhism, described as liberation from the cycle of birth, death, and rebirth.

numinous: related to an intense feeling of unknowingly knowing that there is something that cannot be seen.

Orthodox: pertaining to, or conforming to ideologies, beliefs, attitudes, or modes of conduct that are generally approved. In Judaism, it pertains to the strict interpretation and application of the laws and ethics of the law.

pedophilia: a psychological disorder in which an adult experiences a sexual preference for prepubescent children.

persona: a social role played according to the desired impression an individual wishes to create or manifest in the presence of others.

pogrom: an unprovoked violent attack directed against a particular group, whether ethnic, religious, or other, and characterized by destruction of the homes, businesses, and religious centers of those affiliated with the group; the word was first used to describe the persecution of Jews in Russia during reign of tsar Alexander II.

polyandry: the practice in which women may be married to more than one man.

polygamy: the practice of multiple marriage.

post-traumatic stress: a type of anxiety disorder that is triggered by an extremely traumatic event; the trauma is relived in some manner even though the initial cause is no longer present.

psychosis: a psychiatric term that describes a loss of contact with reality.

psychothenia: the phenomenon that occurs when an individual is so oversaturated with input that the capacity for metabolizing experience diminishes even as the thirst for stimulation increases.

Qu'ran or Koran: the central religious text of Islam.

Reconstructionist Judaism: a modern American-based Jewish movement that views Judaism as a progressively evolving civilization.

reparative (or conversion) therapy: a method of treatment aimed at changing the sexual orientation of homosexuals and bisexuals to heterosexual or at eliminating or diminishing homosexual desires and behaviors. Techniques that have been tried include behavior modification, aversion therapy, psychoanalysis, and religious counseling.

ritual abuse: a sadistic psychological, sexual, spiritual, and/or physical assault on an unwilling human victim, committed by one or more people whose primary motive is to fulfill a prescribed ritual in order to achieve a specific goal or to satisfy the perceived needs of their deity.

roshi: a Zen Buddhist name for a monastic who gives spiritual guidance to a community.

satanic: referring to the worship of Satan, the symbol of evil in Abrahamic religions.

satori: Japanese Buddhist term for enlightenment.

shiv'a: the week-long period of grief and mourning in the Jewish tradition for one's father, mother, son, daughter, brother, sister, or spouse.

shunning: an enforced policy that requires Church members to avoid anyone who leaves or gets expelled from the religion.

simulacrum: term coined by Jean Baudrillard; refers to signs and symbols that replace reality; the models of the real are without origin and yet the perceived reality appears more "real" than the original.

situational narcissism: a condition that appears after an individual reaches a level of power or celebrity so elevated that he believes himself special or beyond the boundaries of ordinary human limits and exhibits the characteristics of ordinary narcissism, including extreme self-involvement and a dependence on the adulation of others.

Stockholm Syndrome: the behavior of kidnap victims who, over time, become sympathetic to their captors.

Sufism: a sect of Islam in the mystical tradition.

swami: an honorific title in Hinduism for master. It is usually a term for one who has set aside worldly pursuits to devote himself to the direct experience of the highest spiritual realization and to the service of others.

tonglen: a meditation practice in Tibetan Buddhism that focuses on connecting with the suffering of others. In the practice, one visualizes taking the suffering of others onto oneself and giving one's own happiness and success to others.

trauma bond: a bond formed after an intense, traumatic experience or betrayal of trust takes place, leading to an equally intense relationship between victim and perpetrator.

tulku: a name for a Tibetan teacher who is thought to reincarnate over a number of generations.

Zen: a meditation school in Buddhism that uses direct, experiential realization to attain enlightenment.

Notes

CHAPTER 1

1. Henry Mencken, *Minority Report: Mencken's Notebooks* (New York: Knopf, 1956), p. 241.

CHAPTER 2

1. John Bradshaw, *Healing the Shame That Binds You* (Deerfield Beach, FL: Health Communications, 1989), p. 14.

2. Gershen Kaufman, *Shame: The Power of Caring* (Cambridge, MA: Schenkman Books, 1992), pp. 182–83.

3. Hazrat Inayat Khan, *The Inner Life* (Boston: Shambhala Books, 1997), p. 173.

4. Mihali Csikszentmihalyi, *Flow, The Psychology of Optimal Experience* (New York: HarperCollins, 1990): "Every flow activity, whether is involved competition, chance or any other dimension of experience, had this in common: It provided a sense of discovery, a creative feeling of transporting the person into a new reality. It pushed the person to higher levels of performance, and led to previously un-dreamed-of states of conscious. In short, it transformed the self by making it more complex" (p. 74).

5. Fourteenth Dalai Lama, et al.. *Sleeping, Dreaming and Dying: An Exploration of Consciousness with the Fourteenth Dalai Lama and Western Scientist, Nuerobiologists, and Psychologists* (Boston: Wisdom Publications, 1997): "All the accounts of death move from darkness into light. The experience of light is what researchers call the core experience, seemingly common across cultures. The light has been described as clear, white, orange, golden or yellow, definitely of a different order than daylight. It is much more brilliant but soothing. One both sees it and simultaneously is caught in it. In other words, there is no distinction between light and mind, as though the mind is actually a matrix for this light. In this moment . . . one seems to comprehend everything" (p. 196).

CHAPTER 3

1. Jean Baudrillard, *Simulacra and Simulation*, trans. Sheila Faria Glaser (Ann Arbor: University of Michigan Press, 1994). "Whereas representation attempts to absorb simulation by interpreting it as a false representation, simulation envelops the whole edifice of representation itself as a simulacrum." p. 3.

2. CBS, *The New French Revolution*, May 16, 2004. Samira Bellil wrote *Dans l'enfer des Tournantes* (translated as *In the hell of the tournantes* [gang-rapes]. She was a French Muslim feminist activist who died of stomach cancer at the age of 31, five months after the CBS news segment.

3. Sara Corbett, "A Cutting Tradition," *New York Times*, January 8, 2008: "In Bandung, Indonesia, female circumcision is performed on girls by a small group of women who swiftly and with apparent affection cut off a small piece of her genitals. The girls are treated gently, and given some small gift at the end of their procedure."

4. Christina Hoff Sommers, "The Subjection of Islamic Women and the Feck-lessness of American Feminism," *The Weekly Standard*, May 21, 2007, p. 2.

5. Ibid., p. 3.

6. Anitra Freeman, *A Psychological Analysis of Fundamentalism*, December 8, 2002, http://www.anitra.net/activism/fundamentalism/psychology.html (a succinct user-friendly look at the subject). Also see "Exiting from the Terrorism-State Terrorism Vicious Cycle: Some Psychological Conditions," Johan Galtung Acceptance Speech, 110th Convention of the American Psychological Association: Peace Division, Chicago, Illinois, August 25, 2002, http://www.webster.edu/peacepsychology/johangaltungaddress.html.

7. Trevor Southley, *The Mormons*, PBS documentary, 2007.

8. Charles Rush, *The Problem with Shame Based Religion*, http://www.christChurchsummit.org/sermons-1998980111.

9. Christina Martin, "Offend Who You Like, Just Don't Mention Religion," *The New Humanist*, http://newhumanist.org.uk1658. In 2006, Ms. Martin was due to perform a set for "The World Stands Up" on the Paramount Comedy Channel, but, after running her jokes past her lawyers, the show's producers felt that she might offend Christians. The cancellation ended up being a blessing in disguise. She was approached by the *New Humanist* magazine to write an article about what happened and has been writing for them ever since.

10. Christina Martin, *The New Humanist*.

11. Sharon Waxman, "Abuse Charges Hit Reservation Church-Run Schools," *Washington Post*, June 2, 2003.

12. *Diaspora* refers to the movement, migration, or scattering of a people away from their ancestral or established homeland. The term has come to be used to refer interchangeably to the historical movements of the dispersed ethnic population of Israel, the cultural development of that population, and the population itself. Some-times refugees of other origins or ethnicities may be called a *diaspora*, but the two terms are far from synonymous. This is a distinction not simply of race or culture, but in the spiritual heart of a group of people. Those who have been oppressed, been ban-ished, or threatened with extinction because of religious beliefs and culture especially outside of their homeland, identify themselves as diaspora. In all cases, the term *Diaspora* carries a sense of displacement; that is, the population so described finds itself

for whatever reason separated from its national territory; usually it has a ⌐ least a desire, to return to its homeland at some point, if the "homeland" stɪₗₗ in any meaningful sense.

13. *Numinous* is a Latin term coined by German theologian Rudolf Otto to describe that which is *wholly other*, or the transcendent.

14. Sharon Lipkin, "Western Muslims' Racist Rape Spree," December 2005, www.FrontPageMagazine.com (p. 1).

15. Paulo Friere, *The Pedagogy of Hope, Reliving the Pedagogy of the Oppressed* (New York: Continuum Books, 2006): "What we cannot do, as imaginative, curious beings, is to cease to learn and to seek, to investigate the 'why' of things. We cannot *exist* without wondering about tomorrow, about what is 'going on,' and going on in favor of what, against what, for whom, against whom. We cannot *exist* without wondering about how to do the concrete or 'untested feasible' that requires us to fight for it" (p. 85).

CHAPTER 4

1. Rinpoche, Dilgo Khyentse, "Seven Point Mind Training Root Text," *Enlightened Courage* (Somerville, MA: Wisdom Publications, 2006), p. 2.

2. Christopher Lasch, *The Culture of Narcissism* (New York: Norton, 1979), p. 15.

3. Michael Downing, *Shoes Outside the Door: Desire, Devotion and Excess at San Francisco Zen Center* (Washington, DC: Counterpoint Books, 2001), pp. 232–33.

4. See www.advocateweb.org. for information about religious abuses across the religious spectrum.

5. *Countertransference* is a condition in which the therapist begins to transfer her own unconscious feelings to the patient. It can be the entire body of feelings that the therapist has toward the patient and includes cases in which the therapist literally takes on the suffering of her patient.

6. Robert Milman of Cornell University speaks of *situational narcissism*, which appears only after the person in question has risen to a stratospheric level of fame and acquired enormous adulation ("Celebrity is a mask that eats into the face": John Updike).

7. Katy Butler, "Encountering the Shadow in Buddhist America," *Common Boundary* (May–June 1990), pp. 14–22: "I recommend never adopting the attitude toward one's spiritual teacher of seeing his or her every action as divine or noble. This may seem a little bit bold, but if one has a teacher who is not qualified, who is engaging in unsuitable or wrong behavior, then it is appropriate for the student to criticize that behavior."

8. Paul Brunton *The Notebooks of Paul Brunton: The Quest* (New York: Larson Publications, 1987), p. 357.

9. Judith L. Herman, *Trauma and Recovery* (New York: Basic Books, 1992, p. 7): "It is very tempting to take the side of the perpetrator. All the perpetrator asks is that the bystander do nothing. He appeals to the universal desire to see, hear and speak no evil. The victim, on the contrary, asks the bystander to share the burden of pain. The victim demands action, engagement and remembering."

10. Lao Tzu, *The Way of Life*, trans. W. Brynner (New York: Perigee Books, 1980), quoted in Frances Vaughn, "Health and Pathology in New Religious Movements,"

Council on Spiritual Practices, http://www.csp.org/communities/docs/vaughan-balance.html.

CHAPTER 5

1. Steven Hassan, *Combating Cult Mind Control: Guide to Protection, Rescue, and Recovery from Destructive Cults* (South Paris, ME: Park Street Press, 1988).

2. The five major world religions are Islam, Christianity, Judaism, Buddhism, and Hinduism.

3. Maxine Hanks, "Perspective on Mormon Women: A Struggle to Reclaim Authority," *Los Angeles Times*, July 10, 1994; K. Loewenthal et al., "Gender and Depression in Anglo Jewry," *Psychological Medicine* (1995), pp. 1051–63.

4. Nathanlie De Fabrique, "Understanding Stockholm Syndrome," *FBI Law Enforcement Bulletin* 76, no. 7 (July 1, 2007), p. 10.

5. *Cultural relativity* is an attempt to understand the cultural development of societies and social groups on their own terms, without trying to impose absolute ideas of moral value or trying to measure different cultural variations in terms of some form of absolute cultural standard.

6. Carol Lee Flinders, *At the Root of this Longing: Reconciling a Spiritual Hunger and a Feminist Thirst* (San Francisco: HarperCollins, 1998), p. 69.

7. Ibid., pp. 108–9.

8. *Opus Dei*, for example, is a society that vows to practice very specific austerities to enhance holiness. Besides silence and fasting, there are practices of mortification by the use of a *cilice*, a spiked chain worn around the upper thigh for two hours a day, and *discipline*, in which one whips oneself; other practices include taking cold showers and sleeping on boards. Women are not allowed to smoke or go to bars. Men are allowed to do so if recruiting for the organization.

9. See Bessel A. van der Kolk et al., eds., *Traumatic Stress, the Effects of Overwhelming Experience on Mind, Body and Society* (New York: Guilford Press, 1996) for a full treatment of trauma and its effects on the body-mind.

10. Frederick Douglass, *Narrative of the Life of Frederick Douglass, American Slave* (New York: Signet, 2005), pp. 6–10.

11. *Abishiktananda, An Interior Voyage, The Life of Dom Henri le Saux*, Inner Directions Films, 1984.

12. Elie Weisel: "The opposite of love is not hate, it's indifference. The opposite of art is not ugliness, it's indifference. The opposite of faith is not heresy, it's indifference. And the opposite of life is not death, it's indifference." New York, October, 1986.

13. Victor Frankl, *Man's Search for Meaning* (Boston: Beacon Press, 2007), p. 172.

CHAPTER 6

1. *Polyandry* is prohibited in Islam, Judaism, and most of Christianity. Historically, in Hinduism and in rural parts of India, Tibet, and Nepal, fraternal polyandry is practiced, allowing several brothers to share marital privileges with one woman.

2. Barbara Bradley Hagarty, "Some Muslims in U.S. Quietly Engage in Polygamy," NPR broadcast, *All Things Considered*, July 19, 2008.

3. Sherif Abdel Azim, at Queens University, reports that the rate of polygamous marriages in the Muslim world is much less than the rate of extramarital affairs in the

West. In other words, men in the Muslim world today are far more strictly monogamous than men in the Western world. Polygamy in fundamentalist sects of Mormonism
appears to be more troubling. It is important to ascertain who benefits from the ar-
rangement. *www.IslamiCity.org*, *Part 14: Polygamy*, http://www.islamicity.com/mosque/
w_islam/poly.htm.

4. Richard Sipe, *A Secret World: Sexuality and the Search for Celibacy* (New York:
Brunner/Mazel, 1990), p. 58.

5. Mary Gail Frawley-O'Dea, *Perversion of Power: Sexual Abuse in the Catholic
Church* (Nashville, TN: Vanderbilt Press, 2007), pp. 50–52.

6. Myra Hidalgo, *Sexual Abuse and the Culture of Catholicism: How Priests and Nuns
Become Perpetrators* (New York: Haworth Maltreatment and Trauma Press, 2007), p. 6.

7. Ibid., p. 7.

8. Richard Sipe, *Sex, Priests, and Power: Anatomy of a Crisis* (New York: Brunner/
Mazel, 1995), p. 162.

9. In 1997, the Dalai Lama met with Western Buddhist teachers, psychologists,
and monastics about the sexual abuse of members by lamas, roshis, and rimpoches
in the European and American communities. In the remarkable documentary, *In the
Spirit of Honest Inquiry*, a bracingly honest dialogue between His Holiness and these
Buddhist leaders revealed what is probably a standard complaint in religious communities of all religions over the globe: that there is little real psychological and spiritual
support to practice their vows and to have an open forum when abuses occur.

10. See www.theawarenesscenter.org.

11. William Persell, "Sexual Abuse by Clergy: A Perfect Panic," Good Friday sermon, March 25, 2008, www.religioustolerance.org/clergy_sex.htm.

12. *The Jerusalem Bible*, Christ's College (Liverpool, 1966).

13. *Antitheist*: one who believes that not only is there no God but that religion
itself is harmful.

14. Christopher Hitchens, Kurtz, Paul (ed.) *Free Inquiry* Magazine 21, no. 4 (2001).

15. "Rule for the Monastery of Compludo," trans. C. W. Barlow, ed., J. Frank Hen-
derson, in *Iberian Fathers*, vol. 2: *Braulio of Saragosa, Fructuosus of Braga* (The Fathers of the Church: A New Translation) (Washington, D.C.: Catholic University of
America Press, 1969), pp. 155–175.

16. Hidalgo, *Sexual Abuse and the Culture of Catholicism*, p. 9.

17. Thich Nhat Hanh, *The Art of Power* (New York: HarperCollins, 2007), p. 161:
"A good spiritual teacher can show us that in our own heart we also have a spiritual
teacher and we have to take refuge in this teacher inside us, rather than becoming attached to a teacher outside us, because the spiritual teacher outside may be a fake."

18. Shirley DuBoulay, *The Cave of the Heart* (New York: Orbis Books, 2005), p. 234.
Swamiji: Un voyage interieur, a film by Patrice Chagnard, Paris, 1984.

19. Mary Gail Frawley O'Dea, "The Long-term Impact of Early Sexual Trauma,"
paper presented to the National Conference of Catholic Bishops, Dallas, Texas,
June 13, 2002.

20. O'Dea, *Perversion of Power, Sexual Abuse in the Catholic Church*, p. 183.

21. Joint Declaration for the United Nations International Day in Support of
Victims of Torture (press release), United Nations, June 25, 2001, http://www.un.org/
News/Press/docs/2006/Reference_Paper_No_45.doc.htm. Also see Jean Sarson and
Linda MacDonald, *Torture and Ritual Abuse-Torture: Perpetrators Who Are "Religious"
Men and Women*, http://www.ritualabusetorture.org/religion.pdf.

22. Satanic ritual abuse is the most extreme form of ritual abuse, using sacrifice, satanic rituals, magic, and mind control.

23. "Report of the Ritual Abuse Task Force," Los Angeles Commission for Women, 1989, a groundbreaking compendium of information, has been updated and expanded by Kathleen Sullivan, *Ritual Abuse and Mind Control.* http://www.mindcon trolforums.com/slvn-rab.htm.

24. Nathalie Goldberg, *The Great Failure: A Bartender, a Monk, and My Unlikely Path to Truth* (San Francisco: Harper, 2002), p. 124. (*Dharma* is a Sanskrit word meaning "one's righteous duty, or any virtuous act.")

CHAPTER 7

1. Thomas Merton, "A Letter on the Contemplative Life," in *Thomas Merton, Spiritual Master,* ed. Lawrence Cunningham (originally published in Merton, *Contemplation in a World of Action* (Notre Dame, IN: University of Notre Dame Press, 1995), pp. 424–25.

2. John Moyne and Coleman Barks (trans.), *Open Secret, Versions of Rumi* (Boston: Shambhala, 1999), p. 22.

3. Jack Kornfield, *A Path with Heart, A Guide through the Perils and Promises of Spiritual Life* (New York: Bantam Books, 1993), p. 190.

4. Leonard Shengold, *Soul Murder, Revisited, Thoughts about Therapy, Hate, Love, and Memory* (New Haven: Yale University Press, 1999): "Pathological doubting is a consequence of child abuse, and sometimes what actually happened cannot be determined" (p. 10).

5. Stephen Levine, "Softening the Belly of Sorrow," in *Unattended Sorrow: Recovering from Loss and Reviving the Heart,* http://www.creationsmagazine.com/articles/ C101/Levine.html.

6. Raymond Blakney, trans., *Meister Echkhart, a Modern Translation* (New York: Harper & Row, 1941): "*God* is where his light is least apparent. Therefore we ought to expect *God* in all manners and all things evenly," pp. 249–50.

7. *Fleeting effect* refers to the sense of the origin, such as a paint stroke. The effect happens even when the representation of that origin can no longer be directly ascertained.

8. Howard Thurman, *The Inward Journey,* Section 20 (New York: Harcourt Brace Jovanovich, 1984), pp. 37–38.

9. See *A Moving Journal, Ongoing Expressions of Authentic Movement,* http://www. movingjournal.org/, a publication devoted to Authentic Movement.

10. Richard Sipe, *A Secret World, Sexuality and the Search for Celibacy* (New York: Brunner/Mazel, 1990), p. 261.

11. *MaleSurvivor* is an organization committed to preventing, healing, and eliminating all forms of sexual victimization of boys and men through support, treatment, research, education, advocacy, and activism. Its Web site is www.malesurvivor.org.

CHAPTER 8

1. Noelle Oxenhandler, "Ah, but the Breezes . . ." in Philip Zalenski, ed., *Best American Spiritual Writing* (New York: Houghton Mifflin Company, 2004), p. 209.

Bibliography

Abhishiktananda. *The Further Shore*. New Delhi: Ispek. 1984.

Adler, Rachel. "A Stumbling Block before the Blind: Sexual Exploitation in Pastoral Counseling." CCAR *Journal: A Reform Jewish Quarterly* (Spring 1993). pp. 13–54.

Akpan, Uwem. *Say You're One of Them*. New York: Little, Brown, 2008.

Ali, Abdullah Yusif (trans.). *The Qur'an, a Translation*. Elmhurst, NY: Tahrike Tarsile Qur'an, 1995.

Anthony, Dick, Bruce Ecker, and Ken Wilber (eds.). *Spiritual Choices: The Problems of Recognizing Authentic Paths to Inner Transformation*. New York: Paragon House, 1986.

Armstrong, Karen. *The Battle for God*. New York: Knopf, 2000.

Armstrong, Karen. *A History of God: The 4,000 Year Quest of Judaism, Christianity, and Islam*. New York: Ballantine Books, 1993.

Armstrong, Karen. *The Spiral Staircase, My Climb Out of Darkness*. New York: Knopf, 2001.

Azim, Sharif Abdel. "Women in Islam versus Women in the Judaeo-Christian Tradition: The Myth and the Reality," IslamiCity.org, http://www.islamicity.com/mosque/w_islam/poly.htm.

Bailey, Charles. *In the Shadow of the Cross, The True Account of Sexual and Ritual Abuse at the Hands of a Roman Catholic Priest*. New York: iUniverse, 2000.

Baldwin, Michael (ed.). "The Tyranny of Faith, Reflections on the Death of a Patriarch," *Beyond the Tyranny of Belief*, April 8, 2005. Available at http://www.metahistory.org/FaithlessAndFree.php.

Barks, Coleman. *Say I Am You: Poetry Interspersed with Stories of Rumi and Shams*. Athens, GA: Maypop, 1994.

Barlow, C. W. "Rule for the Monastery of Compludo," in *Iberian Fathers*, vol. 2: *Braulio of Saragosa, Fructuosus of Braga*. (The Fathers of the Church: A New Translation.) Washington: Catholic University of America Press, 1969.

Batchelor, Stephen. "Shaping the Future? Western Buddhist Teachers Meet the Dalai Lama in Dharmasala, India," *Zen Buddhism Virtual Library*, March 22, 1993, www.thezensite.com.

Baudrillard, Jean. *Similacra and Simulation*, trans. Sheila Glaser. Ann Arbor: University of Michigan Press, 1994.

Beah, Ishmael. *A Long Way Gone, Memoirs of a Boy Soldier*. New York: Farrar, Straus and Giroux, 2007.

Berke, Joseph K. *The Tyranny of Malice, Exploring the Dark Side of Character and Culture*. New York: Summit Books, 2000.

Berry, Jason. *Lead Us Not into Temptation: Catholic Priests and the Sexual Abuse of Children*. New York: Doubleday, 2000.

Bhutto, Benazir. *Reconciliation, Islam, Democracy, and the West*. New York: Harper-Collins, 2008.

Blakney, Raymond B. (trans.). *Meister Eckhart, A Modern Translation*. New York: Harper and Row, 1941.

Blue, Ken. *Healing Spiritual Abuse, How to Break Free from Bad Church Experiences*. Downers Grove, IL: InterVarsity Press, 1993.

Boerree, C. George. "Towards a Buddhist Psychotherapy," 1997, http://webspace.ship.edu/cgboer/buddhapsych.html.

Booth, Leo. *Breaking the Chains: Understanding Religious Addiction and Religious Abuse*. Long Beach, CA: Emmaus, 1989.

Boston Globe Investigative Team. *Betrayal: Crisis in the Catholic Church*. Boston: Little, Brown, 2002.

Bouclin, Marie Evans. *Seeking Wholeness, Women Dealing with Abuse of Power in the Catholic Church*. Collegeville, MN: Liturgical Press, 2006.

Bradshaw, John, *Healing the Shame That Binds You*. Deerfield Beach, FL: Health Communications, 1989.

Brown, J. B., J. R. Noblitt, and P. S. Perskin (eds.). "A Therapeutic Relationship: Shifting Boundaries in the Service of Healing." In *Ritual Abuse in the Twenty-first Century: Psychological, Forensic, Social and Political Considerations*. Brandon, OR: Robert D. Reed, 2008.

Browne, Joanne Carson, and Carole R. Bohn. *Christianity, Patriarch, and Abuse: A Feminist Critique*. Berea, OH: Pilgrim Press, 1989.

Burchett, Dave. *Bring 'Em Back Alive: A Healing Plan for Those Wounded by the Church*. New York: WaterBook Press, 2002.

Cameron, Julia. *Transitions, Prayers and Declarations for a Changing Life*. New York: Jeremy Tercher and Putnam, 2008.

Campbell, June. "The Emperor's Tantric Robes." *Tricycle Magazine* 6, no. 2 (Winter 1996). Available at http://www.anandainfo.com/tantric_robes.html.

Campbell, June. *Travelers in Space: Gender, Identity and Tibetian Buddhism*. London: Continuum, 2002.

Chodren, Pema. *The Places That Scare You: A Guide to Fearlessness in Difficult Times*. Boston: Shambhala, 2001.

Conner, Randy P. *Blossom of Bone: Reclaiming the Connections between Homoeroticism and the Sacred*. San Francisco: Harper Books, 1993.

Corwin, Marla A. "Meaning in Suffering." Columbine Unitarian-Universalist Church guest sermon, January 31, 2005.

Council on Spiritual Practices. "Code of Ethic for Spiritual Guides," www.csp.org.

Cozzens, Donald B. *The Changing Face of the Priesthood*, Collegeville, MN: The Liturgical Press, 1984.

Csikszentmihalyi, Mihaly. *Flow: The Psychology of Optimal Experience*. New York: HarperCollins, 1990.

Dalai Lama. *Healing Anger: The Power of Patience from a Buddhist Perspective*. New York: Snow Lion, 1997.

Dalai Lama and Victor Chan. *The Wisdom of Forgiveness: Intimate Conversations and Journeys*. New York: Riverhead Books, 2004.

Davies, J. M., and M. G. Frawley. *Treating the Adult Survivor of Child Sexual Abuse: A Psychoanalytic Perspective*. New York: Basic Books, 1992.

Devorah, Carrie. "Sexual Abuse in the Jewish Community." *The Jewish Magazine*, 2005, http://www.jewishmag.com/89mag/abuse/abuse.htm.

Dillard, Annie. "Pilgrim at Tinker Creek." *Three*. New York: HarperCollins Perennial Books, 2001.

Downing, Michael. *Shoes Outside the Door: Desire, Devotion and Excess at San Francisco Zen Center*. Washington, DC: Counterpoint Books, 2001.

Doyle, Thomas, Sipe and Wall, *Sex, Priests, and Secret Codes: The Catholic 2000 Year Paper Trail of Sexual Abuse*. Los Angeles: Volt Press, 2006.

du Boulay, Shirley. *The Cave of the Heart*. New York: Orbis, 2005.

Eberle, Gary. *Dangerous Words: Talking about God in an Age of Fundamentalism*. Boston: Trumpeter Books, 2007.

Eckhart, Meister. *Meister Eckhart, From Whom God Hid Nothing: Sermons, Writings and Sayings*. Boston: New Seeds, 1996.

Flinders, Carol Lee. *At the Root of This Longing: Reconciling a Spiritual Hunger and a Feminist Thirst*. San Francisco: HarperCollins, 1998.

Fortune, M., and C. Enger. *Violence against Women and the Role of Religion*. Harrisburg, PA: VAWnet, a project of the National Resource Center on Domestic Violence/ Pennsylvania Coalition against Domestic Violence, March 2006, http://www. vawnet.org.

Fortune, Marie M. *Is Nothing Sacred? The Story of a Pastor, the Women He Sexually Abused, and the Congregation He Nearly Destroyed*. Cleveland: United Church Press, 1989.

Fortune, Marie M. *Love Does No Harm: Sexual Ethics for the Rest of Us*. New York: Continuum, 2003.

Fourteenth Dalai Lama, et al. *Sleeping, Dreaming and Dying: An Exploration of Consciousness with the Dalai Lama*. Boston: Wisdom Publications, 1997.

Fowler, James W. *Stages of Faith: The Psychology of Human Development and the Quest for Meaning*. San Francisco: Harper, 1981.

Frankl, Victor. *Man's Search for Meaning*. Boston: Beacon Press, 2006.

Frawley-O'Dea, Mary Gail. *The Long-term Impact of Early Sexual Trauma*, paper presented to the National Conference of Catholic Bishops, Dallas, Texas, June 13, 2002.

Frawley-O'Dea, Mary Gail. *Perversion of Power: Sexual Abuse in the Catholic Church*. Nashville, TN: Vanderbilt Press, 2007.

Friere, Pablo. *Pedagogy of Hope, Reliving the Pedagogy of the Oppressed*. New York: Continuum, 2006.

Freire, Pablo. *Pedagogy of the Oppressed*. New York: Continuum, 1997.

Galtung, Johan. "Acceptance Speech, Morton Deutsch Conflict Resolution Award." 110th Convention of the American Psychological Association, Peace Division, Chicago, IL, August 2002.

Garland, Diana. "When Wolves Wear Shepherd's Clothing: Healing Women Survive Clergy Sexual Abuse," *Social Work and Christianity, An International Journal* 33, no. 1 (Spring 2006). pp. 1–35.

Gartner, Richard. *Betrayed as Boys: Psychodynamic Treatment of Sexually Abused Men.* New York: Guilford Press, 1999.

Germer, Christopher K. *Psychotherapy and Mindfulness.* New York: Guilford Press, 2005.

Gil, Eliana. *Treating Abused Adolescents.* New York: Guilford Press, 1996.

Goldberg, Natalie. *The Great Failure: A Bartender, a Monk, and My Unlikely Path to Truth.* San Francisco: Harper, 2002.

Goldman, Daniel (ed.). *Healing Emotions: Conversations with the Dalai Lama on Mindfulness, Emotions, and Health,* Boston: Shambhala, 1997.

Goldman, Russell. "Two Studies Find Depression Widespread in Utah. Study Calling Utah Most Depressed Renews Debate on Root Causes." *ABC Evening News,* March 7, 2008.

Goodwin, Jan. *Price of Honor: Muslim Women Lift the Veil of Silence on the Islamic World.* New York. Plume Books, 1995.

Grossman David. *Sleeping on a Wire: Conversations with Palestinians in Israel.* New York: Farrar, Straus and Giroux, 2003.

Hafiz. *The Gift, Poems by Hafiz the Great Sufi Master.* New York: Penguin Press, 1999.

Hanks, Maxine. "Perspective on Mormon Women: A Struggle to Reclaim Authority: The Priesthood they Exercised in the Early Church has been Lost, but the Voice of Feminism Will Not Be Silenced." *Los Angeles Times,* Home Edition Opinion, July 10, 1994, p. 7.

Hassan, Steven. *Combating Cult Mind Control: Guide to Protection, Rescue, and Recovery from Destructive Cults.* South Paris, ME: Park Street Press, 1990.

Haule, John Ryan. *The Ecstasies of St. Francis, The Way of Lady Poverty.* Herndon, VA: Lindisfarne Books, 2004.

Hayden, Tom. *The Lost Gospel of the Earth: A Call for Renewing Nature, Spirit, and Politics: Reclaiming the Ecological Wisdom of Christianity, Judaism, Buddhism and Native Traditions for the Next Century.* San Francisco: Sierra Club Books, 2006.

Hedges, Chris. *I Don't Believe in Atheists.* New York: Free Press, 2008.

Herman, Judith L. *Trauma and Recovery.* New York: Basic Books, 1992.

Hidalgo, Myra L. *Sexual Abuse and the Culture of Catholicism: How Priests and Nuns Become Perpetrators.* New York: Haworth Maltreatment and Trauma Press, 2007.

Hillesum, Etty. *An Interrupted Life & Letters from Westerbork.* New York: Holt, 1996.

Hillman, James. *The Force of Character and the Lasting Life.* New York: Ballantine Books, 1999.

Hitchens, Christopher. *God Is Not Great: How Religion Poisons Everything.* New York: Hachette, 2007.

Hoffman, Richard, "The Hatred of Innocence," *Boston Globe,* November 23, 1998.

Hopkins, Nancy Myer, and Mark Laaser (eds.). *Restoring the Soul of a Church: Healing Congregations Wounded by Clergy Sexual Misconduct.* Collegeville, MN: Interfaith Sexual Trauma Institute, 1995.

Horst, Elisabeth. *Recovering the Lost Self: Shame Healing for Victims of Clergy Sexual Abuse.* Collegeville, MN: Liturgical Press, 1998.

Hunter, Mic. *The Sexually Abused Male: Prevalence, Impact, and Treatment.* New York: Lexington Books, 1990.

Jacoby Mario. *Shame and the Origins of Self Esteem: A Jungian Approach.* London: Routledge, 1997.

Johanson, Greg, and Ron Kurtz. *Grace Unfolding: Psychotherapy and the Spirit of the Tao-te Ching.* New York: Bell Tower, 1991.

John Jay College. *The Nature and Scope of the Problem of Sexual Abuse of Minors by Catholic Priests and Deacons in the United States,* 2004, www.usccb.org/hrb/johnjaystudy/.

Johnson, David, and Jeff VanVonderen. *The Subtle Power of Spiritual Abuse: Recognizing and Escaping Spiritual Manipulation and False Spiritual Authority within the Church.* Minneapolis, MN: Bethan House, 1991.

Jordan, Mark D. *The Silence of Sodom: Homosexuality in Modern Catholicism.* Chicago: University of Chicago Press, 2000.

Kain, John. *A Rare and Precious Thing: The Possibilities and Pitfalls of Working with a Spiritual Teacher.* New York: Bell Tower, 2006.

Kapleau, Philip. *The Zen of Living and Dying: A Practical and Spiritual Guide.* Boston: Shambhala, 1997.

Kaufman, Gershen. *Shame: The Power of Caring.* Cambridge, MA: Schenkman Books, 1992.

Keleman, Stanley. *Your Body Speaks Its Mind.* Berkeley, CA: Center Press, 1981.

Kennedy, Eugene. *The Unhealed Wound: The Church, the Priesthood, and the Question of Sexuality.* New York: St. Martin's Griffin, 2001.

Khan, Hazrat Inayat. *The Inner Life.* Boston: Shambhala, 1997.

Killian, Rob. "The Personal Cost of LDS Social Services' Theories and Practices," speech originally given at the Sunstone Symposium, Salt Lake City, August 1996, http://www.affirmation.org/learning/personal_cost.shtml.

Kimball, Charles. *When Religion Becomes Evil.* New York: HarperCollins, 2002.

Kondrath, William M. *God's Tapestry: Understanding and Celebrating Differences.* Herndon, VA: Alban Institute, 2008.

Kornfield, Jack. *The Art of Forgiveness: Loving Kindness and Peace.* New York: Bantam Books, 2008.

Kornfield, Jack. *A Path with Heart: A Guide through the Perils and Promises of Spiritual Life.* New York: Bantam Books, 1993.

Kornfield, Jack. *The Wise Heart: A Guide to the Universal Teachings of Buddhist Psychology.* New York: Random House, 2008.

Kramer, Joe, and Diana Alstad. *The Guru Papers, Masks of Authoritarian Power.* Berkeley, CA: Frog, 1993.

Khyentse, Dilgo Rinpoche. *Enlightened Courage.* Boulder, CO: Snow Lion, 2006.

Lachs, Stuart. "Richard Baker and the Myth of the Zen Roshi," *Dark Zen* (October 2002).

Lacter, E., and K. Lehman. Guidelines to Diagnosis of Ritual Abuse/Mind Control Traumatic Stress. Attachment—*New Directions in Psychotherapy and Relational Psychoanalysis.* Volume 2 (July 2008).

Ladner, Lorne. *The Lost Art of Compassion: Discovering the Practice of Happiness in the Meeting of Buddhism and Psychology.* San Francisco: Harper Books, 2004.

L'Africain, Joseph Andre. "Re-Reading Fieire and Re-Reading the World through Critical Constructivist Lens" (unpublished essay).

Lao Tzu. *The Way of Life*, trans. W. Brynner. New York: Perigee Books, 1980.

Lasch, Christopher. *The Culture of Narcissism*. New York: Norton, 1979.

Levine, Mark. *Heavy Metal: Rock, Resistance, and the Struggle for the Soul of Islam*. New York: Three Rivers Press, 2008.

Levov, Greg. *Callings, Finding and Following an Authentic Life*. New York. Harmony Books, 1997.

Lew, Mike. *Victims No Longer*. New York: Quill, 2004.

Lisak, David. "Psychological Impact of Sexual Abuse: Content Analysis of Interviews with Male Survivors." *Journal of Traumatic Stress* 7, no. 4, pp. 525–548.

Loewenthal, K., V., Goldblatt, T. Gordon, G. Lubitch, H. Bichnell, D. Fellowes, and A. Sowden. "Gender and Depression in Anglo Jewry." *Psychological Medicine* 25 (5).

Lothstein, Leslie. "Nueropsychological Findings in Clergy who Sexually Abuse," *Bless Me Father for I Have Sinned: Perspectives on Sexual Abuse Committed by Roman Catholic Priests*, Westport, CT: Praeger Publishers, 1999.

Love, Patrick, and Donna Tolbot. "Defining Spiritual Development: A Missing Consideration for Student Affairs." *NASPA Journal* 37, no. 1 (Fall 1999). pp. 361–375.

Macy, Joanna. *Coming Back to Life: Practices to Reconnect Our Lives, Our World*. Gabiorla Island, BC, Canada: New Society, 1994.

Maharshi, Ramana. *The Spiritual Teaching of Ramana Maharshi*. Boston: Shambhala Classics, 2004.

Manseau, Peter, and Jeff Sharlet. *Killing the Buddha. A Heretic's Bible*. New York: Free Press, 2005.

Mansfield, Victor. "The Guru-Disciple Relationship: Making Connections and Withdrawing Projections," lecture given at Hamilton College, New York, 1996, www.lightlink.com.

Martin, Philip. *The Zen Path through Depression*. San Francisco: HarperCollins, 1999.

McGinley, James E. "Suffering: A Search for Meaning." *Journal of Creative Work* 2, no. 1 (2008). pp. 1–10.

Merton, Thomas. *Contemplation in a World of Action: Gethsemani Studies in Psychological and Religious Anthropology*. Notre Dame, IN: University of Notre Dame Press, 1995.

Merton, Thomas. *Turning Toward the World: The Pivotal Years, Journals, 1960–63*. New York: HarperCollins, 1997.

Meston, Daja Wangchuk. *My Journey to Forgiveness Comes the Peace*. New York: Free Press, 2007.

Miller, Alice, Hannam, Hildegard and Hunter (trans.). *For Your Own Good: Hidden Cruelty in Child-Rearing and the Roots of Violence*. New York: Farrar Straus Giroux, 1990.

Miller, Alice. *The Body Never Lies: The Lingering Effects of Cruel Parenting*. New York: Norton, 2005.

Miller, Alice. *Thou Shalt Not Be Aware: Society's Betrayal of the Child*. New York: New American Library, 1986.

Moyne, John, and Coleman Barks (trans.). *Open Secret: Versions of Rumi*. Boston: Shambhala, 1999.

Muster, Nori J. *Betrayal of the Spirit: My Life behind the Headlines of the Hare Krishna Movement*. Chicago: University of Illinois Press, 1997.

Myren, Ann, and Dorothy Madison (eds.). *Living at the Source: Teachings of Vivekananda*. Boston: Shambhala, 1993.

Nation, Ihla F. "Confronting the Guru-Disciple Relationship." *Gnosis* (Spring 1996), http://www.leavingsiddhayoga.net/gnosis.htm.

Neihardt and Black Elk. *Black Elk Speaks*. Lincoln: University of Nebraska Press, 1979.

Noblitt, R., and Noblitt, Perskin (eds.). *Ritual Abuse in the Twenty-First Century: Psychological, Forensic, Social, and Political Considerations*. Bandon, OR: Robert D. Reed, 2008.

Nozick R. *The Examined Life: Philosophical Meditations*. New York: Simon and Schuster, 1987.

Orsi, Robert A. *Between Heaven and Earth: The Religious Worlds People Make and the Scholars Who Study Them*. Princeton: Princeton University Press, 2005.

Patel, Eboo. *Acts of Faith: The Story of an American Muslim, the Struggle for the Soul of a Generation*. Boston: Beacon Press, 2007.

Patton, Kimberley C. "When the Wounded Emerge as Healers, the Study of Religion Is Like a Labyrinth." *Harvard Divinity School Bulletin* 34, no. 1 (Winter 2005). Available at http://www.hds.harvard.edu/news/bulletin_mag/articles/34-1_patton.html.

Peck, M. Scott. "Stages of Spiritual Growth." In *The Different Drum: Community Making*. New York: Touchstone, 1987.

Persell, William. "Sexual Abuse by Clergy: A Perfect Panic," Good Friday sermon, March 25, 2002, http://www.religioustolerance.org/clergy_sex.htm.

Pope, Alan. "'Is There a Difference?' Iconic Images of Suffering in Buddhism and Christianity." In *Janus Head*. Amherst, NY: Triviium Publications, 2007, pp. 247–260.

Pritchard, Evan. *No Word for Time: The Way of the Algonquin People*. Tulsa, OK: Council Oak Books, 1997.

Prothero, Stephen. *Religious Literacy: What Every American Needs to Know—and Doesn't*. San Francisco: HarperCollins, 2007.

Rachels, James. *The Challenge of Cultural Relativism, the Elements of Moral Philosophy*. New York: McGraw-Hill, 1999.

Radke, Andrea G. "The Place of Mormon Women: Perceptions, Prozac, Polygamy, Priesthood, Patriarchy, and Peace," *FAIR*, June 2006, www.fairlds.org/FAIR Conferences/2004_Place_of_Mormon_Women.html.

Rahner, Karl. "What It Means to Be a Priest Today," National Institute for the Renewal of Priesthood, 2002. http://www.jknirp.com/rahner2.htm.

Ratzinger, Joseph Cardinal. "Liberation Theology." Private document that preceded the Instruction of Fall, *The Ratzinger Report*. San Francisco: Ignatius Press, 1984.

Rauch, Mikele. "Dissecting the Lamb of God: The Other Devastation of Clergy Sexual Abuse." *Cross Currents* 54, no. 3 (Fall 2004), pp. 7–14.

Ricard, Matthieu. *Happiness: A Guide to Developing Life's Most Important Skill*. New York: Little, Brown, 2006.

Richards, Scott, and Allen E. Berrgin (eds.). *Handbook of Psychotherapy and Religious Diversity*. Baltimore, MD: American Psychological Association, 2000.

Robinson, Bishop Geoffrey. *Confronting Power and Sex in the Catholic Church*. Collegeville, MN: Liturgical Press, 2007.

Rogers, Annie. *A Shining Affliction: A Story of Harm and Healing in Psychotherapy*. New York: Penguin, 2006.

Rosen, Mark. *Thank You for Being Such a Pain: Spiritual Guidance for Dealing with Difficult People*. New York: Three Rivers Press, 1998.

Ruland, Vernon. *Sacred Lies and Silences, A Psychology of Religious Disguise*. Collegeville, MN: Liturgical Press, 1994.

Rumi, Jalauddin. *Open Secret*, trans. Coleman Barks and John Moyne. Putney, VT: Threshold Books, 1991.

Rumi, Jalaluddin, John Moyne, and Coleman Barks. *Say I Am You: Poetry Interspersed with Stories of Rumi and Shams*. Athens, GA: Maypop, 1994.

Rutz, Carol. *A Nation Betrayed (Ritual Abuse)*. Grass Lake, MI: Fidelity, 1999.

Scales, Peter. "Early Spirituality and Religious Participation Linked to Later Adolescent Well-Being." *The Center for Spiritual Development in Childhood & Adolescence*, 2006. http://www.spiritualdevelopmentcenter.org//Display.asp? Page=FastFacts2.

Schaef, Anne Wilson, and Fassel, Dianne. *The Addictive Organization, Why We Overwork, Cover Up, Pick up the Pieces, Please the Boss, and Perpetuate Sick Organizations*. New York: Harperone, 1990.

Scott, Wayne. "Lost in Our Own Saintliness: The Home Life of the Trauma Therapist." *Treating Abuse Today*, Vol. 8, Jg. H. 1. pp. 27–28 and 31–34, 1998.

Shengold, Leonard. *Soul Murder Revisited: Thoughts about Therapy, Hate, Love and Memory*. New Haven: Yale University Press, 1999.

Simpkinson, Anne A. "Soul Betrayal." *Common Boundary Inc*. (November–December 1996).

Sipe, Richard. *A Secret World: Sexuality and the Search for Celibacy*. New York: Brunner/Mazel, 1990.

Sipe, Richard. *Sex, Priests and Power: Anatomy of a Crisis*. New York: Brunner/Mazel, 1995.

Smith, Caroline E., Reinert, Duane F., Horne, Maryanne, Greer, Joanne M., and Wicks, Robert "Childhood Abuse and Spiritual Development among Women Religious," *Journal of Religion and Health* 35, no. 4 (December 1999).

Smith, Huston. *Why Religion Matters: The Fate of the Human Spirit in an Age of Disbelief*. San Francisco: HarperCollins, 2001.

Sogyal, Rinpoche. *The Tibetan Book of Living and Dying*. San Francisco: HarperCollins, 1993.

Spiegel, Marcia Cohn. "Spirituality for Survival: Jewish Women Healing Themselves." *Journal of Feminist Studies in Religion* 12, no. 2 (Fall 1996).

Strong, Mary. *Letters of the Scattered Brotherhood*. New York: Harper and Row, 1948.

Switankowsky, Irene. "Sympathy and Empathy." *Philosophy Today* 44, no. 1 (Spring 2000). pp. 86–93.

Taylor, A.J.W. "Spirituality and Personal Values: Neglected Components of Trauma Treatment." *Traumatology* 7, no. 3 (September 2001). pp. 111–119.

Thandeka. *Learning to Be White: Money, Race, and God in America*. New York: Continuum, 2001.

Thich Nhat Hahn. *Anger: Wisdom for Cooling the Flames*. New York: Riverhead Books, 2001.

Thich Nhat Hahn. *The Art of Power*. San Francisco: Harper One, 2007.

Thich Nhat Hanh. *The Miracle of Mindfulness*. Boston: Beacon Press, 2005.

Thich Nhat Hanh and Jack Kornfield. *Being Peace*. Berkeley, CA: Parallax Press, 2005.

Thurman, Howard. *A Strange Freedom: The Best of Howard Thurman on Religious Experience and Public Life*. Boston: Beacon Press, 1998.

Tyagananda, Swami. "Why Celibacy? A Hindu Perspective" (Lecture Series, The Church in the 21st Century Initiative and by the Comparative Theology Area. Boston College: March 25, 2003).

United Nations Populations Fund, "Ending Violence against Women and Girls, a Human rights and Health Priority." *State of World Population, 2000*, http://www.unfpa.org/swp/2000/english/ch03.html.

Vallina, Danielle. "Pastoral Care for a Church in Crisis." *Pastoral Care*, 301, Northern Baptist Theological Seminary, http://www.thehopeofsurvivors.com/pastoral_care_church_crisis.asp.

van der Kolk, Bessel A., Alexander C. McFarlane, and Lars Weisaeth (eds.). *Traumatic Stress: The Effects of Overwhelming Experience on Mind, Body, and Society*. New York: Guilford Press, 1996.

Vaughan, Frances. *The Inward Arc: Healing Wholeness in Psychotherapy and Spirituality*. Boston: Shambhala, 1986.

Vaughan, Frances. "A Question of Balance: Health and Pathology in New Religious Movements." *Journal of Humanistic Psychology* 23, no. 3 (1983), pp. 20–41.

Washburn, Michael. "Life's Three Stages: Infancy, Ego and Transcendence" (interview by Paul Bernstein). *Online Noetic Network*, Spring 1998, http://members.tripod.com/~pbernste/life3.htm.

Waskow, Arthur. "Ecstasy, Frenzy, Domination, and Sexual Abuse in Spirit's Name." *The Shalom CenterWebsite*, May 2006. http://www.shalomctr.org/node/1118.

Weintraub, Simkha Y. (ed.). *Healing of Soul, Healing of Body: Spiritual Leaders Unfold the Strength and Solace in Psalms*. Woodstock, VT: Jewish Lights, 1999.

Wilber, Ken. *Integral Psychology: Consciousness, Spirit, Psychology, and Therapy*. Boston: Shambhala, 2000.

Wills, Garry. *Papal, Sins: Structures of Deceit*. New York: Doubleday, 2000.

Wills, Garry. *What Jesus Meant*. New York: Viking, 2006.

Wilmer, Harry A. (ed.). *Closeness in Personal and Professional Relationships*, Boston: Shambhala, 2001.

Wink, P. "Spiritual Development across the Adult Life Course." *Journal of Adult Development* 9, no. 1 (January 2002). pp. 79–94.

Wolkstein, D., and Kramer, S. N. *Innana, Queen of Heaven and Earth: Her Stories and Hymns from Sumer*. San Francisco: Harper and Row. 1983.

Yusef, Umm. "Muslims and Emotional Stress." *A Glimpse into the Life of a Muslimah*, October 24, 2004, http://southernmuslimah.wordpress.com/.

Index

About the Author

MIKELE RAUCH is a licensed marriage, family, and child therapist with Brookline Psychological Services dealing with trauma, male and female sexual abuse, and clergy abuse. In 2004, she served on the Victims Rights Committee as a part of an Independent Review Board overseeing the Catholic Church's policies and procedures regarding survivors of clergy sexual abuse. She is a psychotherapist specializing in psychotherapy with male and female survivors of physical, sexual, and clergy abuse. She is a member of MaleSurvivor, the National Organization against Male Sexual Victimization and its International Retreat Team. She has written for the *Missouri Review*, the *National Catholic Reporter*, *Cross Currents Magazine*, *Healing Ministry*, and *The New Therapist*.